WILD GAME

By the same author

Non Fiction: Fiction:

Pack and Rifle   Fawn
Hunter by Profession   Stag
Backblocks   White Patch
The Deer Hunters   Razorback
Seasons of a Hunter
Outdoors in Australia
On Target
The Wild Pig in New Zealand
The Golden Years of Hunting in New Zealand
The Golden Years of Fishing in New Zealand
New Zealand: Hunters' Paradise
Holden on Hunting
The Deerstalkers
A Guide to Hunting in New Zealand
The Hunting Experience
Hunt South

WILD GAME

Hunting Gamebirds,
Small and Feral Game
in New Zealand

Philip Holden

Hodder & Stoughton

AUCKLAND LONDON SYDNEY TORONTO

For the Acclimatisation Societies of New Zealand —
what they initially stood for and what they stand for today.

Typeset by Glenfield Graphics Ltd, Auckland.
Printed and bound by Singapore National Printers Ltd for
Hodder & Stoughton Ltd, 44-46 View Road, Glenfield,
Auckland, New Zealand.

CONTENTS

Where relevant the author has used imperial measurements throughout this guide, so for those more familiar with metric, the following conversions are applicable:

1 inch	25.4 millimetres
1 foot (12 inches)	0.3048 metre
1 yard (3 feet)	0.9144 metre
1 mile (1,760 yards)	1.609 kilometres
1 acre (4,840 sq yards)	0.405 hectare
1 sq mile (640 acres)	259 hectares
1 pound	0.4536 kilogram

AUTHOR'S NOTE

Assembling a work such as this would have been impossible without a great deal of co-operation from a number of sources. My present-day research in the field, including photography, was made possible only by the generous assistance of the following people: Stuart Capil, Russell Evans (and family), Stella Sanders, Don McKenzie, Henry Maunder, Ron Munro, Ray and Olwyn Gibb, Graeme Middendorf, Peter Smits, Les Moody, Huia Prince, Hugh Creasy, and Carol Morrow, who, through her Southland business contacts, pointed my nose in the right direction on more than one occasion. I offer them all my heartfelt appreciation.

Generous assistance was again provided by Department of Conservation personnel: Roly Martin, Dick Marquand and Tom Kroos in Queenstown; Dick Veitch in Auckland; Kerry Potts, Mike Jebson, Barry Insull, Philip Brady and Jeff Flavell in Wellington.

Special thanks are also due to Pat Montgomery of the New Zealand Kennel Club; to Christine Grounsell and Lyn Nicholls of the Agricultural Pests Destruction Council; to Aldous McIvor of Landcorp; to R.B. Horsburgh and K.G. Patterson of the South Canterbury Wallaby Board; to Sid Hanson, National Secretary, NZ Clay Target Association; to Robbie Danks, President, Kennels Gun Club, Taradale; to Doug Dawson, Secretary, NZ Smallbore Rifle Association; to Brian Shepard, Secretary, Seddon Districts Gundog Society; to Ian Sarney, Secretary, New Zealand Small Game Shooters Association; and to Bob Badland of the NZ Mountain Safety Council.

To the many acclimatisation societies, whose most recent annual reports proved invaluable, very special thanks for responding so quickly to my requests for material. In particular, I should like to acknowledge Maurice Rodway (Southland), Brian Webb (North Canterbury), Niall Watson (Otago), and the Wellington-based trio of Bryce Johnson, Ralph Sutton and Brad Parkes. Importantly, the Wellington Acclimatisation Society granted me permission to use the maps of Lake Ellesmere and the West Coast forests of the lower North Island.

With regard to the photographs, a very warm greeting goes to both Simon Ayton and Les Hoffman for allowing me to join them on a duck hunting expedition up the Oreti River one freezing Southland morning. Believe me, the piping hot oyster soup — prepared by Les's father, Bob — was much appreciated! Similarly, Sean Boswell of the Alexandra Pest Destruction Board, now amalgamated into the Central Otago Pest Destruction District, couldn't have been more helpful while I was checking out the incredible rabbit situation in his part of the country.

At Glenorchy, Ron Stewart's expertise on Canada geese proved invaluable. An account of my delightful trip there is told in *Hunt South*. Also at Glenorchy, Peter 'Stretch' Lucas more than generously offered his assistance.

My thanks must also go to hunting guide, Joe Houghton, shown with a trophy wild ram taken by myself in the upper Mohaka River catchment early in 1986.

While the red-legged partridge is not yet a recognised gamebird in this country, it seems only a matter of time before it becomes one. Consequently, I considered it essential to include this exciting species in this work. The material relating to red-legged partridge was gathered and compiled from a variety of sources, the most significant being John Dyer, field officer with the Auckland Acclimatisation Society.

In closing, may I draw your attention to Appendix 9, which includes the reading matter to which I constantly referred. My appreciation to those authors, past and present, whose names appear there.

Philip Holden
Wellington, 1989

INTRODUCTION

Through necessity, our ancestors were hunters of birds and small animals, which both fed and clothed them. Waterfowl, for instance, were relentlessly pursued because of their abundance and edibility. Such birds are flightless for a short period — around three to four weeks — during the warmest season and, while they are 'moulting', can be easily rounded up and killed. Eskimos still round up geese when they are moulting and salt down huge numbers for use over winter.

We may presume that our ancestors initially killed their quarry in the most basic fashion — with small rocks or throwing sticks or clubs. Later came the bow and arrow, and nets. Ancient Egyptian wall paintings, dating back to around 1500 BC, depict ducks — some of which appear to be ruddy shelduck and marbled teal — being hunted with nets, throwing sticks, and bows and arrows.

Increasingly, hunters became more adept at taking waterfowl. Duck decoys, for example, were almost certainly in use during the reign of King John (1177-1216). Among the first decoys was a netted pipe, which contained a fox-like decoy dog or 'piper'. Naturally curious, ducks were lured from secluded ponds, swam into the mouth of the pipe, and inquisitively followed the decoy as it appeared round each successive screen. A similar decoy may have been used to catch the teal which were served in seven of the courses at the feast to celebrate William Warham becoming Archbishop of Canterbury in 1504.

Hunting waterfowl today may be undertaken on land or on water. A hunter can be in a hide, behind a blind or screen, in a pit, lying in low cover, or crouched under the low branches of bare willows along a known 'flightlane' for 'pass' shooting. Waterfowl can be actively stalked on or off their feeding or roosting grounds. They can be 'jump-shot' off a river or stream, called down, or lured to ground by decoys.

Expert stalkers of waterfowl are particularly familiar with their game. Their hunting is meticulously planned well in advance of the hunting season's opening day, and they know the feeding habits and roosting grounds of their chosen quarry.

They know, too, how the birds react to wind. In coastal areas, they are aware of how much influence the tides can have on the birds' behaviour. Enormous satisfaction can be gained by such knowledge. Indeed, for many such hunters the actual shooting becomes almost incidental. In the field, hunters need a fast, accurate shot. They also have the ability to recognise an approaching bird by its wingbeat and the general shape of its body against the indistinct light of dawn or late evening. They will demand and receive the utmost from their indispensable companions — their dogs. Down through the centuries hunter and dog have successfully teamed together to participate in a sport heavily steeped in tradition. Like the age-old pursuits of the red stag and wild boar, hunting waterfowl is the sport of Kings!

In Chapter 1, we look at the various waterfowl available to the New Zealand hunter. Covered here are their range, physical description, liberations and distribution, habitat and habits. Chapter 2 outlines what a hunter of waterfowl needs to know to succeed in the field. Subsequent chapters follow the same format and sequence for the other quarry covered in this book — upland gamebirds, small game animals, and goats and sheep.

1 WATERFOWL

MALLARD
(Anas platyrhynchos)

Male: Drake   Female: Duck   Young: Duckling

Range
This native of the cold or temperate regions of the northern hemisphere is the most widely distributed and certainly the best known duck in the world. Essentially, it is resident wherever climatic conditions are not too severe, thus the northern parts of Siberia and Alaska as well as a great deal of Canada (east of the Mackenzie River) can be excluded from its range.

The mallard is thought to breed from the Arctic Circle south to north-west Africa, the Azores, northern and temperate Asia, and North America. In the British Isles, where it is evenly distributed, it is a resident, a passing migrant, and a wintering visitor. Some northern hemisphere mallards winter as far south as the Canaries, northern Africa, southern Asia, and Central America.

The mallard is considered the ancestor of the common domestic duck, a possible reason why both may be frequently seen together on ponds of farms or on waters in parks and ornamental gardens. Other direct relations include:

Greenland mallard — A larger and lighter coloured bird than the common mallard, this breeds in southern Greenland and winters along the south-western coastline.

Hawaiian duck — The drake bears a striking resemblance to the female common mallard, both having a green wing-mirror. An endangered species found only in the Hawaiian Islands.

13

Mexican duck — Comparable in size to the common mallard. Again the drake is similar to the female common mallard. It is found from northern Mexico to the Rio Grande Valley, New Mexico.

Florida duck — Resembles the Mexican duck, and ranges from southern Florida, Louisiana and Texas through to the Gulf Coast of the Mexican border.

Liberations and Distribution in New Zealand
The first introduction of mallards into this country took place in 1867 when the Otago Acclimatisation Society obtained a pair from Melbourne. The same society took delivery of a further five birds in 1869, four in 1870, three in 1876, and nine in 1881. A number of these birds were taken north to Kakanui; others were sent to Riverton in Southland. Commenting on these early introductions, G.M. Thomson (1922) wrote: 'Apparently none of these introductions throve, for there is no record of their increase or distribution'.

Meanwhile, the Auckland Acclimatisation Society imported two in 1870 and four in 1886. All were retained for breeding purposes in the Domain. By 1873 the Canterbury society had 12 in their gardens. In 1893 the Wellington society imported 19, but unfortunately stoats and weasels eliminated almost all in their Masterton enclosures. The Otago society imported a further 21 in 1896, 10 of which were sent to Southland. Then between 1910 and 1918 the Southland society liberated about 1350 birds in its district. But, despite such vigorous attempts to firmly establish the world's most adaptable duck in various parts of the country, the overall results were considered extremely disappointing.

A possible explanation for this was the fact that all of the stock so far imported, including those from Melbourne in 1867, were of British origin. All had proved of a decidedly sedentary nature. They lacked the strongly developed migratory habits that were essential if the mallard was to become one of the principal gamebirds of the country.

The obvious answer was to import birds which were largely migratory — North American stock, say. This was first done in the 1930s by the Auckland society. Later, their captive-raised progeny were liberated throughout the entire district administered by that society. Birds were also distributed to the other societies for breeding and/or immediate release. From that point on, the mallard population exploded in all parts of the country, including the Chatham Islands (self-introduced).

Today, the mallard population is estimated to be about five million. Found in every acclimatisation society district in the country, the mallard is undoubtedly the mainstay of duck hunting in this country.

Physical Description

The average length of the mallard is 23-24 inches; the average weight of both sexes is 2½ pounds.

In full breeding attire, the male mallard cuts a dashing figure. His metallic-green head and neck are neatly separated from his body by a clear-cut white ring. The upper breast runs towards a rusty chestnut, while the underparts are delicately streaked with silver-grey. The upper wings are mostly grey-brown; the underwing cream. In the middle of the upper wing is a distinctive marking — an iridescent blue speculum bordered both front and back by a wide white stripe. The bill is an olive-brown, the iris dark brown, and the legs orange. The tail feathers, some of which curl upwards into a tight curl, are mostly black.

The overall colour of the female is a mottled buffy-brown, spotted with lighter and sometimes black markings. She has pale eyebrows and a dark irregular line running through her brown iris. Her wing also displays a blue mirror, although not as bright as that of the male. The bill is olive-brown, mottled with orange towards the tip. The legs are orange, except during the moult when they fade to an olive-brown. Unlike the male, the tail does not curl.

Immature birds are less strongly marked and considerably duller than the adults.

Habitat and Habits

Mallards have adapted better than any other species of duck to the changes made by humans. They are basically birds of fresh rather than salt water and are found on natural and artificial ponds, marshlands, streams, estuaries, and shallow lakes. Unless moulting or avoiding hunters, they shy away from deep water.

Normally they breed at one year old. Breeding follows an intricate mate selection ritual, consisting of elaborate plumage and swimming displays, which may begin as early as mid-March. Pairs team up in June. The territory is chosen close to water and the nest — a simple scrape in the ground — is located in long grasses, under bushes, logs, or among tree roots or not uncommonly, under a deserted farm building or a haystack.

The female makes herself comfortable on the nest, and with her mate on guard duty, she begins laying in July. She does so at daily intervals, usually in the early morning. She leaves the nest twice daily to feed for short intervals, hiding the buff-green eggs under a layer of down stripped from her tail feathers. Oddly enough, the male soon abandons his partner, leaving to the female the sole responsibility of raising the ducklings.

On average she will lay 13-14 eggs and incubation takes 27-28 days. Should a clutch be lost — flooding is a common cause — she will re-nest. The ducklings are taken to water within hours of hatching. They are attractively marked with black-brown tones above and bright yellow faces, underparts, and sides.

The food preferences of the species consist of the seeds and stems of aquatic and pond-edge plants. Like geese, mallards also graze on agricultural crops — ie, ripening grain, corn stubble, and newly sown grasses. They may also grub up crops under the soil, such as potatoes. Insects are readily taken.

The fledgling period lasts 10 weeks, with about six ducklings per clutch surviving to take to the air. This ratio equals that of breeding mallards in Europe and is higher than that recorded for the species in the United States. Certainly it is the highest reproduction rate of any of New Zealand's wetland gamebirds.

Following the breeding season, which may extend to December, the moult takes place. Flightless for about three weeks, mallards gather for safety in countless numbers on large expanses of water. After dark they venture ashore, feeding alertly about the water's edge.

Mallards are extremely strong fliers. They can lift or jump straight up off the water into immediate flight. At top speed they can attain 80 km/h.

GREY DUCK
(*Anas superciliosa*)

Male: Drake Female: Duck Young: Duckling

Range
The grey duck — also known by its Maori name of parera — is native to New Zealand. Two closely related subspecies are also found in the southern hemisphere:

Black duck — While it is very similar in size and appearance to the grey duck, the black duck of Australia is not as strikingly marked, particularly about the face. Found throughout Australia, it is especially numerous in the Riverina and on the East Coast.

Lesser grey duck — Similar in appearance, but smaller than the other two related subspecies, the lesser grey duck inhabits the northern highlands and Orange Mountains of New Guinea, as well as many islands to the north of New Zealand and east of Australia, among them New Caledonia, Samoa, Fiji, Vanuatu and Tonga.

Distribution in New Zealand
Today, it is extremely difficult to realise how prolific the grey duck once was in this country. In pre-European times, for instance, it occupied virtually every type of wetland. The Pakeha's traumatic impact on the land, in particular the transformation of natural wetlands to highly developed regions, was a disaster for the species. Over 90 per cent of its food is obtained in wetlands and unlike the mallard, it does not feed on agricultural land.

Nevertheless, the grey duck was still extremely numerous when the various acclimatisation societies held their first shooting season. As recently as the late 1950s they still remained the most common of all New Zealand's wetlands gamebirds, and few hunters failed to take their daily bag limits. Indeed, at that time they made up 95 per cent of the overall dabbling duck population.

But gradually, and certainly from 1960 onwards, the more aggressive and certainly more adaptable mallard took control of the habitat that the grey duck may have adapted to in time — stock ponds, for instance. As a consequence, the shyer grey duck retreated along with the declining wetlands. Today, only 14 per cent of the natural wetlands which existed a mere century ago remain.

By 1970, the grey duck numbered about 1.5 million, a decade later 1.2 million. Now they may number one million, a fifth of which are shot each hunting season. As long as wetlands remain, their future is not in doubt.

While they are listed as a legal gamebird in every district controlled by the various acclimatisation societies, they are rare in areas where agriculture is prominent. The wild wetlands of the West Coast and parts of Northland spring readily to mind as places where the grey duck can still be considered common. This also applies to the extensive areas of swamps, rivers, and lakes found in the Waikato.

Physical Description
The grey duck may be described as a dark brown bird. The male is a little larger than the female, with a body length of around 21-23 inches. He may weigh up to 2½ pounds, about 10 to 15 per cent heavier than the female.

The sexes are similar in appearance. The top of the head and the back of the neck are dark brown. The light creamy face is marked with two prominent black stripes, the most significant one running from the top of the bill through the eye to behind the ear, while the other one angles across the lower face from the bottom of the bill. These conspicuous facial markings readily distinguish the species from the female mallard, which, while marked with similar stripes, lacks the creamy face and throat.

The body feathers are dull brown with paler edges; underparts are a lighter brown, again with similar greyish or buffy white edges. The upper surface of the wing is dark, a contrasting background to a glossy green patch — the speculum. This is set in the middle of the wing, and has black borders and a fine white bar on the trailing edge. In contrast, the speculum of the mallard is blue. The grey duck's underwing is mostly white.

The iris is reddish-brown, the bill is grey-green with a black tip, and the legs are yellow-green with dusky webs. Immature birds are similar, but perhaps a little duller, than adults.

Habitat and Habits

We have already briefly discussed the preferred habitat of the grey duck — ie, wetlands well away from human interference. There they occupy shallow water. Like a mallard, they take their food on the surface or just below, but are just as likely to up-end themselves to dredge from the bottom. The design of their bills — with rough, knife-like serrations on the upper and lower bill — permits them to feed either by biting or filtering.

Grey ducks eat a wide range of aquatic plantlife. Native pondweeds are easily clipped off with their bills. Also eagerly sought after are the seeds of the various sedges, and below the surface, the bulbous fruits of the underwater growth. Animal matter makes up perhaps 10 per cent of their intake. Highly rated are the tiny freshwater crabs and snails, and the larvae of midges and caddis flies. They are ever on the alert for tasty flies, moths, beetles, caterpillars and worms. Like all wetland gamebirds they partake of freshwater crustacea and molluscs.

Like other species of wild duck, grey ducks are a gregarious lot. They often mix with mallards, and some interbreeding takes place. As a rule, they breed a little later than mallards, starting in the second or third week of August. The entire process of their breeding season — the courtship displays, selecting of a mate and nest-site, the way in which the male leaves his mate while she is incubating the eggs — is so similar to that of the mallard that we need only comment on those few points where we know they differ.

Firstly, they appear to be more secretive than the mallard at this time of the year. They may also nest above the ground in a tree trunk or in the fork of a branch. Nests have been found as high as 10 metres above the ground. However, they prefer to nest on the ground. Secondly, the size of the clutch is usually 10, and the eggs are a creamy-white.

NEW ZEALAND SHOVELER
(Anas rhyncotis)

Male: Drake   Female: Duck   Young: Duckling

Range

The New Zealand shoveler belongs to a rather select group of four species of dabbling ducks with long spatulate (spoon-shaped) bills:

Northern shoveler — Considered extremely difficult to distinguish from the local variety of shoveler, this is the only species found in the northern hemisphere. It breeds in Europe, Asia, and North America. Common in the British Isles, it is, like the mallard, a resident, partial migrant, and winter visitor. The European and Asian populations winter in tropical Africa, India, Burma, Ceylon, Vietnam, southern China, and Japan. North American birds head to the southern states, Mexico, the West Indies and Colombia.

Red shoveler — Regarded as the most graceful of shovelers, it is found in the southern half of South America, ranging from Cuzco in Peru, through Bolivia, southern Brazil, Paraguay, Uruguay, Chile, and Argentina (excluding the Andes), then south to Tierra del Fuego. It is an infrequent visitor to the Falkland Islands. The more southern populations move north to a warmer climate in winter.

Blue-winged (or Australian) shoveler — Again remarkably like the New Zealand shoveler, this species has a broad range and extends from Cape York in Queensland, south-west throughout New South Wales, Victoria, Tasmania, the south-eastern half of South Australia, and south-west Australia. Since Australian shovelers frequently make landfall in New Zealand, it is possible that, like the pukeko, the New Zealand shoveler had its origins on the other side of the Tasman Sea.

Distribution in New Zealand

Known to the Maori as kuru whengi, and by the Pakeha as spoonbill or spoonie, the shoveler is a far-ranging species. Sedentary they most certainly are not! For example, birds banded at Invercargill have turned up as far away as Kaitaia in Northland. Young birds banded in the Waikato have been recorded as far south as the Taieri wetlands in Otago. Later they returned home to breed. Little wonder then that stragglers have turned up on the Chatham Islands from time to time, and that three birds have been recorded on Auckland Island.

The shoveler, normally found well below 300 metres, is widespread in this country where suitable habitat occurs. They are estimated to number 150,000, of which about 30,000 are shot each year. They are legal game in every district controlled by acclimatisation societies.

Physical Description

Of all the ducks found in New Zealand, the male shoveler in full plumage is undoubtedly the most brightly garbed. A little larger than the female, he has a body length of 19-21 inches and weighs a little more than half that of the adult mallard — about 1½ pounds. His head is a bluish or steely blue-grey with a green gloss, the base of the bill is black, and a prominent white crescent line is in front of the eyes. His chest is dark brown with white and light-brown flecking; the abdomen is a striking rich chestnut. The back and rump are black; the tail dark brown, again with a dark-green gloss. A distinct white mark, like a patch, is found on the flank. The upper wing coverts are pale blue, the speculum dark green with a white triangular band in front of it; the underwing is white. The iris is red, or possibly running towards yellow, and the legs and feet are a bright orange.

Uniformly mottled, the adult female is mainly buff or dark brown, with yellowish feet and legs and brown iris. Immature birds resemble the adult female but with less conspicuous markings.

Habitat and Habits

Like all of the previously mentioned dabbling ducks, shovelers are naturally drawn to shallow water. They prefer lowland, freshwater ponds, lagoons, lakes, and heavily vegetated swamp-lands. Seldom are they seen on fast-flowing water.

Shovelers are almost exclusively protein feeders, filtering water or mud with their broad, sieve-like bills for freshwater invertebrates. Tiny snails and crabs are a special delicacy. Small aquatic plantlife — ie, the common duckweed (lemna) — is regularly eaten. On flooded pasture shovelers seek worms and other insects not found in the water.

For much of the year they are seen in small groups or pairs. They are quiet, largely unobtrusive birds, considerably more wary than mallards or grey ducks. Often they choose to rest in thick cover during the day, and they never perch in trees.

In June or early July, however, they gather together in large flocks around low-lying ponds and lagoons. Here they will pair up after the normal courtship displays and the inevitable fighting, which breaks out among the males if only because they outnumber the females by two to one.

Once male and female have paired up, they seek a quiet area to breed — possibly near a secluded pond with plenty of natural cover around it. With quite remarkable ferocity the male will defend both it and his mate from the attentions of frustrated males unfortunate enough not to have a partner.

Both male and female seek a nest site. It is a simple affair, a mere depression in the ground lined with dry grass. Definitely it will be well concealed, and a spot not likely to be flooded.

Eggs are laid in October or November. The females lay one creamy-white egg (with an occasional greenish tinge) a day. The normal clutch size is 9-13. Only when she has finished laying does the incubation period begin. The male will have none of this and, like the male mallard and grey duck, soon flies off to live the carefree life of a bachelor bird.

For about 25 days the female leads a very restricted life, taking a break from her sole responsibility to feed only once or twice a day. But at last it's all over and the eggs break. The ducklings are dressed mostly in dark down. The female looks after them well, often keeping them hidden in thick cover.

The young birds fledge at 8-10 weeks. Once they can fly, they team up with other similarly aged birds and, more likely than not, wander far from where they were born.

PUKEKO
(Porphyrio porphyrio)

Male: Cock   Female: Hen   Young: Chick

Range
The pukeko belongs to the Gruiformes family, which includes many cranes and rails in various parts of the world. Although it is classified as a native bird, the pukeko in all probability arrived here from Australia some 10-15,000 years ago. Known as the swamp hen (*Porphyrio porphyrio*) in Australia, where it is found in every state, the species is particularly widespread in New South Wales, Victoria, and Tasmania. Allied forms occur in South America, Africa, southern Europe, India, parts of the Middle East, south-east Asia, and some Pacific Islands. In the British Isles, the common water hen (*Gallinula chloropus*) bears a striking resemblance to the pukeko, while its habits and clutch-size of similarly marked eggs is wellnigh identical.

Distribution in New Zealand
The pukeko is found throughout New Zealand, a situation that almost certainly existed when the Maori arrived here. They also called it 'pukaki' or 'pakura', and all of these may be found in numerous Maori placenames.

Today the species — estimated to number in excess of 600,000 — is by far the most widespread of all New Zealand's wetland gamebirds. Essentially a bird of lowland swamps, they naturally favour low-lying, high rainfall areas. This is why they are even more plentiful in the wetter, western regions of both the North and South islands than they are in the eastern districts.

Physical Description
About the size of a small hen, the male pukeko has a body length of 20-21 inches and weighs about 2½ pounds; the female is only a little smaller.

23

The sexes are alike in appearance. The most prominent feature is the bright red bill and frontal shield, and the iridescent purplish-blue neck, throat and chest. The upper part of the body, including the head, is sooty black, occasionally glossed over with green or turquoise. A purplish-blue tinge may extend to the otherwise black flanks and belly. A conspicuous white patch is found under the tail. The underwing is a glossy black, the iris is red, and the long legs are a brownish-red.

Immature birds differ from adults in that their bill and frontal shield are a reddish-black, while their legs are dark brown, tinged with orange. The iris is a different colour — a brownish-black to olive tone. Their chest, although mostly blue, lacks the glossiness characteristic of the adult bird.

Habitat and Habits
Essentially, suitable habitat is fresh or brackish water, including lakes, ponds, streams, creeks and rivers.

Like the paradise shelduck, the pukeko also adapted to the drastic changes Europeans made to New Zealand's heavily forested landscape. They learned to exploit agricultural regions, so that crops and pasturelands also became popular places to forage. Unlike the grey duck, they wisely utilised artificial stock ponds; basically any type of wet area, however small, will suffice this most versatile species. Consequently, huge areas of previously unsuitable habitat opened up for them; the central parts of the North Island are a typical example.

Pukeko have the longest breeding season of any wetland gamebird in this country. It extends from August to February and peaks in September through to December. Occasionally newly hatched chicks may be observed as late as March.

Territories are chosen in late July or early August. They may be occupied by birds of strong territorial instincts, or, more commonly, by those in favour of a communal lifestyle — three to six birds as a rule.

Competition for prime nesting areas is fierce, particularly where lone males are concerned. Fighting may also break out in communal areas before a male has established himself in a dominant role. Surprisingly they use their sharply clawed feet, rather than their murderously designed beaks, to fight with.

Nest sites are chosen in long rushes or in other dense vegetation. The nest is a large, bulky affair fashioned from loose vegetation, best described as a bowl-like platform that, while incubation takes place, is constantly added to.

The female lays five or six eggs. Buff coloured, they are marked with irregular blotches and smeared with grey and brown, and, possibly, mauve tonings. Birds in groups may even share nests and it is not unusual for two or three broods to be raised in a season.

The male shares the incubation. During this period, his behaviour towards his mate is in direct contrast to that shown by the male mallard and grey duck. Indeed, the pukeko mating pair carry on pretty much as they did during their mate-selection process, with much mutual preening and bill-nibbling.

Incubation takes 24 days. The chicks are dressed in black down. They are watched over with concern during the first week of their lives and are usually well concealed from predators. The adults bring food to them — initially the flesh of animals, which, of course, is rich in protein. Stealthfully the adults stalk their prey, armed with a formidable weapon — a large, razor-edged beak that is capable of slicing through the toughest vegetation or holding small birds and fish in a vice-like grip.

Around the country, pukeko — like other gamebirds — arouse the anger of horticulturists and orchardists by feeding on crops and fruits. For example, within the Auckland district between 1 September 1986 and 31 August 1987 pukeko caused damage to sweetcorn at Dairy Flat, potatoes and sweetcorn at Paremoremo, Bombay and Manurewa, Asian pears at Cambridge, export flower crops at Drury, strawberries at Clevedon, tree seedlings at Ngaruawahia and watermelons at Tuakau. In addition, they fouled horse-feed bins at Pukekohe and Whitford as well as stock water troughs at Clevedon and Whitford.

The chicks begin to forage with their parents in their second week. They soon discover that their scissor-like beak is a versatile tool. With it they can neatly clip off grasses and clover (a special favourite), wrench off shoots, strip seeds from plants, and dig up roots or whatever else they may fancy under the ground.

Animal matter will figure prominently in their food intake

— insects, snails, flies, moths, and spiders are but a few examples of what they regularly feed on.

The young birds also learn that it makes sense to eat in the manner of a parrot, with their food held firmly between the long, flexible toes (or claws) of one foot. Again, like a parrot, they tend to nibble rather than bite at their food.

Pukeko are known to feed on carrion and some duck hunters swear they prey heavily on eggs and ducklings. It is difficult to believe that such an indiscriminate feeder would choose to ignore such helpless offerings should it stumble across them. This, I feel, would especially hold true when adult birds are hunting live game to feed their ravenous young. How could they resist a duckling?

At about three months, the young birds can fly. When summer ranges tend to dry up, many juvenile birds will look elsewhere for more suitable habitat.

PARADISE SHELDUCK
(*Tadorna variegata*)

Male: Drake   Female: Duck   Young: Duckling

Range
Shelducks belong to a select group of seven species of waterfowl considered intermediate between ducks and geese. They are:

Common shelduck — Breeds in the British Isles, northern France, the Netherlands, Germany, Denmark, Scandinavia, the Balkans, the Caucasus, and across central Asia to northern China. Wintering areas include Spain, the Mediterranean, north Africa, Iran, northern India, southern China and Japan.

Ruddy shelduck — Breeds in the Atlas region of Morocco and Algeria, Greece, Romania, Turkey, Iraq, Iran, most of central Asia east to Mongolia and China, south to Tibet. Wintering ranges include Spain, the Nile Valley, Burma, Thailand, Vietnam, and Korea.

South African shelduck — Widespread in South Africa — ie, Cape Province, Orange Free State, and southern Transvaal.

Moluccan Radjah shelduck — Confined to the Moluccas, Aru Islands, and New Guinea.

Australian Radjah — Found along the north and north-east coasts from Derby in Western Australia to Rockhampton in Queensland.

Australian shelduck or mountain duck — Found in Western Australia (including offshore islands), south-east New South Wales, western Victoria, and Tasmania.

Paradise shelduck — Native to New Zealand (refer 'Distribution in New Zealand' for range).

27

Distribution in New Zealand

When the first European settlers arrived in this country, the paradise shelduck was mostly confined to the Wairarapa and eastern parts of the South Island. But the ensuing transformation of the land — from forest to pasture — would gradually open up an entirely new habitat for the species. Succulent clover and rye grew where trees once stood tall or dense scrub had choked the land. The paradise shelduck took full advantage of this and progressively increased its range.

By the latter part of the nineteenth century the paradise shelduck, due to large-scale slaughter, was thought to be declining in numbers over much of its range. To offset this they were granted intermittent protection.

As pointed out by M. Williams (1981), it is not generally realised that North Island liberations of paradise shelduck — from Southland stock — were made on the central Volcanic Plateau (National Park) between the years 1916-1921. They increased dramatically in numbers and soon spread towards Wanganui, Taihape, and east to Hawke's Bay. The establishment of stock ponds — a linking chain, in effect — provided them with ideal places about which to claim their territories and bring up their ducklings. By about 1944 they had spread to Gisborne. In the late 1960s, about 500 birds were transplanted from the Gisborne district to North Auckland. The results were spectacular.

Today the paradise shelduck has a broad range in this country, also inhabiting Stewart, Great Barrier, Kapiti, and D'Urville islands. Periodically, stragglers turn up on the Chatham Islands, where, just prior to European settlement taking place, they were exterminated. There is every possibility they will re-establish themselves there naturally.

Strong concentrations of paradise shelduck are found over much of Northland, where in 1988 the Department of Conservation carried out an aerial survey of moulting birds. They considered that the Hobson and Whangarei population had reached a new high, possibly numbering upwards of 5000.

Poverty Bay has also seen a dramatic increase in their numbers, as has the Tauranga district.

The same can be said for much of Hawke's Bay, where

in 1988 the local acclimatisation society considered the shelducks 'were holding their own' around Taihape (with its abundance of artificial stock ponds); and Wanganui, where in the same year, that society reported:

> The capture and leg banding identification programme continued this year in conjunction with the Department of Conservation. The assistance from councillors and volunteers ensured that this research work was carried out efficiently and well. A significant increase of numbers on moulting sites was later confirmed in a larger number of paradise shelduck kill returns.

Paradise ducks, according to the Stratford society, are now established throughout that district. Over 1,000 birds were banded there by the society and DOC in February 1988. In his wildlife report for that year the president of that society, T.H. Sinclair, wrote: 'We must keep control of the Paradise duck to make sure it does not become a nuisance.'

This same trend continues in the Wellington district as evidenced by the good returns for the 1988 gamebird season. Also in the same year the Nelson society reported:

> The population of Paradise has remained fairly constant over the last eight years and the birds were there before the season started. Usually a lot are taken on the opening weekend on the Matakitaki Station and in the Maruia Valley. The birds were not in these places in their usual numbers on opening day but for some reason or other they returned later when some good bags were taken in all these areas as well as in the Tutaki Valley and around the Howard where on one occasion a party took 46 birds for the day.

In nearby Marlborough the population was thought to number 11,000. As can be seen from this extract from the Waitaki Valley (1988 Otago Acclimatisation Society annual reports) the same trend continues well to the south:

> It is encouraging to hear of hunting parties concentrating some of their efforts on Paradise Shelduck. In the Hakataramea Valley and in high country areas large flocks of these birds cause problems on newly emerging pastures or on greenfeed crops.
>
> Because of the upward trend in population the bag limit was increased for the 1988-89 season. Affected landowners believe that the increase in the bagged limit has had little impact on the Shelduck population.
>
> On one property in the Haka Valley during the season 1,050

Shelduck were observed feeding in one barley stubble paddock. Other smaller populations were observed in the vicinity. It is estimated that over 2,000 Shelduck were feeding in the lower half of the Haka Valley. In the Omarama-Ohau region flocks of up to 400 were hunted during the season.

Strong concentrations of paradise shelduck also occur in Canterbury — near the Southern Alps but not on the Canterbury Plains — and in other parts of Otago.

Beyond the Southern Alps, hunters in Westland place much emphasis on this species, as the 1987 acclimatisation society report indicates:

> Paradise Shelduck remain an important component of local hunters' bags. It is interesting to note that the importance of this species increases as the season progresses with parrys making up only 15 per cent of birds shot at opening weekend. By the end of the season this figure has risen to give a whole season average of 30 per cent, the highest for any species. Trend counts carried out by the society over the past six years indicate that the population may be stabilising at a figure of around 6000 birds, following a peak in 1984 of 8157 birds.

During the 1987 summer moult, shelduck were rounded up and banded at four traditional moulting sites within the Westland district:

Banding Station	Total Banded	Number Recovered
L. Brunner	253	10
L. Haupiri	400	17
Ikamatua	521	11
Orwell Creek	583	15
	1757	53

In commenting on this (and previous banding programmes carried out in 1985/86) the society published results of how far some 'recaptured' birds had travelled. Generally birds were recovered within 60 kilometres of the banding site. A few birds travelled greater distances. Two birds banded at Lake Brunner were recovered at Tadmor and Mataki Station near Murchison, distances of 165 and 100 kilometres respectively. A bird banded at Lake Brunner in 1987 was recovered this game season at Waiau Ferry, near Hanmer, a distance of 120 kilometres.

During my own recent field forays in Southland, I soon

realised how large the paradise shelduck population was there. So it came as no surprise when I read this extract from that acclimatisation society's 1987 annual report:

Paradise Shelduck Management

The population of paradise shelduck in Southland is now at a very healthy level and this can be attributed to two factors. One is the restricted hunting regulations imposed by the Society and the other is the massive land development programme that has been carried out in Northern and Western Southland in recent years. The breeding population in the traditional areas is now at saturation point and this is evidenced by the appearance of breeding pairs throughout Southland.

Of all gamebirds we deal with the paradise shelduck is the easiest for us to manage for the following reasons:

1. An accurate count of the non-breeding population (moult count) can be made each summer.
2. The paradise duck is easily decoyed and therefore numbers can be regulated by shooting.
3. Banding results show the birds are largely sedentary.

As our hunter numbers are nearly static we only have to alter season length or bag limit to increase or decrease our kill and we can monitor the effect by our moult counts. One complication to this is hunter attitudes which change over the years. Staff are pleased to report more shooters are using decoys and hunting the mobs of young birds rather than chasing the old pairs around. A breeding pair is far more valuable to the future population than two young birds. Preliminary results from 1987 diary returns indicate that in excess of 10,000 paradise shelducks were harvested in Southland this season. With careful management there is no reason why this cannot continue.

Presently, then, the future of paradise shelduck in this country couldn't be more assured. We are indeed fortunate that this is the case. A native species that 'pairs' for life must be conserved for future generations of naturalists and hunters at all costs.

Physical Description

The adult male paradise shelduck has a body length of 25-27 inches and weighs around 3¼ pounds. The adult female has a body length of 23-24 inches and weighs up to 3 pounds.

Called the 'painted duck' by Captain Cook, the paradise shelduck is a strikingly attired bird. Of the sexes the female is by far the more conspicuous — her pure white head and neck contrast sharply against her rich chestnut breast and belly, and dark-grey back and tail. The male is much more sombre in appearance — his head, neck, and back are black. His back, however, is finely lined with pale grey. His belly, flecked with pale yellow, is only a little lighter in colour than his back.

In all other aspects the sexes are the same — the upper and lower wing coverts are white, the primaries black, and the secondaries metallic green. The iris and bill are also black, while the legs are best described as being a shiny blackish-grey. The undertail is chestnut, possibly brighter on the female.

Immature birds of both sexes look like young males from a distance. The female, however, already has a large white patch at the base of her bill. As she grows, this patch enlarges. Eventually, it will encompass both her head and neck.

Newly hatched ducklings are mostly white, with a brown head, a brown stripe running from the base of the head to the tail, and another brown mark on both flanks and wings.

Habitat and Habits
Big South Island river systems, with their wide gravel and grassy flats, are favoured habitat of the paradise shelduck. So too are the high country lakes, where, for instance, you will also find Canada geese. In *Hunt South* I told of visiting Diamond Lake in Otago. Like the Canada geese that lived there all year, the paradise shelduck were also moulting. It is typical for them to gather at such places around the country when — for roughly a three to four-week period — they are unable to fly. Large stretches of water — dams, tarns, rivers, and of course, lakes — offer them a far greater degree of safety while they are so handicapped.

Moving closer to the coastal regions of both sides of the Southern Alps, paradise shelduck are less common. But isolated pairs can be readily observed along stream banks, swampy soaks, and natural wetlands. Some may be well inland, feeding on pastures and crops. This is especially true of the North Island, where they are mostly found on grazed pastures near stock ponds or lagoons. Farmers are often distressed by the way in which they foul the land, although not to the same extent as Canada geese.

Wetlands are essential for the survival of waterfowl.
This attractive spot, called Redcliffs Wildlife Refuge,
is one of 11 such wildlife sanctuaries in Southland.

The mallard is the world's most prominent dabbling duck,
and the mainstay of waterfowl hunting in New Zealand.
The male bird is shown here in full plumage.

In contrast to the male, the female mallard is a drab-
coloured bird. Here, in mid-December, her brown,
down-covered chicks have striking facial markings;
the fledgling period lasts about 10 weeks.

Hunting the grey teal (*below*) is prohibited, but many
are killed by mistake for grey ducks or shovelers.

Looking out over Lake Rotoiti, near Rotorua, on a gloomy summer's morning. All types of waterfowl readily congregate here, including the grey duck (*below*). Once common throughout New Zealand's vast wetlands regions the grey duck is, by its conspicuous facial markings, easily identified in the field. Its green speculum, a distinct patch in the middle of the wing, differs from the blue marking of the mallard.

The New Zealand shoveler is also known as the spoonbill or spoonie. The male bird, shown here with its mate, is the most brightly coloured of all New Zealand waterfowl. A shyer bird than the mallard, they show a marked preference for lowland, freshwater ponds and lakes, and are seldom seen on fast-flowing water.

The glossy-garbed pukeko is the most widespread of New Zealand's wetlands gamebirds. Unlike the less adaptable grey duck, they have learned how best to exploit the European impact on the landscape.

Paradise shelduck first feel the urge to mate in their second or third year. Females nearing maturity set great store in teaming up with a strong, aggressive male. To find one they engage in ritualistic courtship displays and incite the poor young fellows with high-pitched, excited calls to do battle with one another. The females then choose a mate from among the more successful fighters.

There are deep-rooted reasons for this process: paradise shelduck mate for life and, as they are strictly 'territorial' for about 10 months of the year (the remaining time is spent at communal moulting sites), it is essential for the female's sense of well-being that her partner is more than adequate to protect both her and their specific patch of turf. They remain faithful to each other, only choosing a new mate should the other die. Which is all too likely during the hunting season when approximately 8,000-10,000 birds are shot.

With the October-November breeding season fast drawing to a close, a 'new' pair of paradise shelduck seek out unoccupied territory. It must contain a body of water and suitably damp areas where various grasses flourish. Paradise shelduck are essentially grass-eaters — ie, their bill is designed for cutting vegetation.

Feeling a strong desire for privacy — they are young lovers, after all — a pair will select an area that allows them and other birds in the same general vicinity plenty of elbow-room, which explains why pairs of paradise shelduck are generally well spaced out in a river valley.

They set about looking for a nest-site the following August, selecting a well-concealed spot under a fallen haystack, even a deserted building. Other birds prefer the enclosed space of a rocky crevice, below a bank, inside a hollow log. Only rarely will they nest in the hole of a tree well above ground level.

At a rate of one a day, the female lays 8-10 eggs directly onto the ground. Ten eggs is a very common number, but as many as 15 have been recorded. She alone incubates them for a period of 30-32 days. At this time, she also plucks down from her breast. This is used to cover the eggs when she is away from the nest, which both conceals them and also retains heat.

The female takes an essential break from her duties every four or five hours for an hour's duration. The male will remain by her side, ever watchful. They return together to the nest, the male usually alighting on a nearby vantage point in the middle of the territory.

Once the eggs are hatched, the male watches over the ducklings while the female is away — an easy chore for they are only in the nest for about a day before proud parents take them to water. The fledgling stage lasts about 8 weeks. In the early stages the youngsters feed mostly on aquatic insects, but it isn't long before they are feeding alongside their parents. Apart from aquatic insects, other preferred foods include swamp and pond grasses, young rye grass, clover shoots (a special delight), grains, seedheads, wheat and maize stubble, earthworms, and, near the coast, crustaceans.

There is a high mortality rate among ducklings and, before the family leaves for the moulting site, approximately half of them will have died. When the moulting period is over, the older birds return to their territory and the young birds mingle together, forming large flocks. Those in the vast empty spaces of the South Island travel greater distances than those in the more settled country far to the north. They will remain in flocks until the age-old instinct to team up with a suitable partner becomes too strong to ignore.

BLACK SWAN
(*Cygnus atratus*)

Male: Cob   Female: Pen   Young: Cygnet

Range

There are six true swans in the world — that is, those birds which belong to the genus Cygnus. They are:

Mute swan — Breeding range includes the British Isles, Denmark, the Netherlands, southern Sweden, Germany, Romania, Russia, and east to Mongolia and Manchuria. It was introduced as a park bird to a number of countries, including New Zealand (1866), Australia, and the United States.

Bewick's swan — Almost all breeding occurs in the tundra regions of northern Russia and Siberia. Birds found in the eastern regions of this range winter over in China and Japan, while those inhabiting the western portions do so in the British Isles, France, the Netherlands, West Germany and Denmark.

Whooper swan — Breeding takes place over an extensive area of northern Europe and Asia. In winter they may be found as far south as the Mediterranean, the Black Sea, and the Caspian Sea.

Trumpeter swan — Breeds in the northern parts of the United States — ie, Montana, Idaho, and Wyoming — and in Canada and Alaska (the present-day stronghold of the species). The Alaskan population tends to be more migratory, spending winters along the coastline of British Columbia.

Black-necked swan — Found in the southern half of South America, with breeding taking place in Brazil, Uruguay, Paraguay, Argentina, Chile, and the Falkland Islands. Apart from the Falkland Islands population (which is non-migratory), the species, and especially those birds breeding in the southernmost parts of this range, head north during winter.

Black swan — Australia's only native swan has a wide range and particularly large concentrations are found in the south-east and south-western parts of the country. Vagrants also occur in the drier central parts and, while it is not classified as a tropical bird, it may also turn up in the far north.

Liberations and Distribution in New Zealand
The Nelson Acclimatisation Society was behind the first introduction of black swans into this country. The actual consignment of five birds arrived from Sydney on board the *Prince Alfred* in December 1863. They were placed in the Eel Pond, the site of the present-day Queen's Gardens. Society officials issued stern warnings to curious boys against harming or disturbing the new arrivals.

Undisturbed, then, the black swans quickly settled into their new environment. They bred well. By April 1867 they numbered 23. They continued to breed until early in 1873, at which time all but one bird took wing in search of new pastures.

Left on its own, and apparently unconcerned, the remaining bird became extremely tame. Soon it took to wandering away from its watery home. It would, however, have been better advised to fly off in search of its mates, as this extract from the *Examiner* of 26 June 1873 proves:

A Wanton Outrage
On Wednesday last, a man named James Sutherland was charged under the Protection of Animals Act, with killing in Trafalgar Street a Black Swan.

Often of an evening it would walk down Bridge Street, up Trafalgar Street and back by way of Hardy Street, calling at the hotels, or at houses where he found street doors open, getting fed with bread. The harmless creature was caught by Sutherland in the passage between Joseph's and the Masonic Hotel in Trafalgar Street, on Monday evening and killed. Fortunately Constable Shore saw him drive the swan into the passage, where the bird was found dead. Sutherland was fined £5 and 9s costs, and in default of payment, was sentenced to 14 days imprisonment in gaol, with hard labour.

In the meantime, black swans had been introduced into the North Island, presumably by Sir George Grey in 1864. It was again in 1864 that Grey presented two pairs of these birds to the Canterbury Acclimatisation Society, who, in turn, liberated them on the Avon River.

One pair took up residence on a watercress-choked stretch of the river at Riccarton, on the farm of a certain Mrs Deans. It soon became apparent, because of the way they were clearing the succulent growth, that black swans considered watercress extremely tasty fodder.

At this time the Christchurch City Council was faced with the serious undertaking of clearing the river of this prolific growth. The local acclimatisation society viewed it with no less concern — watercress was a major deterrent to the development of the trout they intended to liberate there.

At any rate, the idea of using swans as a means of controlling watercress was first voiced at a meeting of the council in August 1864. A special 'Committee of Swans' was formed to consider the feasibility of such a proposal. In due course the committee visited the Deans' farm, saw for themselves the grand job the swans were doing, and returned to their council with the strong recommendation that a number of black swans be purchased forthwith. Presently, 13 pairs of black swans arrived from Sydney at a cost of £71.

Further south, the Otago Acclimatisation Society liberated 61 black swans between 1866-1870, and the Southland society released six in 1869. By then the numbers in Canterbury had increased amazingly, especially on Lake Ellesmere. Indeed, the numbers continued to swell in that vicinity — in March 1871 as many as 300 were observed on a lagoon at the mouth of the Halswell River.

Early naturalists, among them Thomas Kirk, believed that the black swan reached this country naturally within this same period of intense acclimatisation. The year 1867, when countless white-eyed ducks and silvereyes crossed the Tasman, may be considered a probable date when this first took place. The occasional swan, or swans, may still make the same journey.

By the early 1880s the black swan was firmly established in the coastal wetlands of much of the South Island and in the lower half of the North Island. An earlier introduction to Chatham Island had also proved successful.

Today, the black swan is widespread in New Zealand.

Numbers are thought to exceed 60,000, with approximately a further 3,000 found at Te Whaanga Lagoon on Chatham Island. A reason for their high numbers is that they are not held in high esteem as a sporting bird by most hunters.

The same lack of interest by hunters continues to the south-east:

> [The black swan is] possibly on a slight increase, due partly to many shooters getting sentimental towards the 'longnecks' and letting them fly on. Nice to know there are conservationists among us.
> — Hawke's Bay Acclimatisation Society, 1988

Again, shooters in the Wanganui district put down 2,624 mallards in 1988, but only 16 black swans were taken, though admittedly a one-bird bag limit applied.

Only in the Wellington area did hunters do something positive about the black swan population:

Black Swan	Opening Weekend	Rest of Season
Manawatu	—	853
Wellington	—	15
Wairarapa	552	2,430
Rangitikei	15	230
	567	3,528

Lake Ellesmere in Canterbury still remains a stronghold of the species in the South Island. Shoreline counts conducted by DOC in February 1988 added up to a staggering 10,385 birds. Shooters in this area seem reluctant to hunt them and the local society fears, with some justification, that, 'unless we control their numbers we could have complaints from the farmers'. A sobering note upon which to end this segment.

Physical Description

As befitting the state bird of Western Australia, the black swan has a most dignified appearance. The male is larger than the female, attaining a body length of up to 60 inches in the case of a large specimen. He will weigh around 14-16 pounds, a good three or four pounds heavier than the female.

While both sexes appear very much the same, the male

38

can be identified by his larger size when in groups. In flight one is aware of the much larger neck of the male and, on water, by the more erect way he carries his supple neck.

Observed on water, a black swan may appear almost entirely black. The black plumage, however, may have a greyish-brown tinge to it. In flight, the striking pure white primaries and secondaries create a brilliant white border to the otherwise dark wings.

The bill is crimson, with a wide whitish band near the broad tip. The iris is red, while the legs and feet are dark grey.

Immature birds are a dull grey-brown, with a dark brownish bill (which reddens in their first year), and grey legs and feet.

Habitat and Habits

Essentially, black swans inhabit lagoons and lakes holding large areas of permanent fresh or brackish water. They may also be found in salt-water estuaries, bays and lagoons, though these are usually non-breeders.

On a magnificent autumn morning in the Dart Valley of Otago I looked through a pair of 7x35 binoculars at several black swans floating gracefully on a vivid blue lagoon within an area known as the Glenorchy Swamp Wildlife Reserve (administered by DOC). This stretch of reed-fringed shallow water containing a ready source of aquatic plantlife was ideal habitat for the species. The depth factor of the lagoon was a critical one, because the swans find most of their food underwater and can reach down only to about three feet.

Presently I moved closer, wanting a 'habitat' photograph to include both the swans and the towering mountains forming the western skyline. Alarmed, the swans began to crowd together. Arching their long, slender necks, they started to make rather musical bugling or honking sounds, a noise they also emit in flight.

Suddenly several took flight, lifting sluggishly into the air. They flew further up the broad valley towards the shining mountains. The sound of their calling drifted back on the wind's gentle breath.

Black swans are basically social birds, congregating in large numbers. This is especially true of the annual moulting ritual.

At Farewell Spit, for instance, up to 10,000 may gather together. About 60 per cent of this number comprises birds from Marlborough and the Wairarapa, the remainder coming from as far afield as the Waikato, Hawke's Bay, Manawatu, Rotorua, Okarito and Lake Ellesmere. Lake Ellesmere is also a traditional moulting ground, as is the Invercargill Estuary, Kaipara Harbour, and prominent lakes such as Lake Wairarapa.

Depending on locality, black swans either nest in a solitary or colonial manner. Traditional nesting colonies exist in many parts of the country, the birds building their nests once the water levels of the big lakes have started to recede and the flush of the new spring growth is apparent.

Solitary nesters have a consistent July to October breeding season. They construct their nests at well-spaced intervals and, territorially inclined, they aggressively defend a large area around it. The nest is fashioned in reeds or sedges. They do not carry nesting materials; rather, once they have selected a suitable site, they simply rake everything together — reeds, grasses, twigs, etc — into a large central pile. A depression, shaped like a shallow bowl, is formed on top of it. Soon it will be lined with down. Considering the circumstances, the end result is a bulky but otherwise neat arrangement.

Laying, then, starts in late July, so that the eggs will hatch early in spring and the chicks can take full advantage of the new growth. The female usually lays 5-6 greenish-white eggs that are soon stained a dirty brown. A particularly large clutch may contain 14 eggs. Either way they are normally laid at daily invervals.

Unlike other swans, the male black swan is a dutiful fellow who takes his turn at incubating the eggs (about 5 weeks). The female normally sits at night, the male during the day. Should the nest be left unattended for a short period, the eggs are concealed with down.

Within a day of hatching, the chicks — snug in light grey down — are led to water. Occasionally the adults, in the manner of mute swans, will carry their young on their backs. The chicks feed heavily on various types of exposed water plants. The species is thought to be entirely vegetarian.

In communal breeding grounds — Ellesmere is a classic

example — the nests are built only a few yards apart. Nevertheless, the immediate area surrounding each is vigorously protected.

Unlike solitary nesting black swans, which are very protective towards their young, the parents of cygnets living in colonial groups have no objections to their young mingling freely with other broods and thus forming creches. Often a creche — perhaps three or four broods — is looked after by one set of parents. This causes all sorts of problems because the cygnets frequently wander away from each other and end up in an entirely different creche. Over several days they become hopelessly lost and their parents end up looking after a completely different brood to that which they started out with.

By the time they are four or five months old the young swans can fly. Prior to breeding they have a marked tendency to inhabit salt-water habitat far from their birthplace. Thus birds from the Waikato may turn up in the sheltered bays of Northland, while those born at Lake Ellesmere could very well find themselves in coastal Southland. But later, feeling the urge to breed, they will mostly wing their way back to their birthplace. In all probability they will remain there for the rest of their lives, which, if fortune favours them, may stretch to 20 or 25 years.

CANADA GOOSE
(*Branta canadensis*)

Male: Gander   Female: Goose   Young: Gosling

Range

Of all North American geese none is better known or more widely hunted than the Canada goose, of which 11 subspecies can be found. One subspecies — *B.c. asiatica* — is now extinct.

Some interesting comments on the naming of various subspecies of Canada geese are contained in M.A. Ogilvie's excellent book, *Wild Geese*:

> The naming of subspecies is not something that can only be done by following rigidly laid down rules. It is largely a matter of personal opinion. It is quite usual to find intergrading in the area where two even quite well marked subspecies meet, while some species show a continuous cline of variation from one end of their range to the other. A few specimens taken arbitrarily out of this cline might well show sufficient different characteristics to warrant description and naming as subspecies. This is essentially what has happened in the case of the Canada goose.

The common Canada goose — *B.c. canadensis* — has the widest distribution of them all, mostly nesting in the vast northern marshlands of the Canadian prairie provinces. Where they spend their summer depends entirely on which traditional 'flyway' they happen to use. For instance, geese taking the Central and Mississippi flyway summer in the central Canadian provinces, and, in winter, fly as far south as the shores of the Gulf of Mexico. Geese choosing the Atlantic flyway summer on the shores of Hudson's Bay in Canada, and also in Labrador. Winter will find them along the eastern coastline from Chesapeake Bay to Florida. For many North Americans the V-shaped flights of the mighty Canada is reason enough for a moment's quiet reflection — it heralds both the beginning and the end of winter.

Among the less common subspecies is the western Canada goose. Classed as a partial migrant, and about the same size as the common Canada goose, it has a restricted range and can be found from Alaska to Vancouver Island.

The lesser Canada goose is a smaller and shorter-necked bird. Found all along the western coastline, this is classed as the commonest of the Canada geese.

At various times Canada geese have been introduced — mostly as a 'park bird' — into Europe. In Britain, for instance, it is thought they were kept from about 1665 onwards on many estates in England. The inevitable result was that many birds took flight — didn't return — and consequently feral populations became established.

Nowadays they are widespread over much of lowland England, but are less common in Scotland and Wales. There is a good population at Strangford Lough in Ireland. Possibly their numbers in Britain exceed 20,000. They are also known to breed in Sweden and may be observed in parts of Norway, Denmark, Holland and France.

Learned opinions differ as to precisely what subspecies of Canada goose were introduced into New Zealand. Popular consensus considers it to be *maxima*, the Giant Canada goose. Until it was rediscovered in Minnesota in 1962, this bird was generally considered extinct in North America.

The author's research leads him to believe that other subspecies may have been introduced too. At any rate, the 'probable' outcome is that today's populations are mixed.

In specifically defining the Giant Canada goose* (*B. c. maxima*), Ogilvie (1978) says:

> There has been a lot of publicity associated with the Giant Canada goose and its rediscovery after supposed extinction, but too much emphasis has been placed on 'largest', to the exclusion of the true size range of the population. For example, hunters naturally boast of all heavy birds they shoot and these have automatically been claimed as 'Giant'. Even the type specimen of maxima was described from the largest available bird.

---

* After comparing a number of photographs and matching several descriptions of the common Canada goose to that of the Giant Canada goose, I find the two subspecies identical.

Liberations and Distribution in New Zealand

The Wellington Acclimatisation Society first introduced the Canada goose into this country in 1876, but the venture failed. The next introduction took place in 1905. This time the Department of Tourist and Health Resorts was responsible. The actual number of birds is again not known. It is, however, generally believed to be less than 40.

At this time that department and, in particular its general manager, T.E. Donne, were determined to make New Zealand *the sportsman's paradise*. The introduction of the Canada goose — even then rated the premier gamebird in North America — was surely a significant step to achieving this worthy aim.

The birds were distributed to the Wellington, Southland, Otago, and North Canterbury Acclimatisation Societies. Eight birds were accepted by North Canterbury, the rest presumably divided up amongst the other societies. While that aspect is unclear, it is certain that once again the Wellington society failed in its attempts to introduce the Canada goose into the North Island.

For two years the geese in the North Canterbury society's grounds on the south side of the Avon River did not breed — a cause for grave concern. Perhaps they would breed better elsewhere? In 1908 six of the eight geese were taken to Glenmark. This proved successful and in 1910 it was judged prudent to take 10 of the geese that had been born there to Lake Sumner; in that same year the remaining pair of geese in the society's grounds reared four pairs. The future of the Canada goose seemed assured. From that point on the society would release a few pairs each year into various parts of the province.

By 1920 flocks of up to 300 geese were reported from several parts of inland Canterbury. John Digby, a ranger with the North Canterbury society, reported in February 1928 that the geese were extremely numerous around lakes Sumner and Taylor. He also noted that they fed in large numbers on the broad river flats in the upper reaches of the Hurunui River.

In 1931 the Department of Internal Affairs removed the Canada goose from the list of protected birds. The obvious reason for this was that the birds were destroying and fouling pastures, but the North Canterbury society viewed this as a grave mistake. A deputation from its council put forward their case to the Minister of Internal Affairs, which resulted in protection of the species being reimposed in 'that part of the society's district lying east of the main Christchurch-Dunedin railway line'. Protection would remain in force from 1 January to 1 August.

During the following years the Canada goose ranged even further afield in the South Island, nesting unchecked in the remote vastness of the highlands, flying effortlessly down to lakes and rivers in the winter. Particularly large concentrations would gather at Lake Ellesmere, which served as both a summer moulting ground and a wintering haven.

Determined to establish the Canada goose in the North Island, the Wildlife Service (a section of the Department of Internal Affairs), took the plunge in 1969-70 when they released 75 birds from Lake Ellesmere at Ngamotu Lagoon near Wairoa in northern Hawke's Bay. While their rate of increase was judged as 'disappointingly slow' by rangers, the birds did establish themselves in acceptable numbers, passing the 400 mark in the early 1980s. Encouraged by the success of this venture, the Wildlife Service again transferred geese from Lake Ellesmere to the North Island in the latter part of the 1970s.

As a direct result of this, today small populations are well entrenched around the Waikato lakes, Tauranga Harbour, and Lake Wairarapa. Ducks Unlimited has also liberated 500 Canada geese in the North Island, where the overall population (steadily growing) is estimated to number 8000 birds.

During the mornings of 16 and 17 June 1988, DOC carried out its annual count of Canada geese. In what were described as 'reasonably good flying conditions' they estimated the numbers in Canterbury to be:

Area	Count
Coastal North Canterbury wetlands	18,234
Upper catchments: Ashley, Waimakariri	649
Upper catchment: Hurunui River/Sumner lakes	1,260
Upper catchment: Hope/Boyle/Lewis rivers	108
Upper catchment: Waiau River	2,165
Upper catchment: Clarence/Acheron rivers	1,193
Hanmer Plains	490
	Total: 24,099

A further 1,091 geese were counted in the upper Rakaia River by DOC staff carrying out the South Canterbury count. With regard to the 'coastal North Canterbury wetlands' count of 18,234 birds, a staggering 16,015 geese were on, or in the vicinity of, Lake Ellesmere. A comparison with the count for the previous year — 20,535 birds — revealed that they had increased in almost all areas, a trend not appreciated by either DOC or the North Canterbury Acclimatisation Society.

Similar aerial counts of Canada geese took place in other parts of the South Island at approximately the same time as the Canterbury survey:

Location	Count
Southland coastland wetlands	210
Te Anau Basin/Waiau River	2,117
Otago-Maniototo/Falls Dam/Styx Basin	409
Wanaka/Hawea/Wakatipu	1,651 +
Tekapo catchment	1,344
Pukaki catchment	503
Ohau catchment	547
Benmore catchment	627
Ahuriri catchment	415
Rangitata catchment	646
Ashburton River catchment	722
Rakaia River catchment (Ashburton count)	1,091
South Canterbury lowlands	698
Waitaki Valley lowlands	2,278

Total: 13,258

All up, then, we have a figure of 37,357 geese in the areas covered, which do not include Nelson and the West Coast. Add the North Island number of 8,000 to this and by the time you're reading this we should have a population of at least 50,000 birds of a species regarded as the finest gamebird in the world.

Physical Description

The Canada goose is an easy bird to recognise because of its large size — a wingspan of up to 6 feet — and contrasting black and white markings on the head and neck.

Both sexes are alike, with the male being a little larger. A big gander, for instance, will weigh 12-14 pounds (in North America large specimens exceed this and an unusually big gander may weigh 20 pounds). An average male, however, will weigh around 10-11 pounds; the female a good pound less. They have a body length of 35-40 inches, so that, in profile, they appear not unlike a black swan in height.

On closer examination, they have a distinct black head and neck; equally well defined is a pure white throat patch that extends up to just behind dark brown eyes. The blackish-grey bill is equipped with a wide nail. The back of the body — upper wing surfaces, etc — is a darkish-brown, with much paler edges forming wave-like bars on the wing coverts. Flanks and belly are creamy white or white; rump and tail are black. Legs and feet are a darkish-grey, tending towards black.

Habitat and Habits
On the Canterbury Plains and the remote high country valleys of the Southern Alps, Canada geese have found the perfect habitat. The isolated lakes and tarns, where they are seldom disturbed, have proven ideal spots to breed and, later, to moult while they tend to their goslings. Indeed, the nature of the terrain is much like that inhabited by their North American cousins. The real difference is the weather, which, in the southern hemisphere, lacks 'extreme' winter conditions. Nor do they have to travel staggering distances in migratory flights between summer and winter habitat.

In fact, the climate is so temperate that, providing the lakes remain unfrozen and the depth of the snow is not too great to prevent feeding, some birds won't follow their instinctive down-country, pre-winter migration pattern and will remain in the same general area throughout the entire year. Such a precedent has occurred in the Mackenzie Country, principally around lakes Ohau, Benmore and Tekapo. This has caused concern among local farmers and runholders because the geese constantly feed on the same favoured pastures, grazing the grass to ground level and thus severely restricting available feed for stock and naturally impeding essential spring growth. They are also known to winter over around lakes Guyon, Bowscale, Heron, Clearwater, Grasmere, and in the upper reaches of the Hurunui River.

47

By and large, however, the seasonal patterns of the Canada goose are highly predictable. Most birds, driven by the urge to mate, head to the high country in early spring. The older birds — the Canada is said to mate for life — are accompanied by their young of the previous year. As soon as the serious business of nesting begins, though, the older birds forsake all their responsibilities for their young and drive them away. No matter. By now the young are well able to fend for themselves, but will not mate until they are three years old.

Each pair of Canada geese has a specific territory during this part of their yearly cycle. Within it will be their nest. The primary concern in choosing a nesting site seems to be that the view obtained from it is not obstructed — this most wary of birds, with the vision of a hawk, is constantly on the lookout for danger.

The actual nest is fashioned mostly from grass, but it is not unusual for Canada geese to use whatever else is nearby in its construction — mosses, sticks and driftwood (almost certainly if a stream is close by). It will be lined with down and feathers.

Laying normally begins around the third week of September and extends right through the following month. The average clutch contains 4 or 5 white eggs. The female alone is responsible for the month-long incubation. It is an exacting time for her; she may lose as much as 27 per cent of her body weight.

In the meantime the gander stands guard — there is no more worthy or possessive husband than he. Constantly on the alert, he will hiss furiously and make other signs of aggression should another male — occupied in the same manner — stray too close to the invisible boundary line of his territory. Not to be outdone in front of its mate, the other gander will reply in a like manner. For the male of the species this too is a stressful time.

Within 24 hours of the eggs hatching, the goslings — attired very attractively in yellow and brown down — troop away from their nest. The territory, as such, ceases to exist. Soon the entire breeding area will revert to common ground.

While they can swim from a very early age, the goslings spend most of their time in marsh and grassland. During their 80 days of development they are watched by their overly

With its distinctive white head, there is no mistaking the female paradise shelduck, shown in the moulting stage (*above*), and in full plumage (*right*).

The male of the species is sombre in appearance. Paradise shelduck mate for life.

In late December a female paradise shelduck — in the Whitemans Valley, near Upper Hutt — keeps a wary eye on her young ones. Like Canada geese, they feed extensively on agricultural land.

Two adult black swans and a cygnet observed in late January on the Ohau channel, linking lakes Rotorua and Rotoiti.

Opposite: Black swan habitat in April in the Dart Valley, Otago. This stretch of water, with the Humboldt Mountains rising impressively in the background, is part of the Glenorchy Swamp Wildlife Management area, where swans are fully protected.

Territorially inclined, black swans choose a suitable nesting site and then simply rake materials within easy reach into a large central pile.

Both male and female Canada geese are alike, the male being a little larger. Gregarious by nature, they are numerous in many parts of the South Island, especially in Canterbury where, on and around Lake Ellesmere, they may be seen in their thousands.

Canada geese are also gaining a foothold in the North Island — the Tauranga district is a typical habitat. This adult bird and juvenile were spotted in a secluded estuary near Katikati.

protective parents. But it is not uncommon for several broods to be taken care of by one set of parents, or, depending on the number of young, by even more adult birds. We could call this a welcome break from parental responsibilities. Such gatherings of goslings are called creches. As many as 45 young birds — protected by three adult pairs — were once sighted at Lake Forsyth.

High-protein spring fodder is the order of the day now. Canada geese are fortunate that so much of their range has been extensively 'top-dressed' by fixed-wing aircraft. This is typical of the vast Molesworth run. Quite apart from improving the food supply of the resident geese, fertilisation increases the protein content relative to fibre. Molesworth country also has within its far-flung boundaries a number of excellent roosting sites that are normally free of ice during winter.

Although almost entirely vegetarian, geese will eat insects and small invertebrates — molluscs and crustacea — living in the water. When feeding in that watery environment they frequently present an amusing sight by up-ending themselves in the manner of ducks.

At night they roost near water — sandbars, shorelines, river flats, or the junction of a stream.

By the time they are three months old the goslings can fly. In flight, as well as on the ground, the Canada goose is an extremely noisy bird — much like the common domestic variety, which could never be described as having a taciturn nature. So they chatter constantly among themselves. In flight their main call is a resounding 'Honk!' It is used to communicate with other birds feeding on the ground. Appropriately enough the name 'honker' is commonly used by North American hunters when referring to the Canada goose.

By April most geese and their goslings have left their high country haunts. They will either go directly to coastal roosting waters or, as already noted, remain to winter over around suitable lakes and tarns.

It is when they are back in the lowlands that Canada geese — precisely as they have done in their homeland — display how very well they can adapt to an agricultural environment. At Lake Ellesmere, for instance, they obtain most of their food from nearby grainfields; grain stubble is an important food supply of the Canada goose in North America. They also feed heavily on clover, rye, lucerne, and root crops, turnips being rated highly. In the process, they extensively foul the land upon which they feed.

One method of frightening geese from crops and pastures is the use of a gas-operated scaregun (using an LPG bottle). Hard-hit areas necessitating such action in the last few years have been the upper Hurunui River Basin, the upper Waimakariri River Basin, the eastern shoreline of Lake Ellesmere, and the northern end of Lake Forsyth.

Over a six-year period (1982-1988) scareguns have been used with mixed results to deter geese and other birds such as black swan, paradise duck and pukeko from what is termed 'crop predation' over much of Canterbury. Crops protected by this method include grass seed, wheat, turnips, lucerne, rape seed, barley, peas, cornfeed, most horticultural crops, maize, clover, linseed, and kale.

In late April 1988, farmers and runholders in the Lake Tekapo district were once again faced with the same old problem of too many geese ruining their pastures — ie, priceless winter feed. Once again they turned to their local society for assistance. To solve the dilemma society rangers set out a linking chain of scareguns. At first they seemed to have worked — the badly frightened geese stayed away for long intervals before picking up sufficient courage to return. Soon, however, the geese became accustomed to a sudden blast at regular intervals and, aware that the noise was only scare tactics, remained where they were, simultaneously feeding and fouling the land.

So drastic action was required. A cull was the answer. This was undertaken in the last week of May, with 125 local shooters, two light aircraft, and 33 boats being used. Total kill was 415 birds. The society was 'reasonably pleased with the result, though a higher number was sought at the time'.

Because of constant pressure from many runholders, DOC has also resorted to aerial culling of geese. Conservation officers I discussed this with in the Southern Lakes district in 1988 deplored the sickening method and openly bemoaned the fact that private shooters were unable to kill sufficient numbers to make such a sickening scenario obsolete in this country.

A typical aerial shoot was carried out by the Ashburton society in June 1988. A Hughes 500 helicopter and Auster fixed-wing aircraft were used. The targeted areas were Denny, Emma, Roundabout, Clearwater, Trinity, and Maori lakes. Later, nine people using outboard-powered craft and rowboats picked up 313 dead birds from these lakes. Total cost of this operation — helicopter and fixed-wing hire, 12-gauge shotgun ammunition, and vehicle expenses — came to $2039.

During the special goose season of 1988, the North Canterbury-based Gameshooter's Club, working with the local society, carried out a two-day culling operation at Lake Ellesmere. On day one — ideal windy conditions — the birds behaved according to plan and 800 were shot. Day two — fine and sunny — saw the birds less predictable and no doubt somewhat wary after yesterday's slaughter. Only 150 were bagged.

On 5 January 1989, 20 DOC field staff and helpers rounded up 5,000 moulting Canada geese at Lake Ellesmere as part of their long-term banding programme. Of these, 1,000 birds were freshly tagged and then released. When hunters return leg-bands to the appropriate source, they greatly assist DOC by providing information as to the individual bird's movements, life expectancy, and harvest rate. Nothing unusual in this, of course.

What was new, however, was that DOC saw fit to transport 3,000 of these birds to Bankside, near Rakaia, for the purpose of fattening them for export. Conservation officer Dick Hutchinson was reported in the *Evening Post* as stating that DOC had explored the commercial prospects of the birds and preferred this method of control to moult drives and, echoing what I'd heard a year ago, helicopter shoots. He hastened to add that commercial use was 'only secondary to achieving effective management through recreational hunting'.

The piece continued:

No payment was made for the birds (described as a Crown resource) at the collection, but if they prove economical the department would be looking to recoup some of the costs of managing the birds. . .The geese will be farmed at Bankside by Tinwald farmer Ray Colville. They will be fed grain and specially prepared pellets and Mr Colville hopes to have them fattened by May.

The birds' wings will be pinioned to prevent them flying.

Mr Colville began farming trials last year with 150 birds caught on Lake Pukaki. Samples of the processed birds were recently sent to West Germany to be assessed as game meat. While Mr Colville is awaiting feedback, he is investigating the possibility of using goose down for sleeping bags.

When I stayed with Ron and Ann Stewart at Glenorchy, I was told by my generous hosts that Canada goose was rather delicious, and that it could be likened to your ordinary domesticated variety as a table bird. In this instance, however, it was not as fatty tasting. Which is what you would expect of a wild, rather than a tame, bird.

Who knows. Maybe all this could be the start of a brand-new industry for the South Island?

Postscript

To encourage hunting Canada geese in the over-populated Lake Ellesmere area, the NZ Acclimatisation Societies have produced a colourful, informative brochure titled *Canada Goose Hunting, Lake Ellesmere, New Zealand*. It covers accommodation (a comfortable 16-bunk cottage is available at the lake's edge), access, hunting tips, and a good map of the lake and surrounding country. For further information contact the Secretary, North Canterbury Acclimatisation Society, 61 Bealey Avenue, Christchurch. Telephone: (03) 669 191.

2 HUNTING WATERFOWL

The Hunting Season

Each year the Minister of Conservation declares an 'open season' for gamebirds in this country. Notification of this is published as a supplement to the *New Zealand Gazette* on or about 28 March. In a concise and comprehensive manner it includes the duration of the hunting season — which may vary from species to species — as it applies to various districts presently administered by the acclimatisation societies, the times of shooting, what species of gamebird may be shot, bag limits, numbers of decoys, and so on. Refer to Appendix 1 for an acclimatisation society directory.

The following chart for the Auckland area will serve as an example:

Auckland Acclimatisation District
Reference to Description: Gazette, No. 62, of 16 October 1947, at page 1680

Game That May be Hunted or Killed	Duration of 1989 Season
Grey, shoveler and mallard duck (except that no duck may be hunted on Great Barrier Island)	6 May to 25 June 1989 incl.
Paradise shelduck (Rodney, Otamatea and Raglan only)	6 May to 25 June 1989 incl.
Paradise shelduck (Otorohanga, Waitomo, Taupo and Taumarunui counties only)	6 May to 28 May 1989 incl.
Paradise shelduck (All other unspecified counties)	6 May to 7 May 1989 incl. 24 June and 25 June 1989 incl.
Pukeko	6 May to 30 July 1989 incl.
Black swan (except that no black swan may be hunted or killed on the Waikato Hydro Lakes, Karapiro, Arapuni and Waipapa)	6 May to 25 June 1989 incl.

Canada goose (Waikato, Waipa and Raglan Counties only)	6 May to 25 June 1989 incl.
California quail	6 May to 30 July 1989 incl.
Cock pheasant	6 May to 30 July 1989 incl.

Daily Bag Limits

Grey duck, 10
Shoveler duck, 3
Mallard duck, 10
Grey, shoveler and mallard duck
   aggregate limits, 10 in all
Paradise shelduck (Otorohanga,
   Taumarunui, Waitomo and
   Taupo Counties), 5
Paradise shelduck (Franklin, Rodney
   & Otamatea counties), 2
Paradise shelduck (Raglan
County), 4
Paradise shelduck (all other
   unspecified counties), 2

Pukeko, 10
Black swan, 3
Canada goose, 2
California quail, no limit
Cock pheasant, 3

Shooting hours: 6.30 a.m. to 6.30 p.m.
Decoy limit: No limit.

Copies of the *New Zealand Gazette* can be seen at acclimatisation society offices, public libraries, police stations, and post offices. It is also on sale from the Government Printing Office, Wellington.

Information relating to the hunting season is also contained on game licences, which include details of local wildlife refuges. The various types of game licences and their cost in 1989 were: Adult $38; junior $19; week $19; day $7.50; adult goose $19; junior goose $9.50.

So you have your game licence and the hunting season is about to begin. You might very well wonder precisely how many wildfowl will fall to hunters' guns before the season is over. An interesting chart prepared by Tom Caithness — a DOC scientist involved in fisheries and gamebird management — provides an 'approximate' figure from 1968 through to 1987. It also includes the 'average bag' per hunter for both the North and South Islands:

Year	North Island	Average Bag	South Island	Average Bag	NZ Total
1968	695,000	25.0	264,000	18.7	959,000
1969	617,000	22.4	240,000	17.9	857,000
1970	572,000	21.0	297,000	21.3	869,000
1971	611,000	22.1	284,000	20.6	895,000
1972	795,000	26.1	311,000	22.4	1,006,000
1973	655,356	21.2	310,590	21.0	966,000
1974	584,656	18.5	350,959	22.2	935,615
1975	723,923	22.6	476,486	27.4	1,200,409
1976	723,267	22.7	378,617	22.1	1,101,884
1977	797,475	25.0	478,261	27.9	1,275,736
1978	771,200	24.1	483,000	29.6	1,254,200
1979	728,000	22.7	486,000	29.9	1,214,200
1980	815,700	26.4	532,000	32.5	1,347,700
1981	865,207	27.9	471,500	30.7	1,336,707
1982	804,200	25.7	495,700	31.6	1,299,900
1983	782,125	25.0	444,030	28.5	1,226,155
1984	806,328	27.0	549,974	35.4	1,356,302
1985	749,050	26.3	496,174	33.2	1,245,224
1986	593,483	21.8	347,160	24.0	940,623
1987	592,669	21.5	329,812	23.3	922,481

The next chart, again compiled by Tom Caithness, shows the 'average' season's bag of mallard and grey duck for each district in 1987:

Bay of Islands	10.1	Nelson	16.4
Maunganui-Whangaroa	14.4	Marlborough	20.1
Hobson	22.6	North Canterbury	16.6
Auckland	20.8	Ashburton	26.5
Tauranga	10.1	South Canterbury	23.3
Central Conservancy	12.7	Waitaki Valley	28.9
Taranaki	17.8	West Coast	18.2
Stratford	13.2	Westland	25.7
Hawera	17.9	Southern Lakes	2.3
Wanganui	25.5	Otago	14.8
Hawke's Bay	21.5	Southland	17.8
Wellington	18.3		

So how many wildfowl hunters are there in this country? The answer is a lot. According to figures made available to me by Brad Parkes of the National Executive of Acclimatisation Societies approximately 41,000 game licences were sold during the 1988 season.

Unfortunately there are no nation-wide figures on record as to how many farmers also participate in the sport. To best clarify the rules on this point, the following notification, prepared by the Otago Acclimatisation Society in time for the 1988 gamebird season, appeared in the *Otago Daily Times*:

Farmer — Duckshooter — Licence Requirements

Farmers who do not live on the property they farm must buy a game licence to hunt waterfowl.

The occupier privilege, allowed under Section 19 of the Wildlife Act, permits occupiers to hunt game without a licence only on the land they farm and on which they live permanently. This privilege also applies to the occupier's wife or husband and one son or daughter.

An occupier is defined, under the Wildlife Act, as the person whose permanent and principal or only place of residence is on the land being hunted. The occupier may be the owner of the land, a lessee of land (where the owner does not reside on the land), the manager of a farming business carried out on the land, or a sharemilker.

In cases where several people could qualify for the occupier privilege, the person who intends to use the privilege must notify the Society in writing.

A person who resides on land that is farmed in conjunction with any other land is legally considered to reside on both areas of land. However the occupier privilege does not apply where the residence is separate from the land which is farmed nor does it apply to land around a weekend or holiday residence.

Occupier privileges do not apply on public land, such as chain strips along rivers and streams, even though those strips may be adjacent to the occupier's land.

Since there is at least one strategically located maimai on almost every farm and station in the country, and given that a father and son can legally hunt without a licence, it should go without saying that the overall number of wildfowl hunters in this country must be considerably higher than the figure given.

Maimai

The ideal maimai or hunting stand is shore-based and a few yards from water — a simple yet highly effective way to conceal oneself from keen-eyed gamebirds above. Perhaps the most effective method of constructing one is to clear sufficient space within a patch of dense cover — rushes, gorse, broom, manuka, etc — so that you can erect the framework. As an example, stout willow poles can be used for this purpose. The maimai will have a low doorway at the back, which can be closed to keep in the gundog. The front will naturally look out over the water, with the main crossbeam at about waist height. In effect, a hunter will have a full 180-degree view of the shooting area.

Over the framework can be placed tightly stretched sacking, hessian, or even hardboard or corrugated iron. Corrugated iron is ideal for the upward sloping roof which extends approximately two-thirds over the structure, thereby mostly concealing a hunter from above but not restricting line of fire in any way. The still-growing vegetation, hemming in the finished maimai, will naturally conceal much of it. But where it doesn't — over the roof, the front, and a few gaps here and there — you can use the same vegetation to hide it better. To retain the 'right' look this must be cut from elsewhere.

Within the maimai emphasis is on comfort; duck hunting can be a lengthy business. So a wide seat fitted with inexpensive foam-rubber padding is a blessing. A few nails come in useful for hanging various items, and shelves — strong wooden boxes with their open tops facing inwards — can be slotted neatly into the front wall during construction. These are within easy reach of the shooters and can be used for holding flasks of warm drink or soup, cartridges, or whatever.

The maimai just described is situated on a low bank above a shallow pond near the Oreti River in Southland. Roughly two by two and a half metres, it is built in a mixed patch of high gorse and broom. On opening day 1988, three guns accounted for 55 gamebirds — 53 mallards, one shoveler and one paradise shelduck.

Of course, such an ideal location as this might not be possible to find — ie, there is no natural cover around the duck pond in question. In this instance, the maimai, or at least the lower part of it, can be built below ground level. This will give it as low a profile as possible. It can be concealed with sods of earth, cultivated grasses or native tussocks. Even locally cut vegetation works well providing the maimai is finished well before opening day. An existing one should likewise be retouched with freshly cut growth well before time. This allows resident birds to become familiar with it. So everything should be completed a month before the hunting season starts. A maimai erected later might spell disaster; the birds will invariably shy away.

Like mallards, Canada geese are inherently suspicious of anything new or unusual in their regular feeding grounds. To hide themselves therefore, most goose hunters dig a small hole in the ground — about two feet deep and wide. It can be easily hidden with clumps of roots, tussock, or similar vegetation, which, providing a good root-base is left attached, will stand up quite well around the hole. Other shooters might use open-weave 'camo' nets to conceal themselves, a method also commonly used when hunting paradise ducks.

Decoys

Decoys are essentially imitation ducks, geese, or other waterfowl made from wood, plastic, cork, canvas, or rubber. They have altered little in concept from those intricately hand carved from hardwoods by early North American Indians. Certainly the fundamental idea remains the same — to entice waterfowl to within effective range of one's particular weapon.

Arguably the more decoys used on opening day the better, as waterfowl are most vulnerable on the opening day of the hunting season. Magnum and super-sized magnum decoys work extremely well. Later on in the season, gamebirds tend to become more wary of decoys and a much smaller number — six or eight, say — will just as easily do the trick.

Only two acclimatisation society districts place stipulations on how many decoys can be used. In Waitaki, it applies to just one area — Wainono Lagoon — where 25 is the limit. Throughout North Canterbury 30 is the maximum number of decoys that can be set out. No matter. That number would be about the most decoys any duck hunter would want to use.

Well-anchored, floating decoys are the most effective. They should resemble the genuine article as realistically as possible. The angle and direction in which they float is governed by where one attaches a weighted cord (nylon fishing line is commonly used) to one of several tethering points. By tying it between the head and center line, for instance, the decoy will face into the wind. Fixing it closer to the tail results in the decoy facing downwind. As a guideline, most decoys should face into the wind — the direction from which ducks invariably appear.

There are no set rules as to how one should place decoys. A well-proven method, however, is to set them out in a 180-degree semicircle, leaving a clear 'landing area' directly in front of the maimai. Place the brighter coloured drake decoys (a ratio of one male per six females is about right) on the imaginary perimeter line. They should be no further than 40-45 metres from the maimai — a sensible 'maximum' range for the type of shotgun choke most commonly used for hunting from stands. Thus decoys serve as an effective 'sighting marker', meaning any live duck level with, or closer than, the outer decoys will be within shotgun range.

A 1981 New Zealand Wildlife Service publication, *Hunting the Canada*, had this to say about decoying Canada geese:

Correct positioning of the decoys is all-important. If you are shooting a known feeding area, arrange your decoys in a rough horseshoe layout with the open end downwind. They should be well spread out facing into the wind and most should have their heads down as though feeding. Alarmed geese bunch up with their necks erect so be careful not to set your decoys in that position. Although geese may approach from any direction they will always land upwind and are most likely to settle behind the decoys. Generally speaking, the more decoys used, the more effective they will be.

When hunting over a rest area the use of decoys will depend on the circumstances. Unlike their behaviour while feeding, when they may settle anywhere in a comparatively large area, geese will return again and again to a well defined rest area which can be identified by the presence of feathers and droppings. The hunter can be fairly confident that by positioning himself in the right place, he can get birds either as they come in to land or on their flight line, even without the use of decoys. This is especially true if they are using a small body of water, a pond or tarn. The more birds are disturbed and the larger the rest area, however, the more effective decoys will be in indicating an apparently safe resting place and bring them within range.

Strict laws apply to decoys and are clearly set out in both

the Wildlife Act 1953, and in the Wildlife Regulations 1955. They are as follows:

(a) Wildlife Act 1953, Section 16(1)(bb): — The Minister, in notifying an open season for game shall specify the numbers of decoys that may be used by any person for the purpose of hunting or killing any game.

    Wildlife Act 1953, Section 18(1)(f)(i) — Save as otherwise expressly provided in this Act, or except in such circumstances and at such times, areas, and places and subject to such conditions as may from time to time be authorised pursuant to a notification given by the Minister, no person shall for the purpose of hunting or killing any game use any live decoys. Section 18(2) defines "decoy" — includes any dead game that is so placed or arranged as to simulate appearance of live game.

(b) Wildlife Regulations 1955 (Reprint), 1962-199: — Regulation 18
    (1) No person shall use any artificial decoy for the purposes of hunting or killing game, unless that decoy is securely anchored.
    (2) No person shall place any artificial decoy within (50 metres) of any other artificial decoy already set out by any other person.
    (3) Every person using artificial decoys shall prevent any of them coming within (50 metres) of any other artificial decoys already set out by any other person in conformity with subclauses (1) and (2) of this regulation.
    (Note: The 50 metres were introduced by amendment 1973/3, Regulation 4, to alter the "60 yard" provision).

Calling Gamebirds

If there is one thing most hunters don't use enough, it is their game call. Wildfowl of all types respond readily to suitable calls providing the caller is fairly skilled in their use. Which means learning how to use one well enough to hoodwink a passing flight that what they're hearing is the real thing. It is of course a simple matter to hear how ducks sound — parks and reserves are chock-a-block with them, especially after the opening weekend of the hunting season. Again, those essential pre-season reconnaissance trips to a hunting area allow one to hear all manner of gamebirds. Another suggestion is to tag along with an expert or two and hear how they do it. As always, one can pick up a great deal by observing.

A wide range of duck and Canada goose calls are made by the North American firms of Olt, Falks, or Scotch. Instruction tapes (sound and video), and booklets on how to call are readily available, too. Experts stress that the only way to learn is to practise, practise, practise! They could also add: at the right time. Which isn't in the maimai on the opening morning of the hunting season. Gamebirds aren't that gullible.

Night Shooting

Most districts in the South Island allow the hunting of Canada geese 24 hours a day; this does not apply to any other gamebird in the country. May I suggest you refer to your local district office for the latest information about shooting times.

Hunting the Canada contains this pertinent paragraph:

Night shooting under the right conditions can be both exciting and successful. The main requirement is to determine where geese are coming in to feed. Suitable areas may be located during daylight by finding evidence such as fresh droppings left during the previous night. The only requirement is to wait in a strategic location where you are not showing any tell-tale silhouette. Merely lying on the ground in dark clothing with darkened face and hands is often adequate but use natural cover if it exists. Do not position yourself facing into the moon and ensure that all light-reflecting articles are covered.

Other Hunting Methods

Wildfowl can of course be stalked successfully on foot, or, in certain areas — check this one out with your local acclimatisation society — from camouflaged boats drifting slowly down the shady edges of rivers, reed-fringed streams, or perhaps across larger stretches of open water.

The hunter afoot knows the area intimately. Warily he sneaks along the well-screened banks of rivers and ponds where he has recently observed birds feeding. Even though it may be poor light, he doesn't take any chances with such alert game and therefore will utilise every bit of cover available. More often than not he will hear the birds before spotting them. Just as likely, he will make doubly sure of success by getting down on hands and knees — or maybe even belly — to cover the last part of the stalk. Only at the last moment will he leap up. As one, the birds take sudden, explosive flight. Great action!

Shotguns

The wise man who once said that 'the right shotgun for you was the one with which you shot best' certainly knew what he was on about. Which means that no one (and definitely not this writer) can be dogmatic on a subject as 'touchy' as a group of hunters discussing the merits of their various calibred rifles over a few too many drinks. Instead, we will attempt to let the facts speak for themselves.

The most commonly used style of shotgun in this country today is the over-and-under. Only a little behind it in popularity is the side-by-side. In a distant third place comes the single barrel, either a gas-operated semi-automatic, or, less common, a slide or pump-action gun.

The sheer versatility of having two barrels with different chokes for instant use are obviously points in favour of purchasing a more 'traditional' side-by-side or over-and-under shotgun. A strong point against 5-shot, semi-automatics is that they are required by law to be securely pinned, allowing the use of only two shots — one in the breach and the other in the magazine. Also, they are not as well balanced as the other types. Another strong argument against them is that it is impossible to tell whether they are loaded or empty; a side-by-side or over and under can be broken open when not in use. In the confines of a maimai, where a close-range blast of shot would make you resemble raw meat, I know what type of gun I'd like the other guys to be using. Having said all this, a great many hunters in this country wouldn't use anything but their semi-automatic shotguns. Which of course harks back to the opening line of this section.

The ever-growing popularity of the over-and-under shotgun has a great deal to do with its single sighting-plane — that is, one barrel superimposed above the other. Those of us who first learned to shoot with a rifle, and that would apply to the vast majority of hunters in New Zealand, find they adapt more easily to a single-barrel shotgun than they do to one offering a much broader sighting plane. But nothing of course can surpass, or come even close to, the elegant looks and the incredibly sweet-handling qualities of a classically made side-by-side. Fundamentally, it remains the same weapon as used by duck hunters in the latter part of the last century. Having stood the test of time, it must remain the 'thoroughbred' of shotgun designs.

Turn up at any maimai in use from Northland to Bluff during the hunting season and chances are every hunter there will be using a 12-gauge calibre shotgun. With less recoil than is generally realised, a 12-gauge can in full-choke barrels deliver up to 1¼ ounces of shot to a maximum killing range of about 55-60 metres. With ammunition on sale throughout the country, the versatile 12-gauge has no serious challenger in this field.

Only one other shotgun gauge — the 20-gauge — can be seriously considered for duck hunting; the 16-gauge has never taken on with the shooting fraternity and at best the 410 is an 'orchard' gun.

Having little recoil, the 20-gauge is well suited to a lightweight shotgun. Unfortunately, its effective killing range and striking power fall short of the performance achieved by the 12-gauge. We could however class it as a sound choice for a woman or for someone who is overly sensitive to recoil.

What is meant by choke? Keeping it simple, a choke is a device fitted in the muzzle of a shotgun which prevents the shot charge from spreading as rapidly as it would have otherwise done. In short, it controls the spread of the shot pattern (pellets) within a 30-inch circle at 40 metres.

The various classifications of chokes used in Britain and their North American equivalents are:

Britain	United States
Full choke	Full choke
¾ choke	Improved modified
½ choke	Modified choke
¼ choke	¼ choke
Improved cylinder	Improved cylinder
True cylinder	Cylinder

Your everyday Spanish side-by-side, for instance, has a ½ choke left barrel and a full-choked right one. At close range — the ducks zooming in over decoys at roughly 25 metres — you would fire the left barrel because it offers wider spread. Many hunters prefer an even more open choke in such a close situation and they may use a ¼ choke or even an improved cylinder. The full-choke, a much 'tighter' pattern at short distances, really comes into its own at 40 metres and beyond. The use of variable chokes fitted to single-barrelled guns brings a great degree of versatility to such weapons.

Recommended shot sizes for waterfowl are:

No. 4/5 — mallard, grey duck, shoveler, and pukeko
No. 3/4 — paradise shelduck
No. 2/4 — Canada goose, black swan

Ideally, shotguns should have dull, non-reflecting barrels and stocks for use in the field. Remember that a shiny barrel can be easily covered with adhesive 'camo' tape.

Anyone about to purchase a shotgun is faced with an almost bewildering selection of various makes. The following list of new and second-hand shotguns, available at Gun City, Christchurch, in early 1989, is a 'guide' to what is currently available:

Shotguns

12g WINCHESTER	Inter Choke 6500
12g WINCHESTER	Inter Choke 5000
12g WINCHESTER	Inter Choke 6000
12g WINCHESTER	Diamond 32''
12g WINCHESTER	Diamond 2 barrel set
12g WINCHESTER	Diamond Inter Choke
12g WINCHESTER	Grand Euro Trap
12g WINCHESTER	Pidgeon Grade Trap
12g BROWNING	A1 Trap
12g BROWNING	B2 Trap

Personifying New Zealand's numerous waterfowl hunters are Simon Ayton and Les Hoffman. Les's labrador, Gunnie, appears to be enjoying the morning sunshine after taking several dips in ice-cold water. The location is on a bank above a small pond, close to the Oreti River, Southland.

Two different styles of hunting stand or maimai. With the 1988 shooting season over, this maimai near Te Anau will need to be concealed with suitable material in time for the following year's duck shooting activities. A well-concealed maimai is shown below on opening day. Note the two decoys — magnum and super magnum (*inset*).

Within the maimai, Les Hoffman lures the mallards (*inset*) to within shooting range by using a duck call, and Simon Ayton swings into action with an Italian-made Bettinsol 12-gauge shotgun. The result can be seen overleaf.

12g BROWNING	B2 (cased)
12g BROWNING	A1 (cased)
12g SKB	500 (cased)
12g SKB	880 2 Stocks Trap
12g SKB	500 Trap
12g FRANCHI	Master Trap
12g NIKKO	5000 ¾ full
12g NIKKO	Shadow Cased
12g KAWAGUCHI	Trap
12g BERETTA	686 Trap
12g BETTINSOLI	Inter Choke Field
12g KILWELL	u/o D/T Field
12g BAIKAL	IJ12 D/T Field
12g BAIKAL	IJ12 D/T Field
12g WINCHESTER	101 S/T Field
12g MIROKU	S/T Field

Skeet

12g SKB	600 Skeet
12g SKB	600 Skeet
12g MIROKU	800W Skeet
12g MIROKU	800 Skeet
12g NIKKO	Shadow Skeet
12g NIKKO	199 Skeet

Semi-Auto

12g BROWNING	A5
12g BROWNING	B80 Ducks Unlimited
12g KTG	5 shot
12g KTG	5 shot
12g WINCHESTER	1400
12g WINCHESTER	1400
12g WINCHESTER	1400
12 KTG	Inter Choke
12g FUJI	5 shot
12g REMINGTON	870
12g WINCHESTER	Super

Pump Action

12g REMINGTON	Wingmaster
12g KTG	Inter Choke
12g KTG	3″ chamber
12g WINCHESTER	Mod 12
12g WINCHESTER	120
12g WINCHESTER	1300
12g WINCHESTER	Defender

12g SMITH & WESSON	3000
12g MOSSBERG	600
12g MOSSBERG	Camo special
12g MOSSBERG	Camo special

20g

REMINGTON	Mod 870 Pump Action
PEDRETTI	u/o

Gun Clubs

Simulated field events held by gun clubs are becoming increasingly popular in this country, offering those participating an excellent way of keeping their shooting skills finely honed throughout the year.

Most shotgun enthusiasts of course belong to a gun club, the majority of which are affiliated to the New Zealand Clay Target Association Inc. From information sent to me by the National Secretary, Sid Hanson, I discovered that there are 98 such clubs in New Zealand and that total membership in early 1989 was 2,840.

The association's well-produced journal, *Gunshot*, is published bi-monthly. It contains a wealth of information relating to the clubs scattered around the country. The 1989 Match Allocations of the association, listed below, reveal how full and eventful their year is:

JANUARY
7/8   Kokatahi: 1989 Westland Provincial Championships
28/29   Waitemata: 1989 North Island DTL Championships

FEBRUARY
12   Eketahuna: North Island Southern Zone Simulated Field
        Match
12   Southland: South Island Southern Zone Simulated Field
        Match
18/19   Rotorua: 1989 Waikato & Central Provincial
        Championships

MARCH
11-18   Waikato: 1989 New Zealand DTL Championships

| 26 | Rotorua: North Island North Zone Simulated Field Match |
| 26 | South Canterbury: SIMULATED FIELD CLUB: South Island North Zone Simulated Field Match |

APRIL
2	Taupo: 1989 North Island Simulated Field Championships
8	Dunedin: 1989 South Island Simulated Field Championships
9	Dunedin: 1989 New Zealand Simulated Field Championships

MAY   No Association Matches

JUNE
| 3/4 | Awatere: 1989 Nelson/Marlborough Provincial Championships |

JULY   No Association Matches

AUGUST
5/6	Dunedin: 1989 Otago Provincial Championships
26	Belfast: 1989 South Island Ball Trap Championships
27	Belfast: 1989 New Zealand Ball Trap Championships

SEPTEMBER
9/10	Waitemata: 1989 Auckland Provincial Championships
17	Taumarunui: 1989 North Island Ball Trap
23/24	Wanganui: ISU Zone Match
23/24	Timaru: 1989 Canterbury Provincial Championships

OCTOBER
7/8	Belfast: ISU Zone Match
14/15	Waitemata: ISU Zone Match
21/22	Wanganui: 1989 Wellington & West Coast Provincial Championships
21/22	Dunedin: ISU Zone Match

NOVEMBER
4/5	Waitemata: 1989 North Island ISU Championships
11/12	Belfast: 1989 South Island DTL Championships
18/19	Gisborne: 1989 Hawkes Bay Provincial Championships
23/24	Belfast: South Island ISU Championships
25/26	Belfast: New Zealand ISU Championships
25/26	Balfour: 1989 South Island ISU Championships

DECEMBER
| 2/3 | Nightcaps: 1989 Southland Provincial Championships |

Appendix 4 lists the postal addresses of gun clubs affiliated to the NZ Clay Target Association Inc. Appendix 5 lists where each club has its grounds, when they meet to shoot, and a contact name and telephone number.

Gun clubs not linked to the NZ Clay Target Association still follow their rulings regarding, for instance, field layout and trap settings. We can point to the Kennels Gun Club, PO Box 7003, Taradale, as an example:

> Our club grounds are situated on the banks of the Tutaekuri River on the southern outskirts of Napier. Our facilities have grown rapidly over the past couple of years and we are currently able to cater for the needs of most clay target shooters. These facilities now include:
> 1 Skeet Field
> 1 Down-the-Line Field
> 1 Simulated Field
> Our membership has also grown accordingly and is expected to top one hundred this year.
>
> Our objective is to provide the greatest possible enjoyment for shooters of all abilities at the cheapest possible price. We view the club as a great place for new shooters to learn gun safety and the skills needed to break targets, as well as providing for the more experienced shooter who is looking for a less competitive atmosphere.

Firearm Safety in the Field

Enough has been published in this country on the correct way to handle firearms (shotguns and rifles) that the author feels it rather pointless to take the risk of boring the pants off his reader. The subject, I believe, is expertly covered in *The New Zealand Firearm Handbook*, by L.H. Harris, published by the Mountain Safety Council.

Instead, may I draw your attention to what can happen when safe gun handling practices are ignored. Take, for instance, opening day of the 1988 season.

A 42-year-old Thames builder went hunting with his 10-year-old son and a 14-year-old boy. They were shooting from a maimai on the banks of the Waipaoa River when disaster struck. Newspaper reports said that 'a gun was accidentally fired, wounding him [the elder man] fatally'. How does someone not yet in their teens come to grips with that tragedy?

Again on opening day, two young Otago men were out

on a farm at Poolburn. They too were shooting from a maimai, this one at the edge of a lake. They were feeling good, having spotted two ducks ready to be plucked. Meanwhile, another man was also in a maimai, this one on the other side of the water. Spotting a duck — but not the other maimai — he fired. Missing the duck, the charge of shot ricocheted off the water. Result? One man blinded for life in one eye, and the other had to have a pellet dug out of his forehead (two stitches) and a much deeper one removed from under his jaw (16 stitches).

A week later, a 35-year-old Te Puke man, while out with three mates near Rotorua, was fatally shot by one of his companions in a moment of lapsed concentration that will haunt the man who pulled the trigger for the rest of his life.

Commenting on the 'ricochet' incident, the manager of the Otago Acclimatisation Society, Neil Watson, said that such ricochets were not uncommon and hunters had to be aware of them. He also pointed out that the society would be investigating the incident, in particular, 'the distance between the two maimais and their positioning'. The law of course states that maimais are required to be 90 metres apart for safety. Safety? Pellets have been known to travel in excess of 200 metres!

One thing I would like to comment on is alcohol. Sure, a nip or two — or three or even four — of rum or Scotch is considered traditional by many duck hunters (more likely to be the older brigade). It's the done thing, they say. Wouldn't be without it.

The trouble is, the hard stuff badly impairs judgement. Hunters make errors they wouldn't otherwise make. They take foolish risks. Certainly they aren't the same person as they are when stone-cold sober. That can easily prove fatal when in charge of a shotgun — a 12-gauge can be lethal. Pulling a trigger inadvertently while in a maimai, with the muzzle pointing at a mate, can be likened to being trapped in a confined space when a hand grenade explodes. Very messy.

The time to drink is when the day's hunting is over and the guns have been cleaned and put well out of the way. Reckon I'd joined you for a drink every time then — great stuff! But in a maimai? Forget it, sport!

Gundogs — Retrievers

When used in the traditional manner, retrievers have no duty until a shot is fired. In a maimai they must be under perfect control, eager for work yet restrained. When a shot is fired and a duck is down, they are commanded to retrieve it. They do so without undue fuss. In the case of wounded game — if only from a humanitarian aspect — they are essential.

The ideal retriever's coat is close, short, and dense — in other words, water-resistant. A number of different breeds are used for this purpose, among them the labrador, golden retriever, English springer spaniel, and the English cocker spaniel. All-purpose breeds used to retrieve waterfowl include the weimaraner and German short-haired pointer. But these last two thrive on work and may by temperament be too restless to sit for lengthy periods in a maimai.

Without question the labrador is the most popular breed for waterfowling in Australasia. Colonel Hawker, a noted British sportsman, said in 1839 that the breed 'is by far the best for any kind of shooting. He is generally black and no bigger than a pointer, very fine in legs, with short smooth hair; is extremely quick running, swimming, and fighting. . .Their sense of smell is hardly to be credited: in finding wounded game there is not a living equal in the canine race'.

Much more recently, and on the local front, Tom Caithness had this to say about the labrador:

> At the risk of offending many hunters I know, I will stick my neck out and say that I consider labradors to be the best all-round hunting dog. They are great retrievers and are especially good in water. They can be trained to point or set. In my experience they are also good watch-dogs and house-dogs and will put up with some incredible torture from children.

And Brad Parkes is equally enthusiastic:

> The fact of the matter is that the labrador is the best breed of gundog to use over water. He/she might tire quicker than other breeds when used on upland game or small game (rabbits, hares, etc) but over water the Lab has no peer, training being equal.

Fundamentally, a gundog must have an instinct to hunt.

This will have been passed on by one or both parents. A good nose is essential — the greatest asset of any retriever. Eyesight and hearing must be perfect. The dog must display nervous energy and yet, like a labrador, have a tractable disposition. In style and appearance it must conform with the breed.

As you will have gathered, the actual training of any gundog is a specialist's role. It demands much of man and dog. The well-trained retriever displays complete obedience to his handler as well as steadiness, a tender mouth, and good delivery of the game. Having a 'hard' mouth is said to be the most serious fault a retriever can have and experienced trainers eventually discard dogs which are unable to break the habit of unduly damaging game.

But whatever is involved in teaching a dog to retrieve correctly, the end result is well worth it: we will never find a better hunting companion.

Certainly it is to the benefit of any gundog owner to join a dog club. Appendix 2 contains a list of Gundog and Specialist Breed Clubs.

The Nelson-based Seddon Districts Gundog Society is, as we can see from the following information provided by the secretary, Brian Shepard, a most active and well-organised club:

Field Trialling

Our Club promotes the sport of field trialling and holds regular training days. We also hold picnic trials and retrieving stakes classes at some ribbon parades. Our training days are very informal and a lot of fun for both handler and dog. We like to encourage ideas on training methods, and we try to help each other with problems that occur in our dog's work. Though we are working towards competitive trialling, we feel that retrieving practice must benefit gamebird shooters. You'll have more control over your dog and it will learn to: mark game, double retrieve, blind retrieve, retrieve from water and land, and direction control. At training days you may use your own or the Club's dummies. For trials we use dead pigeons and blank shot.

Showing

Our Club promotes the showing and breeding of pedigree gundogs. We regularly hold ribbon parades for pure-bred gundogs and open shows for dogs registered with NZ Kennel Club. Hopefully we will be given Championship show status in the near future. Many of our members are involved in all three facets of our Club's activities. Our

members' dogs compete successfully at dog shows throughout New
Zealand.

Obedience

An obedient dog is a happy dog. We encourage gundog owners to
join the local obedience club which will not only teach you how to
control your dog, but give you the basics on commencing show training
and field training, as these all require a measure of obedience work.
Our Club holds special stake classes with most ribbon parades for
gundog obedience.

Zone

Our Club covers the West Coast, Nelson, Marlborough districts, and
though based in Nelson we endeavour to hold activities in all these
areas. Our Club is affiliated to the NZ Kennel Club.

Our Subscriptions are $5 single, $8 double.

We produce a regular Newsletter containing news, views and
information on shows, trials, etc.

Brian has also stated that members are encouraged 'to take
at least basic training courses from an obedience club'. On the
basis of that, Appendix 3 includes the addresses of the many
Associated All Breeds Obedience Societies.

Information relating to purchasing a pure-bred dog is
contained in an explanatory brochure available from NZ Kennel
Club Inc., Private Bag, Porirua.

Ducks Unlimited

Ducks Unlimited (NZ) Incorporated is a private, charitable, non-profit
conservation organisation dedicated to the preservation, restoration,
creation and maintenance of wetland habitat in New Zealand, the
propagation and conservation of the country's rare waterfowl, and the
advocacy of wetlands as a valuable natural resource. This is achieved
through six projects each with specific aims. These are: 'Operation
Pateke', the reduction of the threatened status of the New Zealand
brown teal through the release of captive-bred birds and wise habitat
management; 'Operation Gretel', to increase the number of grey teal
in New Zealand through the provision of suitable nesting habitat;
'Operation Whio', the conservation of blue duck through the release
of captive-bred birds to expand the species range; 'Operation Branta',
to establish the Canada goose in the North Island as a valuable
recreational resource; 'Operation Royal Swan', the conservation of
mute swan through the establishment of a captive breeding population;
and 'Operation Wetlands', to preserve, create and manage wetland

areas through direct funding, technical assistance and public education of wetland values. The scientific study of wetlands and waterfowl is also encouraged through direct funding.

The author is proud to belong to Ducks Unlimited and feels very strongly that all gamebird hunters and conservationists should, too. Membership, in four categories, is open to anyone who supports the organisation's objectives. Junior membership is $11.00 per annum, full membership $27.50 per annum, trade and sponsor membership is $55.00 per annum, and, lastly, life membership is $550.00. Membership carries with it a subscription to *Flight*, the official quarterly publication of Ducks Unlimited. Ducks Unlimited can be contacted at PO Box 44-176, Lower Hutt, Wellington.

Personal Hunting Gear

With heavy emphasis on warmth, the sensible 'maimai' hunter dresses to conceal himself from game. The possibility that they do not distinguish colours accurately in the blue-green range is very strong. Apparently mid-green appears as a mid-grey to them, light green becomes light grey, while dark green appears more like black. But at the other end of the spectrum (reds and yellows) the opposite applies — they instantly recognise such colours.

One cannot stress how vitally important it is to break up the outline and the overall colour of your face and hands with a camouflage paint or cream, burnt cork, or grease paint of the type an actor would use. There is very little point in going to the trouble and expense of kitting yourself out like a guerrilla fighter unless you alter the rest of your appearance. Rangers reckon that the first thing they notice when checking licences in the field is the glaring white faces of hunters peering out of their maimai. It becomes even more noticeable in sunny weather. Oddly enough, even a darkly tanned skin stands out like you know what.

Hunters everywhere have proven time and time again how effective the combination of camouflage clothing and face paint is in the field, sitting motionless near their decoys. They haven't been observed by the feathered ones until it's been too late.

So what else do you need? First of all make sure you've got your licence. The day you forget it is the day a ranger asks the question. Next, a roomy framepack is essential because, for obvious reasons, one's transport is parked some distance from the maimai. A pack (or packs) can be stashed at the back of the maimai — under the seat, say. Cover them with a spare item of clothing if, like so many of today's backpacks, they are brightly coloured.

A change of clothing makes sense. Ammo? Take heaps. Torch? Never forget that. A first-aid kit should be law. Fieldglasses are never a mistake. Mustn't forget a knife and sharpening implement, either. A short-bladed folding knife — carried in a holster at one's waist-belt or on a cartridge belt — is ideal. A good length of string or twine comes in useful for handling downed game. Also, you might require a second game call, since other gamebirds might be on the agenda — ie, a Canada goose call for luring paradise ducks in an area where, like mallards, they too are common. Insect repellent should never be overlooked.

Flasks of tea, coffee, soup, and sandwiches and cake soon became priceless items in a cold maimai. The dog would no doubt appreciate a bite, too. Maybe he'd enjoy a brisk towelling down if some time had passed since he was last in the water or is showing signs of the cold.

Totally incongruous, light-coloured garments are ill advised. So too is red, a colour, oddly enough, which deer are thought to have trouble identifying correctly. Shy away from black, too.

In more recent years there has been an enormous swing in this country towards camouflage clothing. Even your everyday 'swanni' — that long, hooded, and drab-coloured garment so popular with all sorts of back-country types — can be purchased in a camouflaged design. Almost all of the hunters I talked with while working on this book are in favour, and have proven the great advantage of, wearing this type of clothing. The advice given in numerous books and magazines all adds up to the same thing.

It therefore follows that mid-range greens and browns are a sound bet. The previously mentioned olive-green Swanndri works like a charm. A few farming types I've met over the years wear dull-green workman's overalls over layers of warmer clothing and they've mostly shot their limit. For obvious reasons, rubber boots are mostly worn in a maimai — a roomy fitting will allow the use of more than one pair of woollen socks. You'll need them — it is cold waiting in the pre-dawn with the ground under heavy frost and your breath smoking in the slowly changing air. Icy cold, yes. But deeply satisfying, too.

Woollen underwear of the newer and lighter synthetic type, including long johns, will go a long way to keeping you comfortable. As will a woollen shirt or sweater under your outer garment. To keep dry in particularly nasty weather, chest or thigh-length waders can be worn. They are mandatory when a dog isn't used and a man has to do his own retrieving. That isn't recommended — you can easily drown out there in heavy, restricting clothing.

Wide-brimmed hats are popular with some hunters. Most, however, tend to wear balaclavas, which have the advantage of being much warmer. On the other hand, a wide-brimmed hat offers more protection in the rain and naturally wins out in sunny weather. Personally I'd settle for a warmer balaclava. But then, I always did feel the cold too much.

3 UPLAND GAMEBIRDS

PHEASANT
(*Phasianus colchicus*)

Male: Cock   Female: Hen   Young: Chicken

Range

There are 20 species of true pheasants in various parts of the world. Of these, 16 will readily interbreed and produce fertile offspring. Because of such large-scale hybridisation it is virtually impossible in most instances to determine which strain predominates.

The common pheasant (*P. colchicus*) of Asia and the Transcaucasus was introduced into many countries by the early Romans. It can still be found in a true-bred state in those regions to which it is native. But in most countries where it has been introduced — and certainly in Britain — it is considered impossible to find a true-bred common pheasant. Today, the English black-necked pheasant is certain to have a white collar, or at least traces of it, as a result of interbreeding with imported Chinese and Mongolian pheasants.

The two species in question are the Mongolian ring-necked pheasant, of north-eastern Soviet Turkestan, and the Chinese ring-necked pheasant, which is found in Manchuria, Korea, Mongolia, and northern and eastern China (as far south as Canton).

Both of these species, along with the English black-necked pheasant, have been introduced into other parts of the world — North America, Hawaii, New Zealand, Rottnest Island in Western Australia, and King Island in Bass Strait. More recently the pheasant has been relocated to various parts of the Australian mainland — ie, New South Wales, South Australia, and Tasmania.

These populations of stabilised hybrids have produced a larger and more sporting bird than any from the three species alone.

Liberations and Distribution in New Zealand

Four different types of pheasant have been introduced into this country. The most significant of these are the black-necked pheasant from England and the ring-necked pheasant from China.

Black-necked pheasant

The first pheasants of this species to arrive in this country were a cock and three hens, the property of a Mrs Willis who reached Wellington on board the *London* in 1842. A year later, a Mr Petre landed some more at the same port. Unfortunately the subsequent history of these birds has not been recorded.

In 1848 more birds were liberated at Mangonui in Northland by Mr Walter Brodie. They increased rapidly but, it was noted several years later, had not significantly increased their range. Until 1869 they were captured and then released at various North Island locations — Napier, Tolaga Bay, Kawau Island, Tauranga, Raglan, and the Bay of Islands.

Pheasants were first brought into the South Island by Messrs Smith and Robinson, passengers on board the *Monarch* which docked at Lyttelton in 1850. Robinson presented a pair to Mrs Sinclair, the wife of one of the first European settlers on Banks Peninsula. She and her husband lived in Pigeon Bay. The pheasants were kept in a cage, but in the following spring one of them somehow escaped. When it proved impossible to capture the escapee, the Sinclairs let the other one go. The birds were next heard of at nearby Port Levy, where they remained and subsequently bred well. Six years later pheasants would settle in Pigeon Bay, and by 1865 they were said to number 5,000 in Port Levy.

Sir Edwin Dashwood was the first person to bring pheasants to Nelson in 1853. Some were liberated on his property at Lower Moutere and they multiplied swiftly, soon extending their range.

The Otago society liberated pheasants in 1865 and continued to do so almost on a yearly basis until 1877. By then they were so well established that the society issued many shooting licences.

The Auckland society took delivery of seven black-necked pheasants in 1867 and two more a year later. But it was perhaps the Nelson society that persisted more than any other with introducing this variety of pheasant. Between 1879 and 1945, it liberated some 494 birds throughout its district at a cost of £336. About half of these birds were locally bred, while the only overseas-bred birds were 20 that came from England in 1898. The rest were bred in other parts of New Zealand.

Ring-necked pheasant

In 1851, Thomas Henderson imported pheasants directly from China. Two dozen were shipped in the barque *Glencoe*, but only seven reached Auckland alive. The five cocks and two hens were set free in the Waitakere Ranges, where Henderson had a property. Five years later he imported a further six birds from the same source and they too were liberated in the same area.

No other ring-necked pheasants were imported into the Auckland province. As events proved, however, this was all that was required. By 1864-65 they were numerous around Auckland and large numbers were shot. At that time they had ventured into the Waikato. Four years later they were well established in the Waikato and had turned up at Taupo. In a completely different direction, following a general northerly spread, they arrived at Whangarei. The Auckland society would report (1874-75) that the 'Chinese pheasant is the common bird of the province'.

The only other society to directly import this bird from China appears to have been Wellington — 20 in 1874, and four in 1875.

Three birds were sent from the Auckland society to Otago in 1864. Of a further 15 sent in 1877, seven were liberated at Oamaru and five at Tapanui.

Mrs Cracroft Wilson presented a brace of ring-necked pheasants to the Canterbury society in July 1866. They were very much admired in the society's grounds. That same year Mrs Wilson raised 50 ring-necked pheasants at her home in Cashmere (from where she obtained her initial stock is unknown). A year later the Canterbury society obtained three more, presumably from the Auckland society. In 1871 they reported that the ring-necked pheasant was 'thoroughly established' and was 'needing no further importations'. Possibly this statement applies to both species introduced into the province, which, for the record, numbered in their thousands on Cheviot station by 1869.

Certainly the Southland society obtained its Chinese ring-necked pheasants from Auckland between 1869-1870. They liberated them, along with the black-necked pheasants they had acquired, at the same time in various parts of their wide district.

By 1871, then, both the black-necked and ring-necked pheasant had been introduced into many parts of the country, with obvious results. A noted naturalist of the day, T.T. Cheeseman, had this to say about the two species interbreeding:

> Our pheasant is certainly the China pheasant (*P. torquatus*) with a slight mixture of the English pheasant (*P. colchicus*) in the extreme north of the provincial district (Auckland). Such enormous numbers of the Chinese pheasants were distributed from Auckland to other parts of the Colony that I am inclined to doubt the existence of the pure English pheasant in the wild state in New Zealand.

Two more introductions of pheasant were made into this country. The Mongolian pheasant arrived from England in 1923. Then in 1938 a fourth colour type, known as the melanistic mutant pheasant, also arrived from England. This is not a separate race, but a mutation of the black-necked pheasant.

In 1990 the pheasant is well established throughout much of the country, thanks to sensible game management practices and 'releases' into the wild. In the North Island it is listed as a gamebird in every acclimatisation society district.

During 1986, the Mangonui-Whangaroa society, for

instance, was responsible for liberating 152 birds mainly in the Aupouri Forest and Kaeo areas. Some good bags were reported taken from there during the 1989 season.

With its year-round warm climate, the Tauranga district contains a great deal of what might be classed as ideal pheasant habitat. In 1987 the society reported that 'this has been one of the best seasons for years. There have been some excellent bags taken'. The following year, it reported that 'the habitat in a lot of our area is improving to suit the birds'.

The Hawke's Bay society also had encouraging words to say, noting that with time and effort, 'double figures' could be obtained.

During 1988 that society released 414 pheasant hens and 492 pheasant cocks (banded) throughout its district. It also supplied pen breeders with 1,254 eggs and 38 hens.

The Hawera society was also in a mood to release pheasants during the same year:

> Again this year there was very heavy pressure on the pheasant population. There was at least one group of seven guns from outside our area who spent a week shooting over the Waverley area. It is good to know that our efforts to supply birds in the wild is so widely appreciated but it would be nicer to know that the shooters all bought Hawera licences, and thus made a financial contribution.
>
> Last breeding season 2,600 eggs were laid, out of which 1,604 were set, producing 1,090 chicks. There were 934 birds released with 50 hens and 4 cocks retained for breeding.

The coastal 'exotic' forests of the Wellington-Wanganui districts — Harakeke, Lismore, Santoft, Tangimoana, and Waitarere — have long attracted pheasant shooters. In commenting on two of these areas in 1988, the Wanganui society reported:

> Access to Lismore and Harakeke Forests was much appreciated and the extended season in these areas allowed the pheasant shooters ample weekends to obtain birds. The Justice Department land adjacent to Harakeke was also available providing popular coastal shooting areas.

During 1987, some 250 pheasants were taken by Wanganui society hunters, while, in the Wellington district, 1,912 birds were taken.

Canada geese are far from easy targets, appearing to fly much slower than they actually are. Many hunters therefore tend not to give them sufficient lead and thus shoot behind them.

It is permissible in most districts where they are found to hunt Canada geese 24 hours a day (this does not apply to any other species of gamebird). Dusk or night shooting can prove exciting and profitable. In this scene, Peter 'Stretch' Lucas, using a double-barrel Zoil 12-gauge shotgun, has teamed up with Ron Stewart.

Canada geese hunting at Glenorchy, Otago, in winter. Ron Stewart, in his well-concealed maimai, is using a single-barrel Remington Model 1100 12-gauge shotgun. Note the decoys at the water's edge.

For many centuries man and dog have successfully teamed together to participate in the hunting of waterfowl. Ron Stewart's labrador, called Speights, retrieves a 12-pound Canada goose (*right*), and brings it undamaged to his master.

This lightweight net has been erected where Canada geese are feeding regularly. The decoys (*one shown below*) have been positioned among tell-tale droppings, and Ron Stewart begins to use his Canada goose call — a Scotchman Model 1026.

South Island populations of pheasants are mostly found along the warmer eastern coastal belt, where, in certain areas, they may extend well inland. For instance, the Nelson society reported in 1988 that:

> These birds definitely seem to be on the increase throughout the Waimea Plains. This is no doubt due in large part to the increase in horticulture activity. These birds prefer areas of rough weeds etc, such as are found around horticulture boundaries and shelterbelts. Although the season is very short at only three days, many hunters (especially with dogs), enjoy good hunting, on birds which in only three days become very challenging and cunning quarry. . . An extension of the season, with one additional weekend, could well be considered worthwhile with the increasing numbers of birds available. However, because large areas of habitat are not traditionally accessible to shooters, some risk of over-harvesting could occur in huntable areas.

Meantime, the North Canterbury society liberated a total of 147 ring-necked pheasants from their Greenpark Game Farm. It also supplied 213 eggs to private breeders.

Physical Description

Despite various introductions and subsequent hybridisation, the wild pheasant of New Zealand has a fairly uniform appearance. Nevertheless, plumage does vary according to race and degree of interbreeding. Darker plumaged birds, for example, are possibly showing traits of their black-necked background, whereas those with an overall lighter colouration are almost certainly displaying their ring-necked ancestry. Having said that, the ring-necked strain predominates in this country, as it does everywhere else the two species have intermingled.

Generally speaking, then, the adult male is a heavy, fowl-like bird with a long, pointed tail. His head is an iridescent mixture of blue and purple, possibly with greenish undertones. It is enhanced by a large patch of bright, almost scarlet, red skin that completely engulfs the yellow-orange iris, and by a broad white collar about the lower neck.

There are shimmering coppery tones to his mantle, his speckled golden breast has a rich purplish sheen, and he has pale slate-grey or blue wing coverts. The buff to mid-brown tail, marked with black bars, is approximately 22 inches in length and has 18 feathers. His legs and feet are a grey to brown.

The adult female is 22-24 inches in size and her tail is correspondingly shorter. She is a dullish brown, her plumage mottled, spotted, and barred with black and dark-brown bars. The young are like the hen, only much duller.

In its pure form, the male Mongolian pheasant has a broad white ring, broken in front, which extends around his neck. His chest and back are a bronzed orange-red, glossed over with purple or green. On the other hand, the melanistic pheasant lacks a white collar and its quite spectacular plumage is a dark metallic green, with the chest and sides more of a purplish blue. It is thought to breed true.

Habitat and Habits

Only rarely will you observe a pheasant in rough, hilly country above, say, 300 metres. They inhabit low-lying pastoral land of level to undulating form. It must be fertile enough to support 'palatable' crops. Old, well-drained marshlands are ideal. Essential too is cover. Without it there are no pheasants skulking about, or, for that matter, any other gamebirds.

Cover to pheasants means scrub and fern — isolated patches or gullies thickly coated rather than vast unbroken belts. To move undetected from one feeding ground to another they frequently and surreptitiously sneak along linking hedges, windbreaks, and narrow scrubby belts running alongside roads and tracks. If the area is also criss-crossed with ditches, then so much the better. Within all pheasant territories there are well-defined lanes of communication.

Pheasants readily occupy lupin-covered sand dunes such as are found along the Manawatu coastline. They may be on the outskirts of native or exotic forests — Kaingaroa, for instance. But always that vital cover will be there. This is a secretive gamebird by nature.

While they much prefer to run should danger threaten, pheasants are rated among the fastest of flying birds. If suddenly flushed, they are capable of vertical take-off, a heart-stopping affair for unsuspecting humans because of the loud whirring of wings and startled cry.

Although they are essentially ground birds, pheasants will often roost in trees. Apart from the breeding season, they are mostly observed alone or in small numbers — two or three, say. Polygamous by nature, they are sexually mature at six months. They do not breed, however, until they are almost a year old.

In spring, the cock chooses his breeding territory and confirms he has taken up residence by crowing loudly. This warns off (or should) other lusty males, and also attracts females interested enough to see what he has to offer. He will display to them with tail outspread and wings trailing, frequently calling out with a resounding 'kork-kok!' Outside of the breeding season, when he is especially vocal, he usually makes this, or a similar sound, in the early morning or late evening (sunset). At any rate, the hen or hens are (hopefully) suitably impressed with this ritualistic exhibition.

The cock plays no part in selecting a nest site; that is the responsibility of the hen, or hens, that have joined him. The nest is naturally within the cock's territory, which he protects with great zest. The hen is therefore limited to whatever cover it may contain. The nest itself is a basic affair, typical, as you will read in subsequent chapters, of the Phasianidae family.

The hen scratches or scrapes a well-hidden depression in the ground and then lines it with dry grass, vegetation, or whatever is close to hand. It will be located in a hayfield (lucerne, grasses and clover), or in scrub, fern, gorse, under bushes and shrubs, even at times in gardens. A particularly inspired and common choice is under a dense, prickly blackberry bush. A not so intelligent spot is in a hayfield, where, due to farm activity, many nests are destroyed. And should a hen not react quickly enough to a huge mechanical monster looming above her, she will be either killed, or, at least, badly crippled; easy prey for a predator.

On average a hen lays nine olive-brown eggs. She alone incubates them, which takes about 23-24 days. On leaving the nest to feed, she will invariably cover the eggs with grass or leaves. As a further precaution, she will depart and return on the wind, thus leaving no tracks. On the nest, she turns the eggs at regular intervals both day and night.

The newly hatched chickens are alert and well protected in a snug coat of thick down. As soon as they are dry, they leave the nest. They grow very quickly, feeding on small succulent insects rich in protein; essential for their growth. By day 12, their flight feathers have grown so much they are able to fly for shortish distances. By this time they are eating other foods — seeds, in particular. Older birds also enjoy insects — grasshoppers and crickets, fruit, berries, and waste grain. The youngsters gain their drab grey juvenile plumage when they are about five weeks old.

Due to several factors — weather conditions, food availability, predation — chick mortality is high. Possibly only half of the brood will reach adulthood, which they do at about five months of age.

CALIFORNIA QUAIL
(*Lophortyx californicus*)

Male: Cock   Female: Hen   Young: Chicken

Range
There are nearly 100 species of quail around the world, and they may be found in Europe, Asia, Africa, Australia, North and Central America, and the West Indies.

Obviously, then, there are far too many varieties of quail to cover here and so we shall concentrate on the two species introduced into this country that established themselves remarkably well — California and brown. In doing so, both gained gamebird status.

The California quail is mostly called the Californian or valley quail in the United States. It is a native to California and Baja California Norte, and for many years has been a mainstay of hunting along the Pacific coastal regions. Importantly, it is still expanding its range into irrigated areas.

Apart from New Zealand, it has also been successfully introduced into Hawaii, Argentina, central Chile, and Australia (various parts of Victoria in the 1930s).

Liberations and Distribution in New Zealand
California quail were possibly first released in this country by M.W. Hay at Papakura, Auckland, in 1862. What happened to the two pairs remains a mystery.

Two years later, J.R. Hill presented three birds — one cock and two hens — of the same species to the North Canterbury society. In their first breeding season in the society's grounds these hens produced 85 eggs. Most of the eggs were placed under bantam hens, but that proved to be a mistake. Once the quail chicks hatched, many were trampled to death. Nevertheless, 21 chickens reached maturity. But apparently they did not 'thrive well'.

A significant number (113) of California quail were imported from the United States by the Auckland society in 1867. While most were released locally (unrecorded locations), others were auctioned (their destination again unknown). Ten birds were retained by the society and within a year they were breeding. Liberations from this stock were made in subsequent years.

The Nelson society were delighted in April 1865 when Sir George Grey presented them with two pairs of California quail. Records do not state where they came from, so we can only speculate that they came either from Sir George's home on Kawau Island, where he had an ever-growing collection of birds and animals, or were imported from one of Grey's many overseas contacts.

At any rate, Fred Huddleston, the Honorary Secretary of the society, constructed an aviary for his precious charges at his home on Nile Street East, near the mouth of the Maitai River. Four months later a further pair of California quail, which had arrived from Australia on the *Phoebe*, were placed in the same aviary. In November the hens commenced laying. By early 1866 there were 14 healthy birds residing on Nile Street East. Some were released locally; others much further afield.

With Huddleston as its main driving force, the Nelson society would be responsible for introducing many more California quail, mostly from the United States, into the district.

In 1868, the Auckland society imported 78 California quail. A few were set free locally, 10 went to the Waikato, 42 to Nelson, 6 to Poverty Bay, and (possibly) 18 to Otago.

In January 1871, Mr J. Grubb of Christchurch made a gift of 13 California quail to the local society. Also in that year the Otago society obtained 120 birds. Southland acquired 2 in 1873 and 29 in 1874, while Wellington took delivery of 266 in 1874 and a further 18 in 1875.

The North Canterbury society obtained 520 California quail in 1878 from the Nelson society — at 5 shillings a pair it represented the cheapest going rate anywhere in the country or, for that matter, overseas. The first consignment of 300 birds reached the society's gardens in March. The local rats immediately began to create mayhem with the newly arrived stock, so understandably very little time was wasted before the quail were liberated. Fifty were released on a private property at Southbridge, 70 on a plantation a little south of Prebbleton, 85 on another plantation (location unknown), and the rest on the property of Captain J. Parsons of Crust.

A second consignment of California quail from Nelson also spent very little time at the society's grounds before being liberated on the estate of Sir John Cracroft at Cashmere. A year later, California quail were 'very numerous' at Prebbleton, and by and large most of these introductions proved successful, at least in the short term.

Success also applied to the Nelson district. By 1890, California quail were so plentiful that drastic measures were taken to check their numbers. Many thousands were shot. Huge numbers were shipped to London frozen, while a great many were also canned locally.

Two years later, the North Canterbury society noted 'the increase of quail in various parts of the district'. But by 1906 a 'steady decrease' in their numbers is mentioned. Overall, however, California quail were doing remarkably well.

Virtually all parts of the then vast Auckland district contained California quail by 1922. Reports of clutches of up to 18 chickens were not unusual. By 1928 they were considered a 'threat to crops' by farmers in the Ohura and Taumarunui counties. Government permission was sought, and granted, for rangers to shoot them.

Not until 1934 did the North Canterbury society attempt to re-establish this species with a total of 245 birds. A similar number were liberated in 1936, and again in 1937.

Today, the California quail is widespread over the North Island. In the South Island, it has a broad range — especially in the drier northern and eastern regions. The only acclimatisation society not listing it as a gamebird is Westland. A 127-centimetre annual rainfall is too much for any quail to cope with, although the author did find record of one hopeful introduction there in 1910.

Physical Description

The male California quail is around 9½-10 inches in size and has a weight of 6-8 ounces. The female is slightly smaller.

Significantly, they are the only quail to bear a plume. Present in both sexes, it is short, black, and curves forward from the black crown; the female's plume is shorter and straighter.

There are crisp black and white pattern-like markings on the head of the male, including a large black patch on the face and throat. His back is slate-brown, and his chest blue-grey. There is a reddish smudge on his scaly pale-buff underparts. He carries distinct white bars on his flanks, has a dark brown iris, a short black bill, and grey or black legs and toes. The female is similarly marked, but lacks the black throat patch. She is also generally much duller in comparison — ie, more of a drab, brownish colour overall.

Habitat and Habits

Throughout its extensive range, where it is found from sea level to around 2,000 metres (Mount Taranaki and the Southern Alps), the California quail reveals a marked preference for 'borderline' farmlands, where there are cultivated pastures, scrub, fern, and trees, all of which combine to offer feed, cover, and nesting sites within close proximity.

The yearly cycle and habits of the California quail are remarkably similar to those of the chukar — they are both monogamous and deeply social, forming large coveys for much of the year. There are of course definite advantages to this — a large number of birds will feel more secure, have little difficulty in locating a suitable food source, and are able to post several birds on sentry duty at strategic points.

The female California quail chooses to nest in more settled country than does the chukar. Normally it is in deep tussock or other high grasses in marginal country. She forms a rounded depression and lines it with dry grass, stems, roots, but only rarely with feathers. Although the nest is difficult to find it is nevertheless vulnerable. Many nests are deserted simply because someone has inadvertently appeared nearby. Farm machinery no doubt disturbs many nests, also. Certainly the nesting quail is more susceptible to sudden attack — from a cat or ferret — than is the grounded female chukar amid rock-bound heights.

Around late winter or early spring, serious fighting breaks out in the coveys as the breeding season approaches. Soon pairs separate, taking up their own territory. Invariably there are more cocks than hens — an unfortunate ratio — and so a cock fortunate enough to have a mate has little choice but to defend the 'territory' against the advances of unmated birds.

On average a hen lays 14 eggs, although nests containing as many as 22 eggs have been found. Should a clutch be lost for whatever reason, the hen will lay again in another nest, this time for an average 8-9 eggs.

Incubation begins once the last egg is laid and takes 23 days. Should the hen die during this period, the cock will more than likely take responsibility for incubating the eggs.

Only in adverse weather do the chickens remain in the nest for any length of time. They feed on insect matter and perhaps a few small seeds. Mother clucks continuously for her adventurous youngsters. Within a month they can fly well. They attain full growth before they are five months old. As with all ground-nesting birds, the mortality rate is high and only about half of the chickens hatched reach maturity.

Most feeding occurs in the early morning or late evening. In winter, they may favour a later start, often still feeding at noon. Certainly they seek sunny faces to feed in the colder months. They mainly feed on seeds, varying their diet with grasses, insects and clover. Waste grain in stubbly fields is a certain lure.

BROWN QUAIL
(Synoicus ypsilophorus)ˈ

Male: Cock   Female: Hen   Young: Chicken

Range
There are over 30 species of quail in Australia. The most common is the brown quail, which is found in all states, including Tasmania. Apart from New South Wales, where it extends well inland, the brown quail is mostly found in coastal regions and adjacent tablelands. It is also known as the Australian quail, swamp quail, and, where appropriate, Tasmanian quail. Its range extends north of Australia to New Guinea and Indonesia.

Liberations and Distribution in New Zealand
Introductions of brown quail were first made in New Zealand in 1866 when a pair were presented to the North Canterbury society by a Lieutenant-Colonel White. Two years later they obtained four more birds, and an unspecified number in 1871. On all three occasions the quail failed to establish themselves.

The Otago society imported three birds in 1868 and nine in 1870. They were liberated at Green Island, south of Dunedin, but quickly vanished.

When the vessel *Gothenburg* arrived in the port of Nelson in August 1870, the local society took delivery of 10 pairs of brown quail — here again there is no mention of precisely where they came from. Later they were taken to Motueka.

Apparently this was not the first time the species had been liberated in the Nelson district. A short statement in the 1870 annual report of the society mentioned that year's release and said there was 'great hope of them increasing'. A later report, released in 1871 stated that 'a pair of these birds, liberated earlier by Henry Redwood in the Waimeas, had bred and reared a brood of young'. Unfortunately the whole lot had then vanished.

The Motueka 'liberation' were reported as 'doing well' in July 1871. But that was the last heard of them, too. This also happened to 15 pairs of brown quail that the society liberated at Appleby three months later.

The Southland society took delivery of 2 pairs in 1872. They bred. Later, releases would take place on the Awarua Plains (25 birds), and at Mason Bay on Stewart Island (an unknown number). Neither liberation proved successful.

Precisely why brown quail failed in the South Island is unclear. A possible explanation is that they were greatly preyed on by stoats, weasels, ferrets, cats, rats, hawks, and even wekas. Having said that, the South Island societies were not persistent in their attempts to introduce this species. Perhaps they decided to concentrate their efforts on the California quail — a bird far more suited to open tussock grasslands.

Fortunately the same thing did not happen in the North Island. The Auckland society imported either 4 or 10 brown quail (more likely the latter) in 1867. They were kept caged at the aviary in the Domain and bred. A year later, four were taken to Poverty Bay, 10 to the Waikato, and 10 were retained for breeding purposes.

Also in 1868, a further 70 brown quail were distributed in the Auckland district, while 10 were sent to the Waikato and six to Poverty Bay. Writing in *The Centenary History of the Auckland Acclimatisation Society*, C.R. Ashby tells us that a further 42 were sent to Nelson. No mention of this substantial number is made in records pertaining to the history of the Nelson society.

Not content with this, the Auckland society obtained considerably more brown quail in 1871. Their annual report of 1871-1872 tells the story:

The value of the Australian quail as an insectivorous bird, affording sport and food, has long been recognised by the Council, which has devoted a considerable portion of its efforts during the past season to the thorough acclimatisation of this valuable bird. Nearly 500 birds have been obtained by purchase or exchange, and distributed in various places from the Bay of Islands to Upper Waikato. Gratifying accounts of their increase have been received from Whangarei, Mangawai, Kaipara, Kaukapakapa, Waikato, and other localities, where they were liberated sufficiently early in the season to allow of their breeding, and they may now be added to the list of introduced birds thoroughly established in the Province.

In the years that followed many more birds were relocated from one part of the North Island to another. This, combined with a slow but steady natural spread, would eventually see the brown quail plentiful in most suitable habitat.

Physical Description

While it is only 7½ inches in size and weighs a mere 5-6 ounces, the brown quail is nevertheless the largest variety of this type of bird found in Australia.

Male and female are similar in appearance, with, in this instance, the female being slightly larger. They are a brown-looking bird with a short head, short tail, and short, rounded wings. Their general shape could be described as rounded, but, if one were being unkind, dumpy would fit the bill very aptly.

The throat and cheeks are a buff white to light brown, the iris is red, and the bill is blue-grey. The back tends to be more mottled with darker brown and black markings, attractively set off with narrow stripes — white for the male and pale buff for the female. The brown wings are speckled with chestnut and the buff to brown underparts are covered with black, wavy bars. The legs and feet are yellow or tending towards orange. From a distance the birds appear uniformly spotted.

Habitat and Habits

The brown quail differs from the California quail in that it shows a marked preference for low-lying terrain and rarely, if ever, is seen at high altitudes. Particularly favoured habitat are semi-swampy regions close to flat cultivated grasslands and marginal areas profusely covered with coarse grasses and tangled thickets of manuka scrub. They may also be seen in pine plantations, where there is usually plenty of ground cover. In summer it is not unusual to come across them on the sides of back country roads or forest tracks, where they sun and bath themselves in the dust.

The habits and season-to-season events in the lives of brown and California quail are virtually identical.

CHUKAR
(*Alectoris chukar*)

Male: Cock   Female: Hen   Young: Chicken

Range
The chukar — a red-legged partridge — is native to India, Pakistan, Nepal, and Iran. It is found mostly at elevations ranging from 300 to 5,000 metres (Mount Cook, New Zealand's highest mountain, is, for the record, 3,764 metres).

In 1928, chukar from the Himalayan foothills were introduced into the United States. Eventually they would flourish in the western Great Plains and in the Rocky Mountains and Cascades areas. They can be hunted legally in California, Arizona, Colorado, Oregon, Nevada, Ohio, and Connecticut.

Other successful liberations have taken place in the USSR, Canada, Mexico, the Hawaiian Islands, on St Helena, and in Britain (small localised populations on the South Downs, in Sussex, and in parts of Aberdeenshire). Using North American stock, chukar have also been successfully established in France.

Liberations and Distribution in New Zealand
Annual reports of the Auckland Acclimatisation Society indicate that 15 mature chukar birds were liberated as early as 1893 in 'secluded country' near the Kaipara Heads. Two clutches were observed soon after. By 1903, however, it was thought that they no longer existed.

R.C. Todhunter of the Ashburton society was the driving force behind the first introduction of chukar into the South Island; in June 1926, 15 pairs, obtained through the Zoological Society of Calcutta, arrived at Lyttelton in good health. Apparently this was not the full number that had been ordered. Todhunter naturally queried it and received this reply, dated 27 July 1926, from the Honorary Secretary of the Zoological Society:

93

Dear Sir,

I have to acknowledge your letter of 30th ultimo regarding chukar partridges and have noted contents. We shipped 40 birds and got receipt from the Chief Officer for that number. Perhaps the difference is due to four birds having died or escaped unnoticed during the voyage. I therefore confirm that 10 birds have to be shipped to make up the balance of 50.

We have had considerable difficulty in obtaining chukars and those recently collected have practically all died. We do not wish to ship birds to you until we have had them in captivity for some time and are certain they are free from disease and injury and can not therefore ship and per S/S "Sussex" on her next trip. We are making arrangements to collect the birds and shall ship them to you during cold weather.

True to its word, the Calcutta Zoological Society shipped a further 10 chukar partridge in one box to this country. They were found to be 'healthy and free from ticks' by the veterinary surgeon, Norman Gilford, who examined them prior to departure on 2 December 1926. Meantime, the initial 15 pairs had been liberated (August 1926) at Barrosa in the Ashburton Gorge by Captain R.B. Neil.

In January 1927, the annual report of the North Canterbury society stated that 'a further consignment of four chukar arrived for the Ashburton Society'. We may presume that six of the birds shipped from Calcutta did not survive the voyage, a problem, as we will see, that would plague future importations of this species.

Forty-six years after they had first tried to establish chukar, the Auckland society took delivery of 23 birds from Bombay (1929). They were taken to Taumarunui. There it was mistakenly believed they would find the steep, dry high-country habitat similar to the Indian highlands. Subsequent reports indicated the birds had dispersed over a wide area. In the following year two birds were observed.

In 1931 the same society imported a further 19 birds. They were handed over to a Hamilton gamebird breeder for use in experimental breeding programmes. The following year, a considerably more ambitious consignment of 400 chukar was ordered. When they arrived in Auckland in 1932 only 18 birds remained alive. Precisely what happened to these survivors is unknown.

A year later, a further 123 chukar left Horbol in Baluchistan (Pakistan) for Auckland. Eighty-three birds survived this journey, but worse was to come. Within a few weeks a further 50 had died of dysentery, and the remainder were also infected. They continued to die until, six weeks later, only 8 cocks and 4 hens remained alive. Collectively, the hens would produce 22 chickens, 10 of which fell victim to stoats. The rest reached adulthood. The total chukar population in the Auckland district stood at 24 birds. Perhaps all was not lost?

Then winter arrived — cold and wet, and a far cry from the type of weather the species knew at home. All the chukar very quickly died.

Returning to the South Island, in 1931, the North Canterbury society made arrangements to import chukar. One hundred pairs were captured in Baluchistan and placed in crates on board the vessel *Narbada*. During the trip to this country 11 birds died. The *Narbada* reached Lyttelton on 8 January 1932.

These birds were then taken to the society's grounds at Greenpark, where they would be given several weeks to acclimatise. Liberation took place at the following locations in about the second week of February:

Lake Lyndon:	35 pairs	Parau:	5 pairs
Hawkeswood:	17 pairs	Teddington:	5 pairs
Lake Taylor:	10 pairs	Waipara:	2 pairs
Mount White:	10 pairs		

The remaining birds were retained for breeding. About 185 chickens were reared later that year and a further 300 in 1933. Of this number only 117 reached maturity.

Five more liberations of chukar were made by the same society in 1935 — 25 birds at Mendip Hills, 50 in the upper Hurunui River, 25 at Eskhead (south branch of the same river), and 25 at Hanmer.

Meanwhile, the Auckland society persisted in its attempts to establish chukar. In late 1935, they obtained four sitting hens from the North Canterbury society, but again all the birds died.

A year later the North Canterbury society liberated what chukar they had on hand (numbers unknown) at two locations — Mt Herbert and Castle Hill.

Even in 1988 liberations of this species were still taking place. The North Canterbury society released 52 birds — 6 adults at their game farm, 44 young birds at Lake Coleridge, and a further 2 juveniles at Hanmer.

Chukar have also been introduced into Hawke's Bay, where in 1987-1988 56 birds were liberated.

Today we may define chukar range as the eastern slopes of the Southern Alps, extending from the Wairau River in Marlborough through north and south Canterbury, into Central Otago (see map). Within this comparatively narrow landmass the annual rainfall is around 63 centimetres; considerably less in parts of Central Otago — ie, 33 centimetres in high country east of Alexandra. This light rainfall, combined with high summer and low winter temperatures, closely resembles the original habitat of the chukar.

Chukar mostly occur in isolated pockets rather than a general spread. In areas where they are considered common they reach a density of around 10 birds per 60 hectares.

Physical Description
This is a small, rather plumpish fowl-like bird, 13-15 inches in length; a cock weighs 1½ pounds, a female 1 pound. Since the sexes are difficult to tell apart in the field — with the overall size being the only real indication in adult birds — the following description will suffice for both male and female.

The breast and shoulders are a soft ash-grey delicately flecked with an unusual shade of red wine, a pastel tone difficult to describe accurately. The wings tend to be more brown; again they may be tinged with these same reddish shades.

An eye-catching black line — like a distinct bar — runs from directly above the curved red bill, passes through the brownish-yellow iris, and both extends and broadens down each side of the neck, forming a large patch just above the upper breast. Contained within this black 'necklace' are the white cheeks, chin, and throat; they may also be flecked with buff. The flanks are barred vertically with striking black and white bars. The underparts are buff. The legs and feet are a pink to a deep red.

In 1938 the melanistic mutant pheasant was introduced into New Zealand. They are not a separate species, being a mutation of the black-necked pheasant.

The pheasant is New Zealand's foremost upland gamebird. Sensible game management practices have ensured that the species is common over much of its range.

An ideal pheasant habitat fringes coastal sand dunes on the South Kaipara Head, north of Auckland.

In 1987 the Waitaki Valley Acclimatisation Society reported that "some good coveys of California quail were about". This type of hard tussock terrain, north-west of Omarama, is well suited to the species.

The California quail is distinguished from other types of quail by its short black plume, present in both sexes.

New Zealand's most recently introduced gamebird is the red-legged partridge, which should prove a welcome addition to the upland gamebird hunting scene.

Habitat and Habits

Chukar tend to do particularly well in country similar to that of their native range. This explains why they found the rock-strewn high country of Central Otago wellnigh perfect habitat. Much of the land here is over 300 metres (1,000 feet), the temperature hot in summer and cold (but not damp) in winter.

An extremely hardy bird — perhaps the hardiest of all gamebirds — the chukar is found in altitudes of up to 2,000 metres in this country. It has the ability to survive in snow and tests have revealed it can live without free-running water. Having said that, it prefers to remain near fresh water and unless disturbed is seldom found further than 400 metres from it.

Monogamous by nature, chukar first team up in pairs in the early spring when they are almost one year old, having lived in a large communal group until then. Each pair takes up a breeding territory, which, in the case of new pairs, may be some distance away from where they have wintered over. Pairs of long standing return to established breeding grounds.

At any rate, the female chooses the nest-site, normally a well-hidden spot under a rocky ledge or amidst thick scrub such as matagouri or sweet briar. Once she has scratched out a small depression in the ground, she then lines it with roots and dry grass, and overlays this with feathers.

Meanwhile, the cock is arrogantly guarding their territory. He is an aggressive character. Indeed, hill country villagers in the chukar's native range frequently use the male chukar at festivals as substitutes for fighting cocks. Therefore feathers are almost certain to fly should another male enter this sacred ground.

The cock plays no part in incubating the eggs. Nor does he show much interest in the newly hatched chicks, attired in dense, soft down. He will, however, protect them with beak and claw should the need arise.

As soon as they are dry the chicks leave the nest. They are bright-eyed and alert. At first they feed on insects and larvae. Like many types of bird, adult chukar quickly feign injury to lure away any predators or intruders from precisely where their young are. At such a time the precocious chickens have the good sense to remain perfectly still, huddled to the ground, their varicoloured feathers of mostly brownish tones blending very well with the dull shades of the ground and vegetation.

At two weeks the chicks can fly short distances. When separated they peep anxiously until they rejoin the main group. Adult birds are more vocal in the early morning and late evening with a loud vibrating 'chuck-chuck-chuck'.

The chicks eat mostly the same foodstuffs as their parents — the seeds and leaves of matagouri, weed and rose seeds, tussock (they swallow tiny stones and pebbles to help grind down certain hard foods). Later on, in winter, they eat waste grain and other cultivated crops.

The social nature of the species becomes apparent when the chickens are about three weeks old, for the hen merges her brood with those of others in the same general vicinity. In autumn they link up with other such 'extended' families or groups and thus form the large winter coveys.

A serious problem in South Island high country chukar habitat is the use by pest destruction boards of 1080 poison on carrots, oats, and dried pellets. A decline in chukar numbers has been noted from information collated from a survey conducted by the Gamebird Management Section of the Department of Conservation, Southern Lakes, in 1987. The following two paragraphs appeared in a discussion paper prepared by that gamebird section for debate at a public meeting between DOC staff, the Otago Acclimatisation Society and the public in Alexandra on 18 November 1987:

> There is no doubt in our minds that chukar are very partial to carrot baits. We have seen green-dyed pieces in the crops of several chukar that had been shot. These crops were handed in by a successful hunter who was concerned that the birds may have been dangerous to eat.

> We have spoken to hunters who claim to have found both California quail and chukar dead, close to poison lines in recent years. One particular incident apparently occurred on Bendigo Station near Tarras and involved both quail and chukar. These birds had been feeding on green-dyed oats.

The day pest destruction boards cease to use 1080 — and surely that must happen — will be the beginning of a marked increase in the numbers of both chukar and California quail.

RED-LEGGED PARTRIDGE
(*Alectoris rufa*)

Male: Cock   Female: Hen   Young: Chicken

Range

On the Continent, where it is known as the French partridge, this compact, ground-dwelling gamebird is found in north-western Spain, France, Holland, Belgium, northern Portugal, western Germany, north-western Italy, and Corsica. It is unclear whether it is a native of all these areas or, as in the case of western Germany and northern Portugal, if it was introduced there for sporting purposes.

Successful introductions of this species have been made into the Balearic Isles (in the Mediterranean), on the Azores and Canaries, and on Madeira.

The red-legged partridge was first released in England in 1790. Today, with a population estimated at between 100,000 and 200,000 pairs, it is widely spread over a great deal of eastern England and the Midlands, but becoming scarcer in the west — ie, towards Wales. It was also released possibly as late as 1970 as far north as Scotland and west to the Isle of Man. Locally it is known as the French partridge or 'Frenchman'.

Some allied races also occur. These are the Northern Spanish, Southern Spanish, Corsican and Canary Island.

Liberations and Distribution in New Zealand

They are a very engaging, highly attractive bird, which, if they live up to expectations, will be a significant part of the avifauna of the country's grassland/shrubland areas in the very near future.

(P.J. Howard, Senior Field Officer,
Auckland Acclimatisation Society)

The year 1869 was almost certainly the first time that an attempt was made to establish red-legged partridge in this country. In March of that year, the committee of the Nelson Acclimatisation Society decided to introduce a number of

99

gamebirds from England. When the *John Bunyan* sailed from London on 11 December she had on board 48 partridges — a mixture of the red-legged and the common grey varieties.

During the early stages of the voyage a violent storm raged for some days. Normally no problem. In this particular instance, however, little care had been taken with weatherproofing the crates containing the birds, and, as a result, they suffered accordingly.

When the *John Bunyan* reached Nelson, the society were horrified to learn that only four birds were alive, of which one was a red-legged partridge. The sex of all birds is unknown. They were liberated where, some years previously (1864-1865), eight grey partridges had been released on private properties at Waimea West and Appleby. By 1871 none of these two introductions — including Nelson's sole red-legged partridge — were thought to still exist.

A curious extract from the 1897 annual report of the Wellington society reads: 'It is reported from the Rangitikei district that red-legged partridges are increasing, and a few are working north into bush-country.' Curious? Well, there is no mention of release of red-legged partridge prior to the above date in any of the society's reports.

The Southland society took delivery of 18 red-legged partridges in 1899 (20 had been shipped from London). They were liberated on Stewart Island — a dismal choice of habitat, one would think. The birds must have thought so too because they soon perished.

Two more attempts were made by the Nelson society to introduce this bird, in 1906 and 1917, but neither venture got off the ground.

In about 1910 the Auckland society undertook to import red-legged partridges from England. A large number were purchased and held at London prior to the departure of the ship. Then disaster struck: every single bird died while still in England.

The next attempt by the same society was made in 1923 when it shared — with the Feilding and Whangarei societies — a mixed shipment of 178 red-legged and grey partridges. Later, Auckland's share was distributed to pheasant breeders at both Whangarei and Hamilton.

Presumably selective breeding methods were undertaken with these birds. Possibly a number were liberated in the wild. Definitely they did not survive for any length of time, and, as a species, it would be many years before they would again be mentioned in the annual reports of the Auckland society.

In the early to mid-1970s there was much animated discussion within the ranks of the game committee of the Auckland society as to the feasibility of introducing a gamebird ideally suited to the large grassland areas that had evolved locally. The logical and unanimous choice was the red-legged partridge.

There were a number of reasons for this. Quite apart from its sporting characteristics it had been successfully introduced into Britain, where it had learned to cope with a 153-centimetre annual rainfall. Indeed, of all the far-flung partridge family it withstood high rainfall best. In suitable habitat — and surely much of New Zealand's vast agricultural lands were that now? — it was reported as 'abundant' as long as over-hunting didn't take place. Apparently it caused little crop damage. It was also considered easy to rear and propagate in cages.

The difficulties and frustrations experienced by those involved with bringing a species of gamebird into this country are alone worthy of a lengthy chapter; the pertinent details are as follows:

March 1978: Contact was made with the Game Conservancy, Fordingbridge, Hampshire, England, who supplied a list of potential suppliers of red-legged partridge eggs.

September 1978: The Minister of Agriculture stipulated conditions whereby eggs could be imported to meet both British and local customs regulations. Scotland was named as the only suitable egg source.

November 1978: A supplier of eggs in Scotland confirmed eggs would be available to meet stringent MAF quarantine standards in June 1980. Cost: $NZ1.40 per egg.

May 1980: In preparation for the arrival of 1,500 eggs, a special quarantine unit, built at a cost of $52,000, was officially opened at Massey University.

July 1980: The eggs arrived at their destination and were unpacked for the next morning. Approximately 100 eggs were either broken or cracked in transit. Of the remaining 1,400, 580 later proved to be fertile. Of this number, 150 chickens hatched, 40 of which failed exacting tests or died of natural causes.

This was in effect the real start of an attempt to establish the red-legged partridge in this country. A second importation of 638 eggs arrived at Auckland International Airport in July 1981. But it would be three more years before the society actually released the species in the wild. The following chart covers liberations until 1988.

Year	Date	Sub-Society Area	Locality	Qty
1984	17/03/84	Huntly/	Waiterimu	
	31/03/84	Te Kauwhata		
	15/10/84			822
1985	18/02/85	Huntly/	Waiterimu, Mangapiko	
	09/03/85	Te Kauwhata	Matahuru, Waerenga	631
	09/03/85	Putaruru/Tokoroa	Te Whetu, Matarawa	394
	16/03/85	Te Aroha	Wairakau	499
	13/04/85	Waitemata/Kumeu	Wharepapa, Woodhill	
		Helensville	Muriwai	499
	19/04/85	Morrinsville	Kiwitahi	462
	24/06/85	Warkworth/Wellsford	Hoteo, Tauhoa	460
1986	01/03/86	Warkworth/Wellsford	Hoteo, Tauhoa	400
	08/03/86	Franklin	Pollok	500
	05/04/86	Te Aroha	Waiorongamai	200
	19/04/86	Morrinsville	Kiwitahi	200
	07/06/86	Waitemata/Kumeu		
		Helensville	Muriwai-Wharepapa	193
	26/06/86	Putaruru	Ngatira	49
	26/06/86	Tokoroa	Tokoroa North	49
1987	21/02/87	Warkworth	Mangakura	500
	28/02/87	Franklin	Pollok	500
	13/03/87	Wellsford	Tapora	500
	28/03/87	Waitemata/Kumeu		
		Helensville	Parkhurst	500
	11/04/87	Miranda/Patetonga	Mangatarata	250
	11/04/87	Te Kauwhata	Taniwha	250

	24/04/87	Wellsford (No. 2)	Tapora	383
	22/05/87	Morrinsville	Kiwitahi	473
1988	05/03/88	Wellsford	Tapora	400
	12/03/88	Waitemata/Kumeu		
		Helensville	Parkhurst	400
	26/03/88	Franklin	Pollok	400
	30/04/88	Miranda/Patetonga	Mangatarata	200
	21/05/88	Miranda/Patetonga	Mangatarata	143
	10/06/88	Pakihi Island	Hauraki Gulf	16
				10273

Field surveys in the Waiterimu district to determine how red-legged partridge are faring have been carried out every winter since the initial release in 1984. After the 1987 survey, F. Thompson (Northern Field Officer) reported that:

> A total of 33 partridge were seen and 2 were heard but not seen. 18 were leg banded and 15 were unbanded. Of the banded birds 4 were 1984 release and 14 were assumed 1985 release. The unbanded partridge were from 2 successful wild bred broods, the first wild fledged red legs recorded in this country.

Thompson would also note that:

> During the 1987/88 summer months 8 reliable sighting reports of either partridge broods or singular chicks were reported to the Society office from within the survey area.

Meantime, other societies were naturally keen to establish the red-legged partridge in their districts; they would of course receive their initial stock and/or eggs from Auckland. For instance, during 1987 approximately 250 birds were liberated at various points in the Wanganui area and/or adjacent to it. In the following year, that society received reports that birds had been seen 'pairing up' in several areas.

Hawke's Bay appears to offer the species everything they desire in the way of habitat and climate. Liberations were made in that district at the following locations:

Red-legged Partridge Releases (banded)

21/12/87	Poraiti	6	06/04/88	Poraiti	50
24/12/87	Tutaekuri River	72	07/04/88	Waipawa River	50
05/03/88	Tongoio	50	28/06/88	Seafield	50
17/03/88	Summerlee	66	08/09/88	Tongoio	10

The local society reported in 1988:

Following a request from DOC (Gisborne) 5 male and 8 female red-legged partridge juveniles were supplied to supplement their breeders stock for the coming season.

With the 1988-89 breeding season imminent red legs are reported present in good numbers from all release sites except Waipawa River. Little follow-up has been undertaken at the latter site which is in an isolated area with extensive cover.

Also in 1988, the Nelson society were on an optimistic note:

The red-legged partridge breeding programme has continued satisfactorily during the past year. There have been several sightings, in both release areas, of wild bred chicks. Some of these have survived and appear to be good, healthy, full-sized birds. This is encouraging for the future and is some reward for all the time and effort expended by those who have taken part.

Some problems have been experienced which resulted in the loss of some chicks, but over 250 have been banded and released. Releases: Dovedale 142. Brightwater 117.

The neighbouring Marlborough district could not, however, report with similar optimism:

The red-legged partridge programme ran into considerable difficulties during the year since the last report. Several birds in the flock died just before the breeding season and some people lost their breeding pairs just on the point of lay. They really are most difficult to keep in captivity and meticulous care must be taken with feeding and dosing for disease to ensure survival.

However sufficient birds survived to produce some 750 eggs and Wellington society donated a further 100 eggs and on last year's incubation success rate this should have produced the required 500 poults for liberation. But less than 300 hatched for reasons that are not understood.

The breeding birds are now housed at a magnificent complex on land owned by Mr Soper. This facility has been set up by the hard work of Les Crafar and Ross Atkinson with the help of the Rod & Gun Club. This has cost considerably more than the original costings and still does not address the problems of incubation. Hopefully expertise gained overseas will help in this area.

The same year, the South Canterbury society issued this report:

The Society's red-legged partridge programme has moved a step forward with a further release of 120 birds last Autumn, this has now brought the total numbers of birds released in the field to just over two hundred.

The last breeding season was a little disappointing due to the fact that the egg production and fertility were well down on last year, the Society was hoping to release several hundred birds into the field.

This coming season should prove to be interesting as the offspring from the original release should be breeding, once this happens and is successful the partridge population in the area should be assured.

At present the Society are holding 40 pairs of Partridge and the programme is progressing reasonably well. Once again the Society sincerely thanks the breeders who have been involved in this project.

Typically, the North Canterbury society continued to liberate red-legged partridges in 1988, the third year they had done so. Field Officer Lawrence Piper selected the following locations:

Property	Date Banded	Date Released	Age at Release	Number Released	Comment
D. Potts, Greenpark	11/1/88	11/1/88	12 months	19	breeding adults still laying
P. Smail, Hororata	15/2/88	21/2/88	12 weeks	35	
P. Smail, Hororata	22/2/88	28/2/88	12 weeks	36	—
Turners, Southbridge	14/3/88	20/3/88	12 weeks	27	—
Turners, Southbridge	22/3/88	27/3/88	12 weeks	43	—
D. Potts, Greenpark	13/4/88	18/4/88	12 weeks	38	—
D. Potts, Greenpark	19/4/88	24/4/88	12 weeks	31	—
D. Potts, Greenpark	25/4/88	1/5/88	12 weeks	11	—

The sex ratios were: 9 male, 10 female breeding adults; of the 12-week-old juveniles, 2 were not sexed, 114 were males, 105 females, giving a total of 221.

At the present time it is still impossible to say what the long-term future of the red-legged partridge is in this country. But with perseverance and sensible game management practices, should hunting become legal, there is no good reason why the red-legged partridge cannot be as successful a gamebird as the pheasant.

Physical Description

Best described as a small roundish bird, the adult red-legged partridge has an upright rather leggy stance. Mature birds have an approximate length of 13½ inches, with males being slightly larger. Males weigh 1¼ pounds; females 1 pound.

This is a handsomely marked species, with conspicuous black, white, and chestnut bars occurring on lavender-grey flanks. Upper parts are a warm red wine colouring. A recognisable feature is the characteristic head pattern — a distinct black stripe running through the red-ringed iris to form a band on the throat, and enclosing a creamy white chin patch. The breast is marked with black spread over a warm shade of pink; the remaining underparts are orange-yellow. The belly tends to be a shade of buff. Beak, legs and feet are coral red; quite brilliant in some instances.

If anything the female is somewhat duller in appearance and this may assist in differentiating between the otherwise difficult to distinguish sexes. Also, the male tends to be more aggressive-looking than the female bird.

Habitat and Habits

Like chukar, this species displays a marked preference for light soils combined with a dry climate. In their native range they are found from sea level to around 2,100 metres, although rarely at this elevation. Parts of Nelson-Marlborough, inland Canterbury, and, in particular, Central Otago, offer ideal habitat in this country.

Also in their native range they tend to shy away from all types of wetlands, lushly grassed pastures, heavy scrub or brush. Apart from using it as edge cover, or for nesting purposes, the same thing applies to densely forested regions.

Thus they are more likely to be observed in open or semi-open pasturelands, on heaths, in well-cultivated fields, reasonably open woodlands lacking a heavy undergrowth, and even coastal sand dunes. Here, they find the bulk of their preferred food. This may include the shoots of young corn, waste grain, leaves of clover and other choice grasses, seeds of weeds, leaves of shrubs, bulbs, roots, fruit and buds. They are especially partial to over-ripe grapes in vineyards.

It is interesting to note that during 1986 and 1987, red-legged partridge were responsible for causing serious damage to seedling celery plants at Waimauku in the Auckland district. The society's reaction in this instance was a benevolent Category B classification — trapping and moving elsewhere.

In Britain this species is classed, along with pheasant and grey partridge, as a major pest insofar as the British Sugar Corporation is concerned. By pecking at the leaves of seedling sugarbeet they undermine crop yields. By and large, however, the red-legged partridge, as already noted, is not considered a significant threat to crops or agriculture.

As the breeding season approaches, the birds boost their protein intake by feeding more heavily on small snails, spiders, and insects such as grasshoppers, beetles, ants and their eggs, flies, etc. Overseas research indicates that adult birds can survive long periods with little access to fresh water.

Winter coveys tend to break up in early April. Pairs then select a suitable territory; brisk fighting takes place between cock birds until all are well satisfied with their lot.

The nest-site, chosen by either bird (British research indicates this is more likely to be the male), is usually in hedge bottoms, under a tight clump of long grass such as tussock, or admist low bushes scattered alongside the fringes of native or exotic forests. The actual nest, a mere scratching on the ground, is lined with dry leaves and grasses. The female, with comfort in mind, overlays the lining with feathers plucked from her own body.

She will lay on average 10-18 eggs; as many as 28 have been recorded in England. In the manner of ground birds, the eggs are well camouflaged in colour, being a buffish-earth shade, spotted with reddish-brown, rather faintly in some cases.

The female is able to produce more than one clutch. In New Zealand this may take place with as many as 25 per cent of pairs. Apparently the cock goes down on the first batch of eggs, the female the other. Chicks hatch after 23-25 days and depart the nest immediately. The two broods do not intermingle and they are tended by the respective parent.

In Britain, both parents are thought to incubate a single brood. It is possible, however, that some cock birds, finding themselves in this situation, depart the nest-site after perhaps a week and seek out other females or possibly join an all-male group.

The red-legged partridge has a wide range of calls, often uttered from a low perch. By far the most prominent is the male's loud territorial call — a distinct 'chuck-chuck-ar'. Both sexes possess a sharp alarm cry.

4 IN PURSUIT OF UPLAND GAMEBIRDS

Pheasant

With his extremely colourful plumage, there is no more desirable or sought-after gamebird in the world than a cock pheasant. In both appearance and behaviour, he truly epitomises all that is best in upland gamebirds; he, above all, is the ideal gamebird to mount as a trophy.

Once the season is underway a cock pheasant, comparatively tame and easy to locate until then, suddenly becomes ultra-wary and difficult to find. The fact that he can gobble his daily ration of food in less than 15 minutes if so inclined allows him to remain under cover for long periods. (It still takes him a full six hours to digest properly.)

The intelligent hunter will naturally check out a hunting area well before the hunting season starts. This is best undertaken during the breeding period. The cocks are at their least wary then as they seek the opposite sex or perhaps do noisy battle with their brightly garbed counterparts. Quite often they make resonant calls — a distinct three-syllable 'ca-a-ck!' or 'kor-r-rk!' If silent, a cock can often be encouraged to reveal its whereabouts should a hunter be sufficiently adept with a game call. An Olt Regular Pheasant Call is a good choice. The idea when calling all upland game is not to overdo it — you only want to find out their whereabouts.

These home territories, which remain fairly constant over the years providing nothing drastic happens to the habitat, are invariably close to water. Certainly they will be in warm, sunny spots. So knowing precisely where the birds both roost and feed puts the hunter in the box seat once that big day in May at last arrives. At that time, croplands are rated as the most productive areas to hunt.

No serious gamebird hunter would be without a dog.

Indeed, he would be quite lost without it. The ideal gundog tirelessly ranges large tracts of open country in search of the tell-tale scent of winged game either resting or feeding on the ground. Once the warm, intoxicating smell tells him that prey is very close, a matter of a few metres away, he freezes into a majestic pose. Every muscle is tense. His head is held high; his tail aloft. He indicates the bird's position by pointing at it with his nose, hence the term 'pointer'.

Classical pointing dogs include the English setter, Gordon setter, Brittany spaniel (the only pointing spaniel), weimaraner, and munsterlander.

In Britain and the United States, the English springer spaniel is considered the premier pheasant 'flushing' dog. In this part of the world, many hunters believe the German short-haired pointer, with its ability to hunt, point, and then retrieve, is second to none. There is also no good reason why a top-flight waterfowl dog — a labrador, say — will not adjust to this form of hunting. Indeed, they will mostly revel in the change of scene and the opportunity to enjoy a good workout while learning entirely different hunting tactics.

Unlike the waterfowl hunter, who mostly waits patiently in a hide and dresses for warmth and concealment, the upland gamebird hunter is mobile. Either hunting alone or in a small party (the normal way), he wants to be easily seen in the field. For safety's sake he will wear distinctly coloured clothing — reds and blues are ideal. Anything in fact that doesn't blend in well with the surroundings could be considered a good choice.

Four or five men often make up a shooting party. Usually they have hunted together for several seasons, so they both know and trust each other. With the dog ranging ahead, they form a straight line, or shallow U-shaped formation, and head into the wind. This allows the dog to pick up the scent and invariably take off into the wind. They are separated by maximum shotgun range and communicate among themselves with looks and gestures rather than words. It is an unwritten law that they only shoot directly ahead or directly behind their position.

Suddenly, with or without a dog's warning, a cock pheasant explodes right in front of one of the hunters and the air is filled with a clapping of strong wings drumming frantically against a feathered body. The startled cock also emits an angry, raucous cackle, similar to his mating call. Although half-expecting it to happen, the surprised hunter reacts too slowly and the bird escapes without a shot being fired. Taking a deep breath to steady himself, the hunter is aware that his heart is pounding and that for the moment his legs have turned to jelly. He smiles rather ruefully at his nearest companion — the first 'flush' of the season generally affects most hunters that way.

Soon after, the same thing happens further down the line. This time, however, the hunter is mentally prepared. He could have fired before the cock was 15 metres away, but he restrained himself, knowing such a shot would ruin too much edible meat. He fires a split-second or two later when the cock is about 25-30 metres away. A fine shot — the cock crumples and falls limply to the ground. The hunter smiles in a well-satisfied fashion and watches his dog, upon being ordered, bounding eagerly to the first kill of the day.

It may be necessary to work over a patch of cropland or scrub-lined riverbed several times before a cock breaks. As a rule, however, he will not sit 'tight' for too long. Almost certainly he will flush before the hen will. After an initial burst of dazzling speed both sexes, still caught up in their momentum, can glide just above grass level amazingly fast. Back on ground, they will invariably run a short distance before sitting tight again.

While most hunters use 12-gauge shotguns to hunt this game, author Jack Byrne gives his seal of approval to a 20-gauge shotgun, a double-barrelled gun bored in improved cylinder and half-choke. He adds, that he'd 'be happy with a light 12-gauge in the same boring'.

Top areas for pheasants are in the north — ie, North Auckland and Auckland — the principle being that the further north one goes, the better the hunting. Good sport can be enjoyed in parts of Hawke's Bay, the pumice lands of the central North Island, and the long coastal strip extending from Foxton to Waikanae.

Quail

In the North Island both species of quail are found mostly in the middle to outer extremities of pheasant range, although they sometimes share the same general territory. The scrub-coated pumice land around Rotorua and Taupo can serve as no better example. In the South Island look for California quail a little below the lower levels of chukar range.

The two species differ in voice. California quail make a loud and frequently kurr-like sound, which, to some people, might sound more like 'Ha, haa, haa!' They are especially fond of uttering it supposedly after they have given a hunter the slip. During hunting they can be rather noisy.

In contrast, the brown quail's call is a long, drawn-out whistle. Rising in pitch, it sounds very much like 'tu-whee'. Under hunting pressure they are not nearly as vocal as the other type of quail found in this country.

Perhaps the most productive time to venture after quail is the late autumn when they gather in large coveys of 50 to 100 birds. They lie well to pointers and setters, rocketing into the air like miniature jet fighters. Unpredictably, they head to all points of the compass. This is called a 'covey rise' and it adds up to fast, exciting sport. Shotguns need to be fast-handling and swing smoothly. Use No. 7/8 shot and you won't go far wrong with this game.

Single birds can be followed up cautiously after a covey has broken. Like other upland gamebirds, they are apt to run a short distance after alighting — an inbuilt safety device, obviously.

Nationally, a surprisingly high 41 per cent of licence holders hunt quail. They do so for an average of four days (about 70 per cent hunt from one to five days, and 20 per cent from six to 10 days). In Otago, for instance, approximately 40 per cent of licence holders pursue quail.

From research conducted by the Otago Acclimatisation Society from 1985 to 1987, when an upland game diary was supplied to some hunters, a number of interesting facts emerged:

The brown quail is a small, roundish, brown-coloured bird. Despite being introduced into the South Island, its present-day range is confined to the North Island.

The chukar is perhaps the hardiest of all upland gamebirds. Certainly it presents a hunter with his toughest challenge.

In this typical upland gamebird hunting scene, Peter 'Stretch' Lucas is intently watching his English springer spaniel scenting for game.

In England and the United States the English springer spaniel is rated an excellent flushing dog.

Quail			
	1987	1986	1985
Total Guns	460	321	383
Average hours/gun day	4.0	4.1	3.8
Total coveys seen	246	160	162
Total birds seen	6318	4712	3543
Average covey size	26	29.4	22
Total shot	1309	860	707
Total retrieved	1093	771	619
Total lost	216	89	88
Birds retrieved/hour	0.58	0.6	0.42
Average daily bag	2.4	2.4	1.6

Note: a high percentage of Otago society licence holders hunt quail in the Southern Lakes district.

Chukar

One of the most appealing aspects of upland gamebird hunting is its great diversity. Pheasant hunting, for example, usually takes place in low-lying, easy-walking terrain. Chukar hunting takes place in steep, broken country up to high altitudes, which makes top physical fitness, suitable climbing boots and a daypack essential.

How do you find where chukar are? For a start, you could approach the proprietor of a sports shop in any of the small towns within chukar range. After all, they are selling shotguns (possibly) and ammunition (certainly) to those participating in the sport. Acclimatisation society and DOC field staff are another likely avenue to pursue. The same thing can be said of pest destruction board workers. Importantly, almost all chukar are found on private land; big stations as a rule. Permission to hunt there is required, but isn't a real problem if handled correctly.

So you have been given the 'okay' to shoot on a property holding good numbers of birds. Points to remember are that chukar tend to remain in the lower reaches of their territories overnight — warm, sheltered places offering ample cover where they instinctively feel secure from predators. In the early morning they start to drift uphill in small coveys. They will visit water and are said to drink at last three times daily. Look for their green and white droppings around waterholes or small streams.

In the early morning and the late evening, they are rather vocal. Their call is a loud, ringing 'chuck-chuck-chuck' — an unmistakable sound. Later in the day you might require a game call such as an Olt Chukar Call, Model 500, to discover where they are. A single call is often enough to get an answer. Leave it at that. They are suspicious enough as it is.

Best days to hunt chukar are warm with, if possible, a light breeze. This allows the dog to work into the breeze. Chukar lie well to pointers and so, in the manner of quail, it is best to shoot over them.

Frequently, chukar will be disturbed as a hunting party moves steadily uphill. Possibly they will flush, to alight a considerable distance away. If given the choice, however, they much prefer to run. With their strongly developed legs, much heavier in proportion to their body weight than those of other gamebirds, they run, hop, and half-fly from rock to boulder, travelling up steep inclines at a burst of speed far beyond the capabilities of humans.

Alternatively, they may wait silently as man and dog approach — hugging the ground, possibly aware that as long as they remain still they are extremely difficult to spot. In North America they have earned the rather affectionate nickname 'grey ghost' because of their general colouration and extraordinary ability to merge into their surroundings. Given that most chukar range in this country resembles the hilly terrain of California, and even Arizona, the same nickname could very well apply here.

Not given to panic, then, chukar may even allow the hunters to actually pass within a few feet of them before taking to the air. On the other hand, they will just as likely flush under a hunter's feet or flap their wings in a dog's startled face. In a word, unpredictable.

When flushed, chukar explode from a low crouch. They power away as swiftly as the fastest quail and then, suddenly, sweep downhill, accelerating to perhaps 80 km/h. Small wonder there is a marked tendency for many shooters to fire both behind and over such elusive targets which, when pursued by falcons in their native range, have been estimated to reach 130 km/h.

The normal speed they fly at, however, is more like 55-65 km/h, which still represents a lead of at least 2-2.5 metres. Also, you must make a split-second adjustment of about 1-1.5 metres to compensate for that rapid downhill flight.

Because of the climbing involved, and because autumn can get very warm in chukar country, a lightweight shotgun is ideal. Use No. 6/7 shot in either a 12 or 20-gauge. This will prove ideal for those close shots, but, as a precaution, slot a No. 4 shot into the full-choke barrel. Chances are you will put down your chukar at closer to 40 metres.

Certainly, then, chukar represent the toughest upland gamebird hunting this country has to offer. A hunter must be prepared to spend a lot of time simply searching for his game before the opportunity of a shot arrives. This is borne out from research carried out by the Otago Acclimatisation Society:

Chukar

	1987	1986	1985
Total Guns	31	32	43
Average hours/gun day	4.3	3.0	2.3
Total coveys seen	10	14	7
Total birds seen	124	112	127
Average covey size	12.4	8	18
Total shot	41	29	11
Total retrieved	27	21	11
Total lost	14	8	0
Birds retrieved/hour	0.2	0.2	0.11
Average daily bag	0.87	0.65	0.25

Red-legged Partridge

Naturally much of the general advice already given about hunting upland gamebirds can be applied to this species. In the field, the red-legged partridge takes full advantage of its strongly developed runner's legs by refusing to fly when confronted by a dog or beaters. Often they disturb other coveys, which, in turn, also run. Because of this they have a rather bad reputation on the Continent and in Britain. But the fact of the matter is that they do drive well should adequate cover be present — a hedge, for instance, or dense clumps of brush.

Any slander directed at their sporting qualities is very quickly dispensed with when they take flight. They fly fast and low; bullet-like. They also break singly. It is not to any shooter's discredit to miss one of these difficult targets. Only an expert will repeatedly put them down in the field.

In Britain they are normally treated like pheasants on a put-and-take basis — that is, the numbers taken on any given shoot are replaced with new stock before the next shooting season. That may have to be seriously considered in this country eventually.

5 SMALL GAME ANIMALS

RABBIT
(*Oryctolagus cuniculus*)

Male: Buck   Female: Doe   Young: Kitten

Range

Rabbits are classified in the order Lagomorpha, family Leporidae. Indigenous or introduced, they are found on every continent except Antarctica.

The European rabbit is classified as *Oryctolagus* (1758). The subspecies or race we are primarily concerned with is *O.c. cuniculus*, which ranges in a wide band throughout much of Europe except for alpine areas where snow lies on the ground for long periods. Also found in the broad salt marshes of Europe is *O.c. brachyotos*.

Successful introductions of the European rabbit were made into Chile, Africa, Australia, New Zealand, and a number of warm islands in the Atlantic and Pacific Oceans. An interesting fact pertaining to Madeira, Desertas, Salvage Islands, and the Azores — all of which are found in the Atlantic Ocean — is that the introduced rabbits have gradually altered their appearance somewhat. Now broadly classified as *O.c. huxeyi* (1874), they may on the Salvage Islands be the size of a large hare, or, as occurs on Desertas, resemble a dwarf-sized version of the rabbit common to this country.

Three more varieties of the European rabbit are found in north-west Africa while as many as 15 forms of *Silvilagus* range over North, Central and South America, as well as in the West Indies. Among them is the common cottontail. Primarily a farmland dweller, the cottontail (which, incidentally, was the model for Walt Disney's immortal cartoon character, Thumper) inhabits the entire length and breadth of the United States — overlapping into Canada in the north and spilling into Mexico in the south, where a localised version of this species may be found.

The brush rabbit of the western regions is inclined to favour thick scrubby terrain. Also found in some western states is a single species called *Brachylagus*, while in the swampy regions of the south-east states can be found the marsh rabbit.

Liberations and Distribution in New Zealand

Precisely when rabbits first came to this country is unclear. When G.M. Thomson was researching his 1921 publication, *Wild Life In New Zealand*, he was told by the Rev. Richard Taylor (author of *Te Ika a Maui*) that the early missionaries were the first to bring rabbits here. Taylor, however, was unable to provide Thomson with any firm dates. Thomson commented: 'if he is correct, however, they were almost certainly brought from New South Wales to the northern part of the colony between 1820 and 1830.'

By 1844 a few rabbits existed on a small island between the mouths of the Clutha and Mataura rivers in Southland. How they got there is unknown. Four years later they were liberated in the sand hills between Invercargill and Riverton, at Queenstown, and near the Waitaki River in Canterbury. They were possibly first introduced into Nelson and Marlbourough about 1858. In all instances they did not spread, failed to breed in the accepted manner, and mostly disappeared in later years.

The turning point came in the mid-1860s when the Otago Acclimatisation Society liberated 60 rabbits in 1866, a further 26 the following year, and another 18 in 1868. From that period on there was never any question about whether or not they would survive in this country.

By 1878 they had reached Lake Wakatipu, leaving a devastated landscape in their wake. To the east they had reached the Clutha River. Only a few years later they were found over the greater part of Otago and, apart from unsuitable habitat, the same thing could be said of Southland.

Meantime, they had been introduced into the lower half of the North Island, the Wairarapa, in 1863. Because of the climatic conditions (higher rainfall) and the nature of the terrain (considerably more forested), they were slower to spread north. Even so, by 1900 they were well entrenched in most parts of the North Island, finding the East Coast a particularly ideal place in which to breed.

By 1880 the South Island and, in particular, Otago rabbits were so numerous that the fine natural grasses on which sheep and cattle depended were almost totally destroyed. Sheep, for instance, perished from starvation by the hundreds of thousands. It is no exaggeration to say that the majority of squatters were ruined. Eventually immense areas of grazing land were abandoned. For the moment the rabbit had won.

In those days a variety of methods were used by farmers and runholders in an attempt to control the pest — hunting with dogs, shooting, digging out the warren, poisoning with various baits, trapping. Later still, wire netting, the introduction of stoats, weasels, and ferrets, fumigating the burrows with poisonous gases (such as disulphide and hydrocyanic) and the stimulus given to trapping by the export trade in frozen rabbit carcasses, helped reduce their numbers.

The problem of just too many rabbits was no closer to being solved many years later. Indeed, the number of rabbit skins sent overseas between 1938 and 1947 — 13,335,000 — indicates that the rabbit population was possibly on the increase.

The immediate post-war years saw a considerable expansion of the rabbit meat industry, all of which was sold to Britain. The actual preparation of the canned meat was carried out at the big freezing works, mostly located in the South Island. One such firm — S. Ward (NZ) Ltd of Invercargill — described its operation in this manner:

> A fleet of specially fitted trucks is on the move day and night collecting rabbits within a radius of nearly 200 miles from Invercargill. Any rabbiter may erect on the roadside adjoining his property a 'rabbit rail'. On receipt of advice to this effect, it is visited by the truck every day and the rabbits are collected. These trucks operate over the whole of Southland and collect, on the average, 6 rabbits per mile with a total of approximately 2,000 per trip. The price in the summer of 1947 was 2 shillings a pair at the rail. The factory has facilities for both freezing and canning.

As the years went by, the so-called 'rabbit population' showed no signs of abating. By the early 1950s there were 102 rabbit boards in the country — 58 in the North Island and 44 in the South Island. Nearly every district in Central Otago, for instance, had its own rabbit board. The Cromwell board's territory covered 230,000 acres. On average they employed 45 men full-time. Total expenditure in 1951 came to £34,000.

In the meantime a hideous virus called myxomatosis was devastating rabbits in Australia, specifically in those regions where certain types of mosquito were found — the more humid eastern states. The mosquito transmitted the virus from sick to healthy rabbits by carrying it on the mouth parts (once the virus reaches the gut of a mosquito it cannot be passed on). Oddly enough, there is no period of incubating required in the body of a mosquito before the virus becomes effective, nor, as in the case of malaria, is there a build-up of it in the insect. The entire transmission, then, is purely a mechanical one.

With myxomatosis proving so effective a killer in Australia — by 1953 approximately 90 per cent of rabbits there had succumbed to the virus — it was decided to try the same method of elimination in this country. In late 1951 and early 1952, the Department of Agriculture carried out a series of tests, releasing myxomatosis-infected rabbits into areas of heavy rabbit concentrations. Twelve South Island sites and nine North Island locations were used, with a further eight sites in the South Island selected a year later.

On Haldon station in the Mackenzie Country, 753 infected rabbits were set free to mingle with the incredible numbers infesting the large property. Other sites in the Waitaki Valley district were similarly visited. A further 500 rabbits were liberated near Lawrence. By early 1953 the same thing had happened near Ranfurly, Roxburgh, Kurow, and Balclutha. All told some 2,000 plus rabbits were used in the South Island experiments. (Figures for the North Island tests have not been available.)

The virus took off like a bush fire on Haldon station and the rabbit population fell away dramatically. Long-term success? Ironically, no! For the same results were not sustained there, or, for that matter, at any of the other experimental sites. With no suitable carrier — mosquito or sandfly — to successfully transmit the virus, the scheme had to be judged a complete failure.

As a matter of interest, it was also in 1953 that myxomatosis first showed up in rabbits in Britain. It was thought to have arrived there by way of fleas that had attached themselves to migrating birds, which had fed on rabbits deliberately infected with the virus in France. Myxomatosis would ultimately achieve even more devastating results on the rabbit population of Britain than it did in Australia, where much of the drier hinterland was lacking suitable carriers.

In 1954 the exportation of rabbits from New Zealand — for whatever means — was banned by the government. The Rabbit Destruction Council, formed in 1947, was responsible for this. All along it had opposed the rabbit meat and fur industry, rightly regarding it as a farming operation rather than a way of assisting the rabbit boards to eradicate the species. This, then, was a highly significant change in the story of the rabbit in this country — a time when the Rabbit Destruction Council shifted into top gear. It intended to wipe the rabbit from the face of New Zealand. Eventually it would turn to 1080 poison as a method of dealing with the pest.

In baited form, the highly controversial 1080 poison would prove an effective killer of rabbits. It was also just as effective on hares, possums, deer, pigs, goats, birds, and family pets.

Today the various pest destruction boards around the country continue to wage war on the amazingly prolific rabbit. In most districts they do so successfully, keeping them well under control. It is only in the South Island — parts of Southland and much of Central Otago, running up to the Mackenzie Country — where rabbits remain a serious problem.

Let's take Ben Ohau station, near Twizel, as an example. This high-country run is owned by Simon and Priscilla Cameron. The station has been in the family since 1937, when Simon's father took it over. Rabbits were bad then and his father killed by poisoning an estimated 84,000 in that first year. Since then rabbits have been a constant source of worry to the family. Today, Simon estimates they number in their tens of thousands, far outnumbering his 6,000 sheep, 320 cattle, and 200 goats.

And what of 1080? Well, early in 1988 Simon invited a local gun club to shoot on a part of the station that just three months previously had been extensively poisoned. In just two hours they shot 1,200 rabbits. The rabbits had become bait-shy, as indeed they are on most stations where 1080 has been used too much.

At the time of writing, there appears to be no real solution to the 'rabbit problem' that exists in these regions. Since the early 1980s there has been much talk of reintroducing myxomatosis into New Zealand, especially in those areas where it was first tried out in the 1950s. The carrier this time would be the introduced common European rabbit flea.

Many hard-hit runholders are adamant that this virus is the only real solution to the never-ending dilemma. To emphasise their case, they point out its amazing successes in Britain and Europe.

Proposals to reintroduce myxomatosis have been put forward at a number of public meetings in recent years. In a short article in the Waitaki Valley Acclimatisation 1987 Annual Report, G. Hughes, a field management officer, considers that 'it appears unlikely an attempt to introduce the Myxoma Virus, using the European Rabbit Flea as a vector, will eventuate'. His reasons for reaching this conclusion are explained as follows:

> It is interesting to read the Environmental Impact Report, where a survey of views expressed in 1983 through submissions from Pest Boards, the general public, and other organisations show, of the 552 submissions received, 29 submissions favoured the introduction of myxomatosis, 506 opposed the introduction of myxomatosis, six submissions made no comment and 11 took a neutral stance.
>
> It is certain that apart from the moral acceptability or the inhumanity of intentionally inflicting such a disease on one of God's creatures, there will be, if successful, an impact on the environment we have never experienced. The myxomatosis issue in virtually all its aspects, is dominated by controversy, uncertainties and unknowns.

Physical Description

A mature rabbit stands about 6-8 inches high at shoulder height, has a body length of around 16-18 inches, and, in the case of large bucks, may weigh up to 3 pounds.

A rabbit has chisel-like front teeth, with two pairs of upper incisors. All told rabbits have 28 teeth. Sharp claws are attached to powerful feet. The crepuscular eyes (pertaining to twilight) are large. Front and back legs are in proportion to the size of the body.

The soft, densely packed body fur is normally a grey or fawnish-brown and frequently brownish-red about the shoulders. The belly is lighter in colour, tending towards white in some instances. The top of the tail is darker, possibly black or black-tipped, and white below; uplifted it resembles a ball of fluff.

According to R.M. Lockley (*The Private Life of the Rabbit*, 1964) mutations with peculiar colour and other abnormalities occur in rabbits in Britain. He considers that albinos are 'rather rare' while melanistic (black) rabbits are common, sometimes forming up to 100 per cent of some communities — ie, the Islet of Samson, and Sicily. Closer to home, C. Allison (*The Australian Hunter*, 1969) states that in Australia 'albinism is not uncommon; nor is the incidence of black or cream conies'.

In this country, however, we must consider a black rabbit to be rare. For instance, during two years of field operations with a pest destruction board in Hawke's Bay, I observed only one. Around Alexandra and Cromwell, where I made three separate field trips in 1988 and observed an incredible number of rabbits, I again saw only one that was black. For the record, I have never seen an albino in the wild state in this country; which isn't to say they do not exist.

Habitat and Habits
Essentially rabbits are creatures of open country; they do not like long grasses. Given the choice, they much prefer well-drained sandy soil. They are often found adjacent to farmlands, where they find suitable places to burrow in patches of scrub. In cities or towns they may live in reserves and, in particular, on or close to golf courses. Good dry cover is invariably found in both places. As proven in Australia, rabbits have the ability to withstand long periods of drought. They do not tolerate excessive rainfall very well. This acts as an effective means of control, since it swamps many warrens and kills helpless kittens. The East Coast of the North Island is a point in case.

One sultry summer's evening on Matangi station, near Alexandra in Central Otago, I spotted a rabbit dart into its burrow.

I found that the opening was hardly bigger than my fist. Scattered about this, and several other similar-sized entrances to the warren, were heaps of current-sized droppings. From research, I knew there would be no faeces inside the warren; nor would they urinate in there. For rabbits are fastidious creatures — house proud, so to speak. It is just as well they are so inclined. An unhealthy lifestyle in such cramped living quarters — where they spend approximately half of their lives — would ultimately bring disease and, possibly, death.

Driven by the compulsion of her rapidly developing pregnancy a 'queen' doe would have been directly responsible for starting this particular warren — a maze of separate tunnels and roomy chambers where the young are born. Her partner, old Buck himself, is none too enthusiastic when it comes to bending the back and digging. No matter. The doe works industriously enough for both of them and soon excavates a suitable tunnel.

The nesting area may be only a few feet below the surface of the ground; it may be considerably deeper than that in a well-established warren. Her nest, contained in a small chamber, is lined with grasses (mostly) and other dried vegetation. A touch of luxury is provided when she tears fur from her own body — about the belly usually — to spread over the top.

The buck, meanwhile, has galvanised himself into marking out a specific territory by secreting a colourless fluid from the glands under his jaw — a 'chinning' motion which deposits the powerful scent on plants and rocks. The message it conveys to other rabbits — stay off! — couldn't be more clear. It is the buck's role to defend this ground, to mate with the doe, and to protect her from the unwanted advances of sexually orientated males lacking a female of their own. They are usually young, incautious bucks not yet a year old.

The young, incongruously called kittens, are born after a 28-day gestation period. Litters vary in number, ranging from three to as many as a dozen. At birth kittens are blind, deaf, hairless, and weigh around two ounces. Instinctively they attach themselves at regular intervals to one of their mother's eight teats.

By day seven they have doubled in weight. Twenty-four hours later they have a light covering of fur and their teeth and claws are forming. Before day 10 they can see. By three weeks they are well covered with fur and, egged on by mother, poke inquisitive heads above the ground and gaze about them with wondering eyes.

Kittens are suckled for about one month, by which time they are feeding and frolicking near the warren in the late afternoon, overnight, and in the first light of a new day. The doe will abandon them during the latter part of the fourth week. Nevertheless, they will continue to live in the nest. The doe, having mated two days after giving birth, will again give birth shortly after leaving her earlier litter. Usually she will dig another tunnel — quite near as a rule — and prepare a new nesting area. The exception to this is with the latest litter of the season, when they may remain with their parents in the same nest for quite some time.

All told the breeding season lasts about eight months. During the rest of the year (summer months) the bucks are not sexually active because, while they moult, their testes are withdrawn.

A rabbit is sexually mature at 9-12 months of age, though it is not at all uncommon for a doe to conceive when she is much younger, at 5-6 months old. At about 18-20 months a rabbit is fully mature — the peak of its strength. It is mostly downhill, and rapidly, after that.

During the breeding season a doe will litter at about 30-day intervals. She mates around every seventh day — a time when, if the buck isn't forthcoming — she will seek him out and court him. While engaged in the sexual act, a buck may emit low throaty grunts. Apart from when they utter a terrified scream — as they do when caught suddenly in a gin trap, or pounced on by a predator — they are not otherwise vocal amongst themselves.

Naturally most serious fighting takes place at this time of the year, particularly during the first two months of spring. Bucks battle in deadly earnest. Grappling together, each animal will strive with untold vigour and determination to sink its formidable teeth into the head, or, better still, neck of the other.

The double chisel action of rabbit incisors can gnaw through the hardest timber. On the previously mentioned Ohau station, for example, they have been known to chew their way through tanalised fenceposts — rabbitproof fencing blocking their way to ample feed — so that the top half of the post is left hanging in the air, no longer joined to the stump at the bottom. Mostly, however, the bucks fight with their hindlegs. The claws are sharp, honed by constant use. They can cause deep wounds. Indeed, a well-timed blow can disembowel an animal too slow to protect its vulnerable midriff. Many such encounters take place when a young buck foolishly enters the territory of a big dominant fellow. The youngster invariably takes a bloody hiding before skulking off to lick his wounds. This is the accepted order of things. The younger buck's time will surely come.

Male: Buck/Jack   Female: Doe   Young: Leveret

Range

Hares are found in most continents, native or introduced. Thirty species exist world-wide, of which eight occur in Europe. They are found in England and Scotland — especially the lower and more cultivated parts, and north of the Orkney and Shetland islands — and extend through to central Russia. In the north they reach mid-Finland, while in the south they extend to the northern parts of Israel.

The common or brown hare found in Britain is classified as *Lepus europaeus*. This is the species that was introduced into both Australia and New Zealand.

For sporting purposes, the European hare was introduced into the Falklands (1740), the Bahamas (1842), Ireland (1852), Tasmania (1854), the Australian mainland (1859), Sweden (1886), South America (1888), the United States (1888-1893), eastern Canada (1912), and Siberia (1935).

The so-called jack rabbit of North America is in fact a hare. It is found throughout the western parts of the American continent, inhabiting a broad band from Canada to Mexico. Among the various species found there are the white-sided jack, the white-tailed jack, and the black-tailed jack.

Liberations and Distribution in New Zealand

Apparently the first hares (number unknown) to run free in this country were a rather adventurous lot. When their vessel, the *Eagle*, arrived at Lyttelton in 1851, they seized their opportunity to escape by leaping through a porthole into the sea. Being excellent swimmers they would, no matter the distance, have experienced little if any difficulty in reaching dry land. Some months later they were observed on Banks Peninsula. Almost certainly these animals did not survive for any length of time.

In September 1867 the Canterbury Acclimatisation Society had in its fenced grounds in Hagley Park just one hare, a doe. This had been given to them by Dr J. Macdonald, the surgeon on the vessel *Blue Jacket*, which had recently arrived with British immigrants on board. The society regarded this gift as a most 'valuable present'. They certainly would not have taken that attitude had those hares spotted on Banks Peninsula many years previously established themselves. In other words, finding a suitable mate for the society's single hare would have proven a rather simple matter.

A second hare — a doe — was presented to the same society by Captain Rose of the vessel *Mermaid* early in 1868. In December of that year, a third animal — described as 'a fine jack hare' — was received from the Melbourne Acclimatisation Society. Additional animals — from England, but mostly from Australian-bred stock — were obtained by the Canterbury Acclimatisation Society in subsequent years. This pattern of introducing the hare was more or less paralleled in other parts of the country.

For the record, the Otago Acclimatisation Society obtained three hares from Victoria in 1867. In Nelson, the local society liberated two hares — a buck and doe — on the low hills overlooking the northern suburbs. Again they were Australian-bred animals.

It is worth noting that when the *John Bunyan* sailed for this country from London in 1869 it had 40 hares on board. For reasons unknown to the author only one animal survived this journey; however it should be pointed out that the hare frequently proved a nervous and temperamental passenger. On voyages from England to Australia, for instance, it was found that if a number of hares were placed in an uncovered cage they would usually panic, either killing one another in insane fury or simply dying of fright.

We can explain this latter phenomenon by first drawing attention to the size of a hare's heart, which, in comparison to its body, is extraordinarily large. It is the heart that activates the hindlegs to a speed few animals can equal. The heart, however, will not support the animal in terror. A hare that has been caught in a rabbit trap, and which as a result has received little more than a bruised leg, can serve as an example. When grasped firmly so that it might be released, it is not uncommon for a hare to let out a terrible screech and then die. An attempt to take nine hares to Tasmania in 1868 failed when the crew — revelling in the arrival of New Year's Day with horns, drums, and much drunken shouting and laughter — caused the hares to panic and again die of fright.

At any rate, the sole survivor of the *John Bunyan* was handed over to the Nelson Acclimatisation Society. It was liberated where the two hares from Victoria had been two years previously.

The Southland Acclimatisation Society also obtained its hares from Victoria — an undisclosed number in 1869, a further two animals in 1871, and as many as 40 in 1887. Meanwhile, the Auckland Acclimatisation Society imported 20 hares in 1868 and a further nine animals three years later. Further south, the Taranaki Acclimatisation Society brought in an unknown number in 1876. Two years before that the Wellington Acclimatisation Society took charge of two hares, an additional 14 animals in 1875, and four more a year later.

So how did some of these liberations fare? Remarkably well it would seem. For instance, the abundant hares of the Nelson district originated from a release of just three animals. Down in Otago, where they had been liberated at Waihola, the society reported they were 'plentiful' just two years after they had been liberated. In 1885 the Wellington Acclimatisation Society reported they were 'numerous in the vicinity of Wellington and the lower end of the Wairarapa Valley'.

But in no part of the country did they increase as quickly as they did in Canterbury. By 1876 they were regarded by farmers in that part of the country as a real menace. The Canterbury Acclimatisation Society found itself inundated with demands from irate land owners that they be allowed to shoot the hares. Despite this, the society still saw fit in that same year to capture 80 hares in the vicinity of Christchurch and then liberate them in outlying districts. They would have an appropriate term for this nowadays — acclimatisation madness!

One landowner with a significant hare problem in the

Canterbury region was Lancelot Walker of Four Peaks station. A few years previously he had imported some hares from Melbourne. He gave them full protection and they multiplied. By 1876 they were running riot on his property. Not only had they destroyed both his kitchen and flower garden, but they had also caused immense havoc in his nursery of 12,000 trees, killing an estimated 9,000 of them. Walker's relief was no doubt monumental when at last the society, after approaching government, granted him and others in the same grim predicament full authority to shoot hares; the required warrant or permit was valid for one month.

Early in 1877 the first coursing club — following deep-rooted traditions established in the old country — was formed in Canterbury. Coursing may be defined as the pursuit of game by dogs using the sense of sight rather than smell to follow the game.

With a surplus of hares on its hands, the Canterbury Acclimatisation Society placed the following advertisement in the Christchurch daily papers of April 1877:

HARES! HARES! HARES!

Persons wishing to purchase hares can do so by applying to the undersigned within 10 days from date. Purchasers to take delivery and provide for their removal from the Society's Gardens immediately after they are caught.

S.C. Farr, Hon. Sec.

Many applications for hares at £1 each were made to the society. Possibly the Canterbury Coursing Club was the largest purchaser with a total of 79 animals.

The inaugural coursing season of 1877 in the Canterbury province aroused intense interest. The rules stated that coursing might take place from sunrise to sunset. The society also stressed that the main aim was 'not for sport or the destruction of hares' but to drive them into outlying districts where they had not yet found a way. The problem was that no one bothered to tell the greyhounds, the dog most commonly used for this purpose, precisely what the intentions of the society were. The greyhound, given the opportunity, is a killer first and foremost.

Now in a fair chase situation (one-to-one basis) a hare, with its magnificent ability to uncannily gauge its pursuer's speed, has every chance of out-running a greyhound. Indeed, it takes an exceptionally fast and long-winded greyhound to catch a hare in full flight. But one greyhound was never used in any coursing event. If a hare was proving a particularly difficult customer to catch up with, then it was just as likely other dogs would join in the hunt. For instance, at a gathering of the Sheffield Coursing Club on the estate of Sir John Hall at Hororata in the early 1880s as many as 29 greyhounds were used.

T.E. Donne, who went coursing several times in Canterbury in this period, recalls in *The Game Animals of New Zealand* that at one meeting he attended greyhounds killed 30 hares, the majority of which, much to Donne's obvious disgust, were left to rot or be eaten by the hawks. According to Donne, coursing clubs were also established in the North Island, and the sport was 'maintained with considerable vitality for many years'. With the passing of the Animals Protection Act 1960, it became a punishable offence to promote or to take part in the coursing of live hares.

After the turn of the century, hares were still being liberated in various districts, but the natural spread of the hare seemed rather slow. Guthrie Smith, of *Tutira* fame, said that it took 11 years before hares liberated at Hastings reached his coastal sheep station 50 kilometres away.

Today, the hare has a wide distribution in this country, where they are found in virtually all suitable habitat. Possibly the largest population occurs along the drier eastern side of the Southern Alps, where densities of two to three hares per one hectare are common. Only on offshore islands are hares absent.

Physical Description

A hare is easily distinguished from its close relative, the rabbit, by its much greater size, by its long black-tipped ears, and by its large and extremely muscular hindquarters.

Both male and female are similar in size. Hares reach maturity at five months, at which time they stand about 12 inches at shoulder height. Overall they may measure 26 inches, with a three-inch tail. Adult animals weigh about 8 pounds, with particularly large specimens attaining 10 pounds. Oddly enough, the female outweighs the male by a good pound. The largest hare I shot while employed as a rabbiter was a doe, and, curious about its weight because it was unusually large, I took it home and found that it weighed a shade over 10 pounds.

The ears normally have a light or whitish inner rim, with broken brownish shades occurring on the insides and backs. The proud-looking face is distinctive in shape. Facial markings are mostly brown; lighter shades, tending towards white in some instances, encircle the prominent brown eyes. The texture of the fur, denser in the winter, and possibly much lighter where heavy snow prevails, is silky soft. Its colour ranges from a mid-brown through to a rich tawny shade, not a great deal unlike the hide of an African lion basking in the sun. The belly might be a light brown, white, or a mixture of both shades. The tail is black on top, white underneath. The front legs are about half the length of the back ones; they appear undeveloped in comparison. Also the back feet are non-padded, which results in a distinct spoor unique to the species.

In summary, the broken facial markings and general body coloration of a hare are wellnigh perfect camouflage for the type of habitat it frequents.

Habitat and Habits

Basically hares are creatures of open grasslands. Only rarely will they be encountered deep in a forest. Should they be, then one would strongly suspect they were merely passing through such a closed-in area to more agreeable habitat. This includes tussock country, farmlands, and broad riverbeds. Nearby cover — essential for their survival — is seldom far away. For this purpose they utilise patches of scrub, swampy areas, and the fringes of both native and exotic forests.

Hare habitat, then, may be found from sea-level to the sub-alpine regions of most of the major mountain ranges in the country. They have been observed as high as 2,100 metres in the Kurow (Otago) district, and they are frequently seen around 2,000 metres in Nelson and Canterbury. Again, they climb to around 2,000 metres on Mount Taranaki's lofty slopes and are commonly spotted on the highest parts of the Tararua, Ruahine, and Kaweka Ranges — all well over 1,500 metres.

Although they are mainly nocturnal, hares can often be seen feeding in the early evening. This is particularly true when daylight hours are extended during the summer months. In the Dart Valley of Otago, for instance, I was able to study at length their behaviour — either feeding contentedly or alarmed — until 9 pm in early January.

When feeding or moving slowly about hares display a distinctly ungainly form of locomotion. Awkward is a mild way of putting it. It is a far cry from their loping, mile-eating run and erratic gymnastics we shall later comment upon.

Strictly vegetarians, hares eat various grasses, ranging from cultivated types to alpine tussock. In snowbound country they may stand on snowdrifts to reach low shrubs. They will eat, and nibble at, the bark of trees — young pines and those found in orchards. Overnight forays take them to crops of kiwifruit, turnips, swedes, oats, barley, wheat, maize, and sweet blue lupins. The vegetable garden, especially if carrots and cabbage are growing there, is also high on their hit list.

Unlike rabbits, hares do not burrow. Instead, they live in hollows on the surface of the ground. This is called a 'form' and they have several within their specific territories. I have noted such places under a thickish bush in Hawke's Bay, under a clump of tussock in South Canterbury, under a deadfall (a fine place in nasty weather) within the fringes of the Rimutaka Forest in southern Wairarapa, and in February 1988 I watched a hare emerge from a big cluster of rocks high on sunblasted terrain south-east of Alexandra in Central Otago.

Apparently hares do not return to their forms in a direct line, a dead give-away should ground-scenting predators be on the immediate prowl. With self-preservation in mind, hares first make a complex pattern of confusing trails before they consider it is safe to enter their forms.

But disturb a resting hare in one of its forms and it is an entirely different story. Then it might explode like a shell-burst — an astonishing burst of initial speed which, if called for, can be sustained over great distance. In North America, for instance, hares are rated second only to the pronghorn antelope (clocked at speeds in excess of 90 km/h).

I once watched a full-grown hare keeping a set distance

ahead of a 4-wheel-drive Austin Gypsy on a fairly straight road in Kaingaroa Forest. This went on for some distance — at least a quarter of a mile — before the hare, tired of the game, took a mighty sideways leap and vanished off into the pines. All the time the speed indicator had been hovering around 93 km/h. Incredibly, the hare had not run in a direct line; rather, to confuse its pursuer, it was weaving from side to side in that familiar jinking run.

Generally speaking, we can class hares as rather solitary animals. In spring, however, with the mating season underway, it is not unusual for a good number of boisterous males to group together. The saying 'Mad March Hare', consistent with the first month of spring in the northern hemisphere, has, with good reason, been in use for many centuries. At this time as many as a dozen bucks may gather together and pursue each other with untold zest. They fight with remarkable vigour, rearing up on spring-loaded hind legs, boxing with their clawed forepaws. And like a wallaby, they deliver with blinding speed a powerful blow with their hind feet.

Some of the male hares killed by the author during the southern hemisphere spring proved how vicious these battles really are. Badly ripped faces, torn ears, and missing fur were commonplace. Field research from every country where hares have been studied reveals that all hares fight in this fashion in the spring.

I think this is worth discussing further. In Britain, it was thought until quite recently that the bucks were merely fighting over the does or, that it was a special part of ritual courtship. It has now been discovered, however, that only 16 per cent of the year's conceptions occur in March in Britain, with around 45 per cent taking place once the bucks have settled down. Naturalists Maurice and Robert Burton put forward the theory in their work, *The Animal World*, that by fighting the bucks are establishing a breeding hierarchy, like that which exists among young baboons. To elucidate further, while young male baboons mate with females at the onset of oestrus, the dominant males mate with them later on, and it is they who are responsible for most of the pregnancies. Thus the young males gain experience but the older males become the fathers. An interesting idea.

In this part of the world the breeding season takes place between mid-July and early March, with the female able to conceive when she is about one year old. Gestation lasts about six weeks. By an unusual process known as supertoetation hares may conceive a second litter up to a week before the first litter is born, with, remarkable as it sounds, the original mating fertilising both litters.

A hare may produce four or five litters during the season. Precisely how many young she gives birth to on average is difficult to ascertain because, as a safety precaution, she will place them in separate forms. It is generally thought in this country, however, that she will produce between two and four young. It is rare for a doe in this country to give birth to more than five leverets but in Holland as many as 10 have been recorded.

The leverets are born in a much more advanced state of development than rabbit kittens. They can see clearly, they have fur, and they can scamper about almost immediately. One would imagine this is because they are born above ground level in what at best can be described as temporary accommodation. In other words, they do not have the underground security of a fox's den or a rabbit's warren, where, in both instances, the newly born are helpless. The doe has no real defence except speed and cunning to defeat a predator — ie, she cannot physically protect her leverets. So the new-borns must be ready to shift camp in an instant should danger threaten. Mother Nature, naturally enough, has made quite sure they are able to.

Certainly the plump little leverets are fair game for any predators lurking about — the sharp-eyed harrier or the stoat or ferret. And despite its size, the adult hare is in danger from predators, too.

Many years ago, when deerculling in the Kaweka Ranges, I was returning to the Lawrence hut via the Tutaekuri River. Suddenly, on a low bank near the water's edge, I observed a jet-black cat in a crouched position. Although I was close to it — about 10 long paces — the predator's attention was such that whatever it was watching behind a big boulder held all of its attention. As I watched with baited breath the cat slowly raised its lean and hungry-looking body, its tail swishing back and forth, back and forth. It might, I would later think, have been a lioness watching an unwary antelope. All at once the cat was airborne — front legs widespread, claws extended. It vanished in an instant from my sight. A high-pitched squeal of absolute terror rang out, but was cut off almost instantly. With stealth, and wondering what the cat had attacked, I sneaked up to the boulder and peered around the edge of it. The answer to my unspoken question — a big hare — was already dead. Holding it by the scruff of the neck, the cat was just starting to drag it away towards the nearby scrub belt. Only when the hunter and its prey had gone from my sight did I move on.

WALLABY

(*Macropodidae family*)

Male: Buck   Female: Doe   Young: Joey

Range
Wallabies, or small kangaroos, are native to Australia. Sixteen
different types and various related sub-species of this marsupial
are found throughout the continent, where they occur in all
states, including Tasmania and several small offshore islands.

Liberations and Distribution in New Zealand
Wallabies were first introduced into this country in the early
1870s. In the South Island three animals — one male and two
females — were liberated at Waimate in South Canterbury.
Known as Bennett's wallaby today (*M. rufogriseus*), they are a
subspecies of the common brush or red-necked wallaby of the
Australian mainland.

In this same period, Sir George Grey was responsible for
liberating an unknown number of wallabies — covering five
species — on Kawau Island. They were:

Parma wallaby (*Macropus parma*)
Swamp wallaby (*Wallabia bicolor*)
Black-striped wallaby (*Macropus dorsalis*)
Dama wallaby (*Macropus eugenii*)
Brush-tailed rock wallaby (*Petrogale penicillata*).

Also in the early to mid-1870s John Reed of Auckland is
said to have liberated the brush-tailed rock wallaby on Motutapu
Island in the Hauraki Gulf. Later they spread to nearby Rangitoto
Island; the two islands are linked by a tidal causeway.

In 1903 the South Canterbury Acclimatisation Society
relocated two animals from Waimate to the lower slopes of

Mount Nimrod, the highest point in the Hunters Hills. Then in 1912 a number of Dama wallabies were liberated in the Rotorua district, presumably from Kawau Island. The last release took place in either 1947 or 1948 when some Bennett's wallabies from the Hunters Hills were released on Mount Burke station between lakes Hawea and Wanaka. Approximately 100 animals are found there today.

On Kawau Island wallabies increased their numbers dramatically on the hilly, heavily wooded landmass. Even in Sir George Grey's time control became essential, and as many as 200 would be shot during a single 'drive'. In the 1880s, after Sir George Grey had sold the island, the wallaby situation was so critical that the owners had no other option but to declare total war on them.

Obviously wallabies on Kawau Island gained a welcome respite from heavy hunting pressure and subsequently built up their numbers again because by 1939 the Auckland Acclimatisation Society was reporting that the wallabies were becoming a great nuisance and had 'increased in an almost incredible manner'.

Since then the Department of Internal Affairs and, later, the Forest Service, have carried out regular control operations on the island. In 1965, for instance, some 3,000 animals were eliminated with 1080 poison, a small number of which (about 200) were later considered to have been the Parma wallaby. An incredible situation, really, because this species had not been recorded in its homeland since 1932. Unaware that the species existed in New Zealand, Australian biologists had all but given up hope of ever seeing them in the wild again or of finding species for breeding purposes at any of the major zoos in the world.

At any rate, an Australian scientist, David Ride, found out in the late 1960s that Parma wallabies were common on Kawau Island; as a direct result the species was granted full protection there in 1969. Upon hearing this, Peter Pigott, a successful businessman, decided that something positive should be done about it. He duly approached the New South Wales National Parks and Wildlife Service; and in 1971 an expedition to Kawau Island took place (also sponsored by Sydney's Taranga Park Zoo and the Macquarie University) with 40 Parma wallabies being captured.

Back in Australia, they were shared among the interested parties, Pigott taking his animals to his secluded property at Mount Wilson in the Blue Mountains. Unfortunately all but the wallabies at Mount Wilson soon died, Pigott himself suffering some losses to foxes. In the following year, Pigott mounted a private expedition to Kawau Island and returned with nine fine animals. From that point on Parma wallaby thrived at Mount Wilson.

Later, the Pigotts gave many of their ever-growing numbers of wallabies to various zoos around Australia. By 1987 they had around 300 at Mount Wilson. Pigott asked the National Parks and Wildlife Service if they would consider liberating a large percentage of this number. Agreeing, the NPWS decided upon the Royal National Park near Sydney as being an ideal location to liberate 200 of the animals. It would be the largest release of an endangered species anywhere in the world.

Today the Dama, Parma (special protection was removed in December 1983) and brush-tailed rock wallaby are considered the most numerous on Kawau Island. The swamp wallaby is in reasonable numbers. Only the future of the black-striped wallaby — extremely low in numbers and obviously endangered — hangs precariously in the balance.

In 1984 the Forest Service surveyed the six species of wallaby found in this country and, with regard to Kawau Island, stated: 'Although wallaby numbers on Kawau are high, there is no farming and no intact forest, so that control is of low priority.'

The same report commented on the brush-tailed rock wallaby inhabiting other islands* in the Hauraki Gulf. On Rangitoto Island: 'Wallabies may be damaging the flora colonising lava flows. This should be assessed to determine whether wallaby control is justified.' On Motutapu Island: 'Wallabies contribute to erosion of coastal cliffs where they

---

* Throughout the islands of the Hauraki Gulf all species of wallaby are fully protected. Information regarding access for field study trips, photography, etc, can be obtained from: Hauraki Gulf Maritime Park Board, 60 Cook St, Auckland, Phone: 371-140.

excavate nest-sites, but do not affect farm production at present densities.'

In South Canterbury, the Bennett's wallaby found its habitat very much to its liking and it, too, quickly increased in numbers. The major stronghold of the species would become the Hunters Hills, which form a watershed between the Waihao River to the south and the Pareora and Otaio Rivers to the east.

Hunting pressure in this region peaked in the early 1920s. The Waimate Acclimatisation Society, fearful for the survival of their precious charges, presented a strong case to government for their full and immediate protection. While the request was rejected, it was perhaps the main reason why far less hunting would take place. By the mid-1930s wallabies were again plentiful.

On 27 March 1946 the Wellington *Evening Post* summed up the wallaby situation in South Canterbury in this manner:

> . . . the damage done by the wallabies is very extensive and comparable to that done by deer and rabbits, for not only do they feed on large areas of good sheep country, but they destroy a large part of the bush in the gullies where they hide in the lower hills behind Waimate.

A year later, following representations of the South Canterbury Catchment Board and of local people (mostly farmers), the Wildlife Division of the Department of Internal Affairs at last moved into the troubled areas. The wallaby, not included in any wildlife legislation, was in the winter of that year hunted in a way it had perhaps never experienced before — by fit, well-seasoned professional hunters. They would account for 4,521 animals.

By the end of the winter of 1957, government shooters had killed approximately 68,000 wallabies in South Canterbury.

Over the next 30 years the red-necked wallaby, due to shooting and poison operations carried out by both the Forest Service and the South Canterbury Wallaby Board (formed in 1959), has more or less remained at controllable levels.

At present, the South Canterbury Wallaby Board employs three men to cover an area defined by board secretary, R.B. Horsburgh, as extending 'from the Tekapo River to Lake Benmore, down the Waitaki River to the sea and by a rather jagged boundary in the north above Tekapo which finds its way to the sea coast'.

For the financial year ending 31 March 1987, a total of 1,596 wallabies were killed by the field staff. Over the next 12 months a further 961 were eliminated. Poisoning operations with 1080 — 'bait and broadleaf' — were judged as 'quite successful' by the chairman of the board, K.G. Patterson. It was found, however, that when 1080-impregnated carrots were used in a combined campaign with the Kurow Pest Destruction Board the results were 'not so successful'.

By way of contrast, wallabies were apparently slow to establish themselves in large numbers in the Rotorua district. Little if any valid information is available regarding their early spread. Today, however, they are well established over most of their range — this extends to the north, north-west, west, and south of Rotorua, and includes lakes Rotoiti, Rotoma, Okatina, Tarawera, and the Green and Blue Lakes.

Physical Description
All wallabies found in this country have naked snouts; some species are partly hairy between the nostrils. The fur-like body hair is both long and thick. They have extremely powerful hindquarters and their hindfeet are long — approximately 6 to 10 inches. The tail is also long. The forefoot has five toes, the hindfoot one less. With the marked exception of the swamp wallaby, which resembles a rather scaled-down version of the large and strongly built wallaroo or hill kangaroo, they are of a medium to slender form.

In the following brief descriptions of the various species found in New Zealand the height of the body on average-sized animals is taken in a direct line from the tip of the nose to the vent (the excretory opening) while the animal is lying on its back. The length of the tail is measured from the vent to the tip of the last bone of the tail and excludes any tufts of hair.

Bennett's wallaby
Body height: 36-38 inches; tail: 26-28 inches. Uniform dark-grey in colour, but lighter variations also occur. Underparts normally lighter, grey-white in some instances. Lower face generally dark,

tending towards black in some aged animals. Indistinct cheek stripe. Ears comparatively long and rounded. Often reddish-brown (rufous) about shoulders and rump. Faint hip stripe. Tail grey with black tip.

Swamp wallaby
Body height: 33-36 inches; tail: 26 inches. Head and body brownish-grey, belly rufous orange. Ears rather short. Faint greyish facial stripe. Base of tail dark grey, the rest black. Fore and hindfeet dark brown.

Black-striped wallaby
Body height: 32-34 inches; tail: 24 inches. Head and body grey, belly grey-white. Rufous about shoulders. Ears medium length. Distinct dorsal stripe. Prominent white stripe on hip. Tail grey with black tip.

Brush-tailed rock wallaby
Body height: 29-31 inches; tail: 23 inches. Stocky build, as are all rock wallabies. Face dark, white cheek stripe. Short, oval-shaped ears. Back grey-brown, underparts yellowish-brown. Small black mark in armpit. Tail bushy — ie, not tapering as are those of the other species found here. Base of tail rufous, the rest black. Feet black.

Parma wallaby
Body height: 25-27 inches; tail: 17 inches. Head and body grey; belly grey-white, extending to throat. Ears medium length. Shoulders and back rufous. Clearly defined white cheek stripe. Tail grey.

Dama wallaby
Body height: 23-25 inches; tail: 17 inches. Head and body grizzled and/or silver grey, possibly with darkish fleck; belly grey-white. Ears medium length. Rufous over shoulders. Faint dorsal stripe. Tail grey with black tip.

As a matter of interest, when government deer hunters Henry Maunder and Bernie Cogan were working in the Hunters Hills in the winter of 1955, they accounted for an extremely large male wallaby. They were curious enough about its weight to carry it to the woolshed of the station they were working on, and, on the scales, discovered it had a live weight of 89 pounds. The skin, for the record, measured just under 40 inches. The author has seen a photograph of this king-sized Bennett's wallaby and watched as Henry Maunder ran a measuring tape over the skin.

Habitat and Habits

In New Zealand wallabies range over a wide diversity of mostly lowland terrain. Unlike their big relatives — the red or plains kangaroo of the harsh Australian interior — they require ample cover to survive, and have found precisely that in this country. Also, they are not troubled by natural predators — dingo, fox, and eagle.

Kawau Island, for instance, is a beautiful spot. The climate is pleasantly warm. Trees and scrub are abundant. One walks through a lush green carpet of grasses, where ferns and shrubbery flourish. The island has an almost park-like atmosphere. The wallabies encountered there give the marked impression that they, as Sir George Grey envisaged, live in an unfenced zoo.

As their name implies, the brush-tailed rock wallaby is an agile climber of rocky habitat. It also chooses to live in caves and in rocky crevices. This was the perfect species to introduce to Motutapu Island, where, because of increasing farm productivity, they have mostly retreated to the coastal cliffs.

The adjacent Rangitoto Island is an even harsher contrast to Kawau Island. There is virtually no soil on this volcanic, scoria-ridden landmass so clearly visible from Auckland. Surface streams are non-existent. Yet somehow, and perhaps miraculously, around 200 species of native plants exist here, finding secure rootholds in cracks and crevices in the rocks. So, too, can one find mature trees such as pohutukawa, northern rata, and native honeysuckle. In summer, when the heat builds oppressively on the faces of the lava rock, the temperature can exceed 70º Celsius. In their well-chosen dens, however, or in the heavy shade of the forest, brush-tailed rock wallabies doze contentedly throughout the uncomfortably hot hours.

Further south in the Rotorua district, wallabies inhabit both native and exotic forests. They frequently live in fringe areas adjacent to farmlands. And they are also found in rough hilly country around Lake Tarawera, where the stock-grazed tops are mostly open and all sorts of palatable growth chokes the many gullies that bisect them.

Mount Nimrod, at 1,525 metres, is the highest point in the Hunters Hills. The lower slopes of this extensive stretch of tussock grassland is wallaby range. Similarly, they use the natural cover in the gullies as a daytime refuge and feed in exotic forest — the Waimate State Forest. As in the Rotorua district, they arouse the intense wrath of foresters by feeding on, for example, young Douglas fir trees.

All marsupials breed prolifically. In the case of the wallaby, gestation lasts 35-40 days. Shortly before giving birth to a single offspring, the doe licks her pouch thoroughly. She then assumes the birth position — squatting on the base of her tail, with her hind legs extended well forward and her tail passing neatly between them. The offspring reaches the pouch in a similar manner to a possum kitten — by following a dampened strip of fur up its mother's belly.

Giving birth has no apparent effect on the doe — the newly born wallaby is minute, after all — and she immediately resumes her everyday life. She may even mate if she so desires. Should such an encounter prove fruitful, the embryo will, because of the duration of the gestation period, be ready to be born while the doe still carries a dependent joey in her pouch. In a process too complex to discuss here, the doe is somehow able to delay the birth process — putting the embryo in limbo, as it were — until the joey is ready to vacate the pouch. Mother Nature is never less than amazing.

Like most hunted creatures, wallabies are very much creatures of habit. They have their favoured feeding and resting areas. They use the same well-established tracks back and forth to such places. Often these lead along main ridges.

Favoured food includes grasses, leaves, the bark of a great variety of native and exotic trees. Pohutukawa trees, for example, have fared rather badly on the southern side of Kawau Island.

Rabbits, hares and possums are common in many parts of the country, often sharing the same general habitat. This applies to the Waihau district of backblocks Hawke's Bay, where Philip Holden worked as a rabbiter for two years. The Kaweka Mountains rise on the horizon, with the smaller Burns Range in the foreground, tending towards Gorge Stream (right).

A semi-dozing rabbit seen on a sunwarmed rock in Central Otago.

An ideal hare habitat can be seen in this stretch of terrain in south-east Marlborough. The 'tight' clumps of tussock scattered about the lower slopes provide perfect spots for their 'forms'.

In the Dart Valley, Otago, an adult hare reveals his fright by displaying his white 'uplifted' tail. Moments later it bounded into the nearby forest.

This heavily forested country within the
Maungataniwha Range, lying south-east
of Kaitaia, is one of many Northland
areas where possums (*right*) abound.

A petite Dama wallaby, seen in the Rotorua district.

The bigger Bennet's wallaby is more 'rufous' in colour than the Dama species.

The Hunter Hills are popular with South Canterbury hunters seeking Bennet's wallaby.

This same pattern of causing extensive damage to native trees and shrubs has also taken place in the Okataina scenic reserve in Rotorua, where, in November 1985, the Forest Service claimed wallaby were 'destroying the indigenous forest floor cover' and were 'considered to be a threat to forest rejuvenation'. On Kawau Island they invade gardens in overnight forays when they feed heavily on vegetables and fruit. It is also true that very few residents require a lawnmower!

A wallaby shows alarm by decisively striking the ground with both its rudder-like tail and its hard-soled hindfeet. The thumping causes ground vibrations. Other animals in the immediate area — wallabies are a gregarious lot — instantly receive the 'danger' warning. They stand nervously at full height, positively quivering with apprehension. They have excellent eyesight and a fine sense of smell. Both faculties are put to immediate use.

Should a wallaby make good its escape from impending danger it will use a form of locomotion — hopping — that is unique to the extended family it belongs to. At pellmell speed and airborne for about 70 per cent of the time, a wallaby keeps its forefeet and tail well clear of the ground. The heavy tail acts as a counterbalance to the head and shoulders, while the tremendous hindlegs propel the animal along in great spring-loaded bounds. A single, soaring bound may cover 4 metres or more. A sudden, sideways hop will usually outmanoeuvre a dog in frantic pursuit. Normally, however, wallabies travel — often in a straight line — in a series of shortish, regulated hops which carry them at a fast clip over rough ground.

When cornered by a dog, a wallaby will lash out with its muscular tail — no mean weapon. Even more deadly are its long, talon-like claws. A powerful kicking blow from the hindfeet, delivered with the consummate skill of an expert in martial arts, can completely disembowel an unwary dog.

Bucks fight savagely among themselves. A master buck, for instance, might resent a younger male's attempts to join his 'harem'. Should the younger animal not retreat, then a battle will commence. The bucks circle each other warily. The object is to grasp the other in a bear-like grip. Whichever buck first achieves this is then in a position to avoid the slashing front-paw attack of his rival. His short, dagger-like fangs invariably come into play now. He might strive to tear open his opponents' jugular vein or, should he fail in the attempt, to sink them into the shoulder muscles.

The bucks break apart feverishly. One, as though falling back on his tail, lashes out savagely with his hindlegs in a murderous attempt to rip open the other's soft belly skin. Many a buck wallaby has died a painful death as a result of disembowelling or because his jugular vein has been torn apart in frenzied attack. Mother Nature, always capricious, can also be needlessly cruel.

POSSUM
(*Trichosurus vulpecula*)

Male: Buck   Female: Doe   Young: Kitten

Range
The true opossum (Didelphidae family) is found in Central and South America. The opossum-like marsupial of Australia (Phalangeridae family) bears only a superficial resemblance to those found on the North American continent, and, at best, can be loosely described as distantly related.

In Australia, where eight species of the genus *Trichosurus* occur, zoologists consider they are the most widely distributed and adaptable of all the indigenous fauna. Significantly, the animal is called a possum rather than an opossum in that country.

Liberations and Distribution in New Zealand
Unlike the introduction of deer and other game animals (such as thar and chamois) into this country, the possum was liberated for material reasons — its profitable fur. The first liberation of the possum into New Zealand took place near Riverton in Southland in 1858. The 42 animals (21 pairs) released there are thought to have been the common brush-tailed possum of the Australian mainland.

Numerous liberations, both private and by acclimatisation societies, continued in the years that followed. They ranged from as far north as the Auckland Province to Stewart Island in the south. Sir George Grey, for instance, linked forces with the Auckland society to introduce the common grey variety of brush-tailed possum to Kawau Island in the Hauraki Gulf between 1869 and 1876. The Wellington society liberated 19 'black' possums from Tasmania in the ranges behind Paraparaumu in 1893, while in Southland the Otago society released 12 silver-grey animals from Victoria in Catlins Forest in 1895. Wherever they were liberated possum invariably thrived and gradually increased their range.

But by the mid-1890s, when 'peak' importations were taking place, it had already become evident that the possum was capable of causing extensive damage to orchards, crops, and gardens. Fruitgrowers and farmers in particular protested vigorously, demanding control, and an end to importations and liberations of locally bred stock. On the other hand, the pro-possum faction, largely consisting of acclimatisation societies, strongly opposed control or restriction. In the latter part of the decade the government regularly heard representations from both sides.

Between 1900 and 1910 some changes in legislation took place — the possum was either protected by closed seasons or, should the need arise, could be taken without restrictions.

The annual report of the Auckland Acclimatisation Society reveals that in 1916-1917 the society was still favouring the unlimited release of the species: 'We shall be doing a great service to the country in stocking these large areas (of rough bush hills) with this valuable and harmless animal.'

In 1919, H.B. Kirk, professor of Botany and Zoology at the then Victoria University College in Wellington, was requested by the government to carry out a field study of the possum. Kirk's findings were presented to Parliament in 1920. To judge by the following telling extracts, his report would have found immense favour with the pro-possum groups:

> The damage to New Zealand forests is negligible, and is far out-weighed by the advantage that already accrues to the community. That advantage might be enormously greater. On the one hand, the damage to orchards and gardens is indisputable. Much annoyance, and a loss statable at hundreds of pounds, is caused. On the other hand, the volume of the present trade in skins is in the thousands, but the loss is borne by one section of the community while the gain from the skin trade is made by another section.
>
> Opossums may, in my opinion, with advantage be liberated in all forest districts except where the forest is fringed by orchards or has plantations of imported tree species in the neighbourhood.

It was also Kirk's opinion that the possum for industry could ultimately reach an annual income of around £200,000. Among his recommendations were that an open season — May to July — be implemented forthwith.

As a direct result of Professor Kirk's findings, the taking of possum skins became legal on 5 May 1931. Importantly, the regulations passed at this time also prohibited the harbouring and/or liberations of them without written consent from the Department of Internal Affairs. In the following year the same department declined any further requests for liberations, as well as cancelling those requests already granted but which had not yet been put into practice.

As the fur trade became more important, a large number of illegal releases continued to be made in most parts of the country. The last 'legal' liberations appear to have been made in the late 1920s at the Kaingaroa Forest and on the Chatham Islands.

Today, the possum is found in almost every environment New Zealand has to offer. Certainly no other introduced animal occupies such a broad and diverse range in this country. It has, however, been almost certainly eliminated on Kapiti Island — where between May 1980 and November 1986 — some 22,500 were killed by conservation officers.

Physical Description
Of a medium to stout build, a possum is a small marsupial with a body length of around 15-18 inches. A healthy adult male will weigh 7-10 pounds. The head is comparatively small; the ears are long and oval. The muzzle is rather blunt; the pinkish nose is often enhanced with a blackish band. The round eyes and cat-like whiskers are characteristic of nocturnal creatures. The forefoot has five toes, each equipped with a sharp claw. The hindfeet differ insomuch as, while they also have five toes, the first is opposable and clawless, the second and third are joined, and the remaining two are normal. Overall the body is covered with a dense woolly fur. The tail is long and bushy, perhaps 12 inches in length, and it has hard, scaly prehensile skin layers which, as in the case of some members of the monkey family, are used to grasp limbs. Its life span is around 9 years.

Because of so many mixed liberations and subsequent interbreeding, a wide variety of fur colours exists. Basically, however, they fall into two main groups — 'blacks' and 'greys'.

The colour of a black adult male may vary from a deep reddish-brown to brown; whereas the female, by way of a contrast, is more likely to have darker (possibly black in some cases) tones to its fur.

The grey adult male is best described as a grizzled grey in colour; the fur will frequently have a distinct silvery aspect to it. Again he is often rufous about the neck, upper chest, and shoulders. His underparts are much lighter, a yellowish or whitish shade. While the same general description applies to the grey female, her rust-coloured markings are not so well defined.

Habitat and Habits

As already stated, possum can be found in virtually every type of habitat. They may, for instance, be observed in suburban gardens, in orchards, on both small farms and huge stations. They are very much at home in exotic and of course native forests, where they might range to the bush-line in high country. They inhabit the dry, rockstrewn, and virtually treeless terrain typical of Central Otago. Only in the rain-sodden, southwestern corner of Fiordland and the very tip of the North Island do they appear to be absent.

At night the possum is a most vocal animal, its voice capable of anything from heart-stopping screeching sounds to a rasping, throaty chatter. By and large they are solitary creatures, insofar as they do not form permanent 'pairs' or lasting family groups. Having said that, it is not unusual to find several possums — male, female, and young — living together in the same nest for much of the year.

With no liking whatsoever for cold, damp conditions, a possum's nest or shelter is a waterproofed affair found in all manner of suitable locations — in hollow trees, under rocks, in recesses or scooped-out hollows below overhanging banks, and admist all sorts of interlocked vegetation such as flax.

In adverse weather, possums tend to remain under cover. During prolonged spells of rain and gale-force winds they only emerge to feed during lulls, restricting their movements to comparatively sheltered positions.

Adult possums do not normally travel too far out of what

can be termed their 'home grounds' or territories. Within such areas there are well-utilised 'runways' in the trees and along the ground. Following rain, they can often be seen in the long cultivated grasses on the backs of properties adjacent to bushlands. Bark is bitten to mark tracks and territories, and may be eaten when more suitable food is scarce.

Apparently it is the younger possums — especially restless males — that are more inclined than their elders to wander away. Indeed, there are documented cases of such animals travelling up to 50 kilometres.

The diet of the possum varies according to the nature of the country it inhabits, and it includes leaves, buds, shoots, the fruits of various trees and shrubs, and all sorts of tasty items cultivated by humans.

Among the large native trees favoured by this species are kohekohe, kamahi, southern and northern rata, and mangeao. Smaller trees include fuchsia, willow-leaved maire, wineberry, five finger, and lacebark. Down among the shrubbery are rangiora, leatherwood and mountain wineberry. Exotic trees to their liking are willows, eucalypts, poplars, oak, Douglas fir and pines (particularly during the August pollen season).

In orchards, possums make a beeline for apples, peaches, plums, pears, lemons and passionfruit. In the garden they sample parsnip, carrot, beans, silverbeet, cabbage, potatoes and lettuce. Flowers that take their fancy include the rose, polyanthus, carnation, cyclamen, gladiolus and godetia.

With regard to crops, they will eat with enormous relish (and to a stage where I feel sure they couldn't cope with another mouthful) rape, swedes, peas, potatoes, mangolds, turnips and chou moellier. Interestingly enough, they have been known to travel up to 3 kilometres overnight to a favoured feeding ground and return to their nests before daybreak.

The breeding season — heralded by great vocal gymnastics — usually begins early in March. It reaches peak activity in April and gradually tapers off thereafter. While a doe only reaches her full reproductive maturity at two years of age, it is common for many yearlings to rear young before then; this is especially true when feed is plentiful. The pregnancy lasts 17-19 days. Most births have been recorded towards the end of April.

The new-born, less than half an inch in length, is both naked and blind. It is, however, equipped with perfectly formed forepaws; the hindlegs, at this stage, are only rudimentary. In the manner of marsupial animals, the doe licks and thereby dampens a narrow strip of her belly skin and the kitten, once it has emerged, instinctively and unerringly claws its way up this damp trail while the doe lies on her back. The kitten is heading for the marsupium (pouch), where, once safely inside, it attaches itself to one of the two teats. It will remain in this warm, musky, dark world for about three months.

Later, it will cling to its mother's back while she goes about her business for a further three months. By this time it will start to accept green fodder, and, while it will soon be too big to return to the pouch, it is nevertheless still suckled. At the end of November it can fend for itself. The family links are strong, however, and it will remain with its mother until the next breeding season.

6 HUNTING SMALL GAME ANIMALS

Rabbit

There is of course a world of difference between controlling rabbits and hunting them on a sporting basis. Control means that the harshest methods are brought into operation — poison, trapping, dogging, ferreting; and, because it offers a mesmerised rabbit very little opportunity to escape, the use of a 12-volt spotlight. The redeeming factor about spotlighting is that a rabbit is usually killed very quickly.

While stalking rabbits on foot can be rewarding, to be perfectly realistic, it requires little skill on the part of a hunter to account for a good number in country where they are common. This was never more apparent than when I spent a memorable afternoon with husky Sean Boswell, Supervisor of the Alexandra Pest Destruction Board, on the high country of Riverside station east of the Clutha River.

Rabbits, we found, were plentiful up there. So it proved a simple matter for Sean to range over much of that rockstrewn, plateau-like country in his Toyota 4-wheel drive. No trouble, too, to either shoot them from the cabin or, if the situation dictated, to sneak closer, worm in behind a large rock and utilise that for a rest for his Brno .22 rifle.

Why, we didn't even have to retrieve the dead ones. No, Sean's big, happy-natured weimaraner, Jed, was more than capable of handling that chore. Indeed, there can be no better way of giving one's gundog a regular workout when the shooting season has ended than by taking it out after rabbits. This is advantageous for its master too. For one thing, it helps keep him in good shape, and, of course, the key to shooting success is to practise regularly.

In areas where rabbits are hunted hard and far from numerous, the foot-hunter is presented with a far greater challenge. In this instance, he must be wary of the wind, keep noise to the absolute minimum, and stay off the skyline. Certainly it pays to squat down in a handy spot and simply look for game. A compact pair of fieldglasses are ideal in this situation.

But even if you are the type of rifleman who tends to keep on the move, chances are you will be offered a standing shot — either spotting a motionless target or by waiting for a flushed rabbit to stop after running frantically for a short distance. Surprisingly, one of a pair of rabbits — a buck and doe, say — is all too likely to remain hugging the ground while its head-shot partner jerks spasmodically alongside it. For some reason, I always found that an unsettling experience when it happened to me while I was employed in the business of killing such small game.

Hare

Once coursing fell away in popularity in New Zealand after the turn of the century, organised 'hare drives' became very much the order of the day. A hare drive is when a team of beaters (without dogs) systematically work over a large tussock paddock and drive any hares towards a line of strategically placed shooters armed with 12-gauge shotguns. Not only did this serve as an effective means of control, but it also became a sport to look forward to. In some districts it became an annual social event, where entire families gathered nearby and a picnic-like atmosphere prevailed. Often the total kill would number several hundred; the dead animals, having a monetary value, would usually be presented to a charitable organisation.

By this time a considerable export trade in frozen hare carcasses had sprung up. The number exported in 1910 was 10,744, and in the following year 11,418. This export trade continued to flourish until the mid-1960s when it became too difficult to comply with new export regulations.

So the 12-gauge shotgun was the first firearm in this country to be used extensively as a means of shooting hares. Today, the personnel of the various pest destruction boards around the country also use the 12-gauge shotgun and, of course, the .22 rifle, in their difficult attempts to control various types of small game. Hares, for instance, are mostly taken at close range with shotguns, using No. 3 or No. 4 shot. It's a wise man who reaches for his scoped .22 rifle when a hare's beyond 40 metres — yes, the limitations of a 12-gauge shotgun are that great.

In Britain and Europe hares are classed as a game animal. So anyone in this country who has only taken hares held captive in the dazzling rays of a 12-volt spotlight and thinks he really knows all there is to hunting this species had really better think again.

Naturally enough, I discovered all this while employed as a rabbiter. In fact, I came to enjoy hunting hares a great deal — they challenged my stalking ability, and tested my marksmanship. And more often than not — mainly because it was a hard-pressed district where all small game had to rely constantly on their wits — they came out on top.

The right time to hunt hares is in the early morning or, better still, in the late evening — the last hour of daylight, say — a magical time for hunting in this country, whatever the game. And if it's been a rainy sort of day and the sun has put in a belated appearance, then so much the better. Those conditions will lure most wild ones out of cover to begin feeding. Of the two periods mentioned I have certainly had much better fortune in the late evening. I don't think it's because I happen to function better then than I do in the early hours — no, I consider it is because hares are not quite as wary then as they are in the morning. Maybe after resting up all day in their forms the hunger pangs are really getting to them.

Serious hare hunting demands the use of fieldglasses because, unless a distant animal is exposed on a bare river flat, they are just too difficult to distinguish at long range. That tawny coat is wellnigh impossible to pick up with the naked eye in similar-coloured grass.

At any rate, once you have spotted a hare the stalking starts in earnest. And it's damn good fun — no real pressure as there is when you have sighted a trophy stag. Meaning if the hare escapes, well, what does it really matter? Incidentally, that's my attitude — a belated one, admittedly — when for one reason or another a fine trophy has earned the right to live another day.

Quite often you can move in with ease on an unsuspecting

hare that is out on a narrow river flat by keeping just inside the edge of the forest. In that situation you hold all the aces. Mostly, however, there is only one way of getting close enough for a shot and that is by crawling across open ground — certainly this is true if you are limited to a .22 rifle. Even if you happen to be spotted in that awkward position, a hare's reaction is very different from how they usually react to the sudden sight of the upright, unmistakable figure of man.

All but two of the dozen hares I observed recently in the Dart Valley hugged the ground when they spotted me belly down or, perhaps, when they simply 'sensed' that all was not right. Motionless, they held their antenna-like ears hard against their skulls. This changed their normal outline and you might have been staring at just another brownish lump on the ground instead of a living creature. It was only when I attempted to move much closer and set up my camera on its tripod that they realised what the story was. So off they went at a fast lope into the nearby forest, where, I suspect, they had hiding places under deadfalls and windfalls. Only one of them stopped before reaching cover — it stood tall, with its tail flared like that of a spooked whitetail deer, the Persil-white underparts clearly revealed. Oddly enough, this was whitetail deer range, too.

One thing you will soon learn about hares is that they are far harder to approach than rabbits. Maybe this is because they are very often solitary animals and have to rely on themselves. Definitely they are more 'edgy' than rabbits. Also, they tend to move around their territories a fair bit and seldom remain in one spot for too long when feeding. Lose sight of one during a difficult stalk and you might not see it motionless again.

The choice of a .22 long rifle cartridge is an arguable one for hunting hares in daylight hours. This isn't because hares are difficult to kill; quite the reverse. Rabbits are a far tougher proposition. A wounded hare will seldom cling to life with that grim tenacity so frequently displayed by hard-hit rabbits. No, the real problem, as hinted at a little earlier, is one of range. By no stretch of the imagination is the .22 rifle suitable for small targets at ranges in excess of, say, 100 metres. With a mv of 1,285 fps its mid-range trajectory, when sighted-in at 100 metres, is 9 centimetres. Beyond 100 metres it falls away rapidly, losing its energy — its life-killing force — just as quickly.

Possibly the .222 is the perfect long-range hare calibre. With its incredible accuracy and negligible recoil a skilled rifleman can consistently drop hares out to 225-250 metres. Most hunting of hares, however, takes place in closely settled areas. So when using a treble-two there is always the noise factor to consider. Nothing upsets people more, I have found, than the sound of a nearby shot, especially if it's a high-powered rifle. There is good reason for this. Guns kill folks, and the .222 does make a fair sort of racket — a vicious, almost non-echoing 'cra-ack!' It is sure to upset your average farming type who, in the main, would much prefer to have the local pest destruction boys roaming over his place rather than varmint hunters.

So perhaps the ideal hare calibre from a sporting point of view is the mild-speaking .22 Hornet; the price of its ammunition makes it too expensive to be used in straight-out control work. Known in Europe as the 5.6x35 Rmm. cartridge, the .22 Hornet was developed in the late 1920s. In North America it quickly established a reputation for superb accuracy at all practical distances to around 175 metres. Using a 45-grain, soft-point projectile, this sweet little number has a mv of 2,690 fps. Sighted in for 100 metres, it has a mid-range trajectory of only 6 millimetres, which compares favourably with the .222's mid-range trajectory of 0.5 at this distance.

Not many firearm companies turn out rifles in this calibre today. There is no good reason for this. Over the years dozens of fine cartridges, for one obscure reason or another, have become obsolete. The .22 Hornet, for instance, came close to this state when the .222 arrived on the scene in 1950. Just as well it didn't. The .22 Hornet is an excellent small game load. It is also deadly on wallabies and will handle goats with well-placed shots. Many a fallow deer has fallen victim to this calibre, too. But then, most fallow taken for the pot at close range aren't any bigger than a goat, are they?

Fortunately, the Brno 'Fox' is readily available in this country. This was designed with the .22 Hornet and .222 specifically in mind. Look no further for your small game rifle than this particular model. The sweet-handling 'Fox' weighs just 5.2 pounds, a true 'lightweight' rifle. It features integral scope bases, a Turkish walnut stock, and double triggers — by pressing the rear one you automatically set the front one on 'hair' trigger. A compact variable scope might not be a bad idea for one's small game rifle. Neither rabbits nor hares are large targets, and, in the case of hares, this is particularly true when they are well past 100 metres.

Wallaby

I must profess to having a rather soft spot where wallabies are concerned, the red-necked species in particular. Back in the mid to late 1950s they were the game animal I most commonly stalked in New South Wales. They taught me much — mostly how very little I really knew about all aspects of the hunting game. Under the circumstances that was to be expected. Each and every one of us has to start somewhere. At one stage in our lives we are all greenhorns or novices; just the way we are when we first pick up a cricket bat or ease behind the wheel of a motor vehicle. These are meant as encouraging words for those would-be hunters just starting off.

In his attractive publication *Rifle Sport in the South Island*, R.V. Francis Smith describes wallaby hunting in the Hunters Hills as 'lively sport'. The late Harry Vipond, a senior environmental officer with the Forest Service in Rotorua, considered in 1985 that wallabies were 'good sport', and he encouraged private hunters to help deal with the problem of just too many wallabies in that district. And in his exceptional work, *The Australian Hunter*, Col Allison states: 'Wallaby stalking is an exciting sport, a nice mat being the outcome of a good shot.' And I, too, found that wallabies were grand sport; no question about it. The only question that might arise is: are they rightly classed as a 'lesser game' animal?

Since they vary greatly in size, one's selection of a suitable calibre must be given careful consideration. The Parma wallaby is a good deal smaller than the Bennett's wallaby. The difference in their respective sizes — to draw an easily recognisable comparison — is as great as that which exists between a mature red stag and a fallow buck of the same age.

Physically speaking, there is very little difference in size (certainly not enough to concern ourselves with here) between the red-necked wallaby of the Australian mainland and the slightly smaller, but chunkier, Bennett's wallaby inhabiting Tasmania and, of course, parts of South Canterbury. I discovered very quickly that the .22 long rifle cartridge is not a good killer of any type of wallaby. Col Allison (1969) sees it exactly that way too:

> The .22 rimfire is not a very good wallaby rifle, since chest shots are usually ineffectual, and the animal runs away, to be lost forever in many cases. The skin quickly folds over a rimfire entrance-hole and the hydraulic shock of the high-powered centrefire round is lacking; hence blood is minimal and tracking difficult. A head-shot is the only way a .22 rimfire is effective and the well-developed faculties of the species prevent one's obtaining many of these.

On paper, the .222, .223, and even the .22/250 appear magical wallaby cartridges. The reality is that they ruin far too many skins, punching gaping holes the size of a man's fist. The reason for this might be explained by the incredibly soft skin of a wallaby, which, like the pelage of a hare, tears so easily.

In the section on hares, I stated that the .22 Hornet was a deadly killer of wallabies. This is based on personal observation. A fellow station-hand I once worked with had a BSA rifle in this calibre — the short-actioned 'Hunter' model. At any rate, we often went out riding together at the weekends, naturally taking our respective rifles with us (mine was a Browning slide-action .22). Watching him shoot was a revelation. Always taking a rest for his rifle, and using a 4x Pecar scope, he grassed them at what to me seemed incredible distances — certainly around 200 metres. Importantly, the little 45-grain, soft-point projectile made only a tiny entrance hole in the skin and shed all of its pent-up energy inside the animal's vital organs. It didn't exit on the far side, either. Perfect.

Sneaking around the edges of native and exotic forests in a familiar early morning or late evening routine is a most productive way of spotting wallabies feeding. So, too, grassy clearings and wide forest tracks are likely places to spot one or more with their heads down.

Later on you must seek your wallaby in thickish cover. Not

easy, no matter how proficient a hunter you are. Often they will break just in front of you, either unseen or with just a glimpse of a brownish coat. Off they go with a loud thump, thump, thump, crashing headlong through the heavy undercover. Don't be at all surprised if your heart stops beating momentarily. Again, you might spot a patch of the same colour at extreme close range. With the naked eye alone it is difficult if not impossible to distinguish precisely what part of the animal you are looking at. This of course is where a scope sight really shines. (I believe they excel in all circumstances.) Using a 3x or 4x scope, or an even lower power on a small variable type, one can quickly ascertain what part of the animal's anatomy is in view.

Because what I have just described happens so many times when stalking wallabies in their daytime habitat, it must be stated that a 12-gauge shotgun has a decided edge over a rifle in this situation. Using a shotgun, one is able to fire instinctively, to get a shot away just that bit faster — a split-second, maybe, but that is very often enough to make all the difference. Load up with No. 2 cartridges for wallabies and you won't go far wrong.

In South Canterbury it is common for men to hunt in teams; a party of four, say. The very nature of the terrain there — pockets of bush and scrub dotted about the gully bottoms or scattered more profusely about the slopes above it — lends itself very nicely to this form of hunting.

It works along these lines: equipped with shotguns, two men and the dogs head off into the cover. They proceed slowly ahead, the dogs there to disturb or flush the resting animals rather than pursue them. On either side of the valley the other hunters, usually armed with scoped rifles, more or less keep pace with their companions below. Once the action starts, the fleeing wallabies, especially if the valley suddenly narrows, have a marked tendency to break out into the open. Frequently, they do so within close shooting range. To hear a wallaby bolting through the bush towards you, and to then have it burst into sight is, I have been told, high excitement indeed.

Sean Boswell and his weimaraner, Jed, among rocky rabbit-infested country typical of Central Otago, where the annual rainfall is about 33 centimetres.

Sean uses a Brno .22 bolt-action rifle, a popular choice for small game hunters.

Jed acts as a retriever, and (*overleaf*) is proud of his success.

The small game hunter is often seen pursuing game on private land close to town or city. By wisely utilising cover on this stretch of farming country near Lumsden, Southland, most shots could be taken at close-to-medium range.

The semi-automatic Winchester is adequate to deal with hares, much larger game than rabbits.

Hares are likely to range more open terrain, such as this sweep of tussock land near Ida Burn, Central Otago. Chukar and California quail are found on the high country in the background — the eastern end of Hawkdun Range.

Essential equipment in this country are a .22 magnum Ansultz, a pair of Nikon 7 x 35 field glasses, a folding knife in a pouch, and a first-aid kit.

Possum

The two most commonly used firearms for hunting possum are the .22 rifle, firing hollow-point, long-rifle cartridges; and the 12-gauge shotgun, loaded up with No. 4 shot. These are what pest destruction board personnel take along with them during regular spotlighting forays into over-populated areas. One cannot hazard even a wild guess at how many possum alone have fallen victim to the most popular .22 rifle utilised by men engaged in this work — the Ruger 10/22 semi-automatic — over, say, the last two decades.

As mentioned earlier, the possum is not a sporting animal — it was introduced for its fur — and that is still the case today. The skills and special techniques required to trap or poison possum on a professional basis are much too involved to go into here. Also, I consider they would be sadly misplaced in this work, which celebrates the sporting, rather than the commercial, aspects of New Zealand's game animals and birds.

Most possum skins are sold at auction. In this instance, the skins are sold for the trapper on a commission basis. Wrightson Dalgety (until recently known as Dalgety Crown NZ Ltd) is by far the largest auctioneer, with a reputable track record dating back to the early 1930s.

Two auction houses operate in the North Island: they are Fur Exchange New Zealand Limited, PO Box 4334, Hull Road, Mount Maunganui; and New Zealand Fur Auctions, PO Box 38-113, Petone, Port Road, Seaview, Lower Hutt.

Quite apart from auction houses, a number of firms spread around the country buy skins direct from the trapper. These include Taimex Trading: Dunedin 770-041; Tauranga 440-985, and Machouse Furs: Rotorua 55-245; Inglewood 68-484.

Anyone who is considering hunting possums for their skins is well advised to refer to these three excellent works:

The Opossum in New Zealand, L.T. Pracy and R.I. Kean, published by the New Zealand Forest Service, Wellington, 1969.

Commercial Opossum Hunting, D.J. Moresby, published by the author, 1984.

Possum Hunting in New Zealand, Graeme Marshal, Halcyon Press, Auckland, 1984.

General Information

All of the small game animals covered in this section are hunted or controlled in various ways by Agricultural Pests Destruction Council field personnel who, if approached correctly, are in a position to offer invaluable advice on whatever species you wish to hunt. Certainly they know on whose property good hunting is to be found.

Obviously it is to the mutual benefit of landowner and shooter alike if an understanding can be reached over gaining access to private land. If that permission is granted, then it is up to the shooter to behave himself in the correct manner. Basically that comes down to common sense, and there is no necessity for me to elaborate further.

As already indicated, most small game hunters use a .22 calibre rifle, particularly when hunting rabbits. May I suggest that anyone who owns a .22 rifle and is seriously thinking of mounting a scope sight to it should do so. There is simply no comparison between them and open sights for field use. Indoor range shooting is, of course, an entirely different field.

Not, I must add, that I would suggest buying the usual scope one sees on a .22 — tinny, cheap, and difficult to sight-in. They are more of a handicap than anything else. Buy a brand name instead, say of 3x or 4x.

I have seen such scopes as Leupold, Pecar, Weaver sitting above the action of a .22; scopes that normally would be found on a high-powered rifle. None looked out of place. Nor did they spoil the overall balance of the piece. And, like most top-quality scopes, they were simple to sight-in.

With a scope-sighted .22, I found I was able to take small game at longer ranges than ever before. By that I mean around the 100 metre mark. Beyond this, unless one is really something else at judging distances and also the drop of a cartridge, which falls away quickly beyond this distance, you may as well forget about trying to connect with anything.

The best range to sight-in a .22 is 75 metres, which means you will be about 2.5 centimetres high at 50 metres and some 9 centimetres low at 100 metres. Beyond this, as I have mentioned, the trouble starts. Sighted-in for this distance the drop of the bullet between 100 and 125 metres is around 20 centimetres. That is a lot when your target is small to begin with, right? There is something else to seriously consider, too. Once past 100 metres the .22 round has lost so much energy that clean kills are an exception.

When it comes to hunting with a .22 there is only one type of cartridge to use — the hollow-point. In the hands of a skilled shot this will often perform out of all proportion to its minute size. On the other hand, a hollow-point will sometimes allow a hard-hit rabbit to reach its burrow. Unpredictable, that's the .22 rifle.

Today, there is a fantastic range of .22s to select from. The following list (Gun City, Christchurch, early 1989) says it all:

RIMFIRE

22mag	ANSCHUTZ	1522 Deluxe 5 shot bolt-action
22mag	ANSCHUTZ	1516 Deluxe 5 shot bolt-action
22mag	STIRLING	5 shot bolt-action incl: scope
22mag	STIRLING	1500 5 shot bolt-action
22mag	BRADLEY	Sport 5 shot bolt-action NZ made
22	ANSCHULTZ	525/51 7 shot semi-auto/scoped
22	ANSCHULTZ	520 7 shot semi-auto incl: scoped
22	REMINGTON	522 Speedmaster 15 shot semi-auto
22	VOERE	Semi-Auto incl: scope/slnr
22	VOERE	Semi-Auto 5 x only
22	MARLIN	60 and 70 semi-autos
22	FRANCHI	semi-auto 15 shot
22	FRANCHI	semi-auto 15 shot
22	STIRLING	20P 15 shot semi-auto
22	STIRLING	20P 15 semi-auto c/wscope
22cal	JAGER	AP80 30 shot semi-auto (scope)
22cal	JAGER	AP47 15 shot semi-auto (scope)
22cal	STIRLING	Armalite 15 shot semi-auto
22cal	STIRLING	Armalite 15 shot semi-auto (scope)
22cal	BROWNING	"Takedown" semi-auto
22	SPORTCO	semi-auto incl: scope
22	SPORTCO	semi-auto 71A 7 shot
22	GEVARM	7 shot semi-auto

22	VENTURINI	semi-auto incl: scope
22	MAHELY	M21 7 shot semi-auto incl: thread
22	SPORTCO	71A semi-auto
22	MOSSBERG	Plinker semi-auto (thread)
22	MOSSBERG	Plinker 15 shot semi-auto

LEVER ACTION

22	WINCHESTER	94122 15 shot
22	WINCHESTER	94122 incl: scope
22	GERMAN	Lever Action incl: scope

BOLT ACTION

22cal	RUGER	M77-222 5 shot incl: mnts
22cal	ANSCHULTZ	1416P 5 shot Deluxe
22cal	ANSCHULTZ	1416DL 5 shot left-handed
22cal	ANSCHULTZ	1450DG incl: silencer thread
22cal	ANSCHULTZ	1450 5 shot bolt-action
22cal	BRNO	452 Deluxe 5 shot bolt-action
22cal	BRNO	452 Standard 5 shot bolt-action
22cal	BRADLEY	Sport incl: silencer
22cal	BRADLEY	Sport 5 shot bolt-action
22cal	STIRLING	14P 10 shot bolt-action
22cal	STIRLING	14P 10 shot bolt-action
22cal	TOZ	5 shot bolt-action
22cal	TOZ	5 shot bolt-action incl: scope
22cal	TOZ	5 shot bolt-action
22cal	TOZ	5 shot bolt-action
22cal	B.S.A.	Sportsman 5 shot
22cal	SPRINGFIELD	5 shot incl: silencer
22cal	STEVENS	5 shot

Useful Addresses

Refer to Appendix 7 for the address list of the New Zealand Smallbore Rifle Association, and to Appendix 8 for the address list of the New Zealand Small Game Shooters Sporting Association. Another private organisation worthy of inclusion here is the fast-growing New Zealand Bowhunters Society, who frequently conduct 'wallaby' field trips in the Rotorua district. The address is C/- Jessie Henwood, 10 Cowan Place, Fairview Downs, Hamilton.

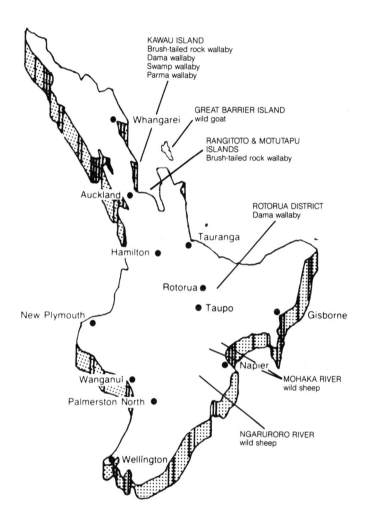

KAWAU ISLAND
Brush-tailed rock wallaby
Dama wallaby
Swamp wallaby
Parma wallaby

GREAT BARRIER ISLAND
wild goat

RANGITOTO & MOTUTAPU
ISLANDS
Brush-tailed rock wallaby

ROTORUA DISTRICT
Dama wallaby

Whangarei

Auckland

Tauranga

Hamilton

Rotorua

Taupo

New Plymouth

Gisborne

Napier

MOHAKA RIVER
wild sheep

Wanganui

Palmerston North

NGARURORO RIVER
wild sheep

Wellington

North Island and offshore island distribution of wallaby, wild sheep and wild goats inhabiting specific regions.

165

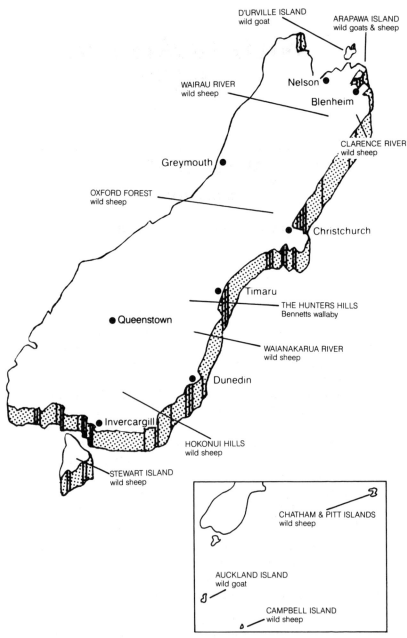

D'URVILLE ISLAND
wild goat

ARAPAWA ISLAND
wild goats & sheep

WAIRAU RIVER
wild sheep

Nelson

Blenheim

CLARENCE RIVER
wild sheep

Greymouth

OXFORD FOREST
wild sheep

Christchurch

Timaru

THE HUNTERS HILLS
Bennetts wallaby

Queenstown

WAIANAKARUA RIVER
wild sheep

Dunedin

Invercargill

HOKONUI HILLS
wild sheep

STEWART ISLAND
wild sheep

CHATHAM & PITT ISLANDS
wild sheep

AUCKLAND ISLAND
wild goat

CAMPBELL ISLAND
wild sheep

South Island and offshore island distribution of wallaby (one species),
wild sheep and wild goats inhabiting specific regions.

166

7 WILD GOATS AND SHEEP

WILD GOAT
(Capra hircus)

Male: Buck   Female: Doe   Young: Kid

Range

Domesticated goats are a common sight in many parts of the world. Almost certainly such breeds as the angora, cashmere, Walliser, and the saanen (thought to be the oldest of domesticated animals) were evolved from a wild species of *Capra hircus* (Persian ibex).

Among the large family of true wild goats the introduced Himalayan thar holds a special significance in New Zealand. Its native range is south of the main Himalayas from Bhutan to Kashmir. A somewhat smaller animal is the endangered Nilgiri thar, which inhabits the mountains of southern India. The smallest of this select group — the Arabian thar — lives in the mountainous regions of south-eastern Saudi Arabia.

The many ibexes are characterised by their long, backward-curved horns. They are:

Ibex — Originally this species ranged throughout the Swiss Alps, northern Italy, and bordering highlands. Today it is restricted to a few small 'protected' herds on the Italian side of Monta Rosa. It has also been introduced into several game reserves in Switzerland.

Spanish ibex — Found today in the mountainous districts of Spain and Portugal, as well as in the Pyrénées.

Persian ibex — Ranges the mountains of south-western Asia from the Caucasus through Iran to Baluchistan and Sind.

Siberian/Asiatic ibex — Found in central Asia from the Tien Shan and the Altai Mountains through to the Himalayas in Kashmir. A number of subspecies are known.

Himalayan ibex — Ranges the Himalayan mountains from Kashmir east through Nepal.

Nubian ibex — Can be found from the Red Sea hills to the coastal mountains of North Africa.

Abyssinian ibex — This species is limited to the mountains of Ethiopia.

Caucasian ibex — This species is also referred to as the Caucasian tur. Found in the Caucasus, it generally resembles the alpine species of ibex.

Interestingly enough, the European chamois, the Rocky Mountain goat of North America, and the serow of eastern India are not classed as true goats but rather as goat-antelopes.

Feral goats are plentiful in various countries around the world. In the British Isles, *Capra hircus* can be found in parts of England — Devon, Isle of Man, Northumberland; Scotland — throughout much of the highlands and a number of offshore islands; Wales — especially Snowdonia National Park; and Ireland — a general spread in the mountainous regions.

They range over much of the Mediterranean, including such notable offshore islands as Crete, Corsica, and Monte Cristo.

Wild goats are also widely distributed, although not in large numbers, over a great deal of North America. They are found in every western state with, it is said, the exception of Washington. Their overall range extends from islands off the Alaskan coastline through to Texas hill country.

They occur in Mexico, the West Indies, Hawaii, Chile, Venezuela, Argentina, the Bonin Islands (belonging to Japan), Galapagos and many other oceanic islands, Australia (where their range is as broad as it is diverse) and, of course, New Zealand.

Liberations and Distribution in New Zealand

It was during Captain Cook's second voyage to New Zealand — specifically, 2 June 1773 — that the first documented liberation of goats took place in this country. Cook's journal states the place was the eastern side of Queen Charlotte Sound and that there were two animals — appropriately enough, a male and female. Much to the good captain's distress, he was later told that these goats had been killed by Maori soon after their release.

With the persistency for which he was noted, Cook again tried to establish goats in Queen Charlotte Sound. The date was 20 February 1777, during his third and last voyage to this country. On this occasion there were three — a male and a female with kid. Wisely, Cook presented them to a Maori elder, making him promise not to kill any until they had greatly increased their numbers. Naturally, we have no way of knowing whether or not these goats are the forebears of the wild goats that today range unchecked throughout this part of the South Island.

Last century, it was common practice for seafarers, especially whalers, to liberate goats as a ready source of food for castaways on various outlying islands. This is thought to have happened on the following islands: Three Kings group (1889-90), Macauley (1836), Raoul (1836), Enderby (1850), Auckland, which includes Ewing and Ocean islands (1850), Kapiti (before 1854), Campbell (1868), Antipodes (1886), Snares (1889) and Adams (1885).

One way or another goats would also inhabit these offshore islands: Cuvier, Mokohinau (Burgess Island), Great Barrier, Cavalli, Great Mercury, Whale, East, D'Urville, Forsyth, Herekopare, Mangere, South-east and Chatham. No dates of release are available.

Without assistance from humans goats died out on Adams, Enderby, Campbell, Antipodes and Snares.

The goats found on Arapawa Island in the Marlborough Sounds are worthy of separate comment. They are considered by expert breeders to be of a most unusual origin, definitely unlike any breed in this country. Research carried out in the 1970s by an American, Betty Rowe, who ran an organic farm on the island, confirms that these goats are the Old English Milk Goat, a breed now extinct in Britain.

169

These findings were backed up by Lawrence Alderton, technical consultant of Britain's Rare Breeds Survival Trust. From the evidence presented to him, he confirmed that the goats inhabiting Arapawa Island most certainly represent an important surviving repository of the genes of this old breed.

Unfortunately, it is not known where these goats came from. One possibility is that they were Captain Cook's introduction of 1773 — any goats taken by Cook on his voyages would almost certainly have been of native British stock — or that they may have descended from the three animals of 1777. Another theory is that they were obtained in New South Wales by whalers and subsequently liberated on the island.

Early European settlers also brought many goats with them to the new land. As with pigs, goats were bartered or given to the Maori. Frequently they escaped into the bushlands. They were reported as running wild as early as 1839 in parts of Northland, and by the mid-1850s in the Maitai Valley, near Nelson, and on the hills about Banks Peninsula in Canterbury.

Goats were also used as a ready source of food by goldminers, prospectors, and by road and railway builders. Often poorly fenced or tethered, many goats escaped into the surrounding countryside, or, just as likely, were left to fend for themselves when the various camps were abandoned. The huge numbers of goats that came to infest the Skippers Canyon country of Central Otago resulted from stock initially brought there by goldminers.

With a view to creating a market for their fine skins, a number of angora and cashmere goats were introduced from Australia in 1867 by the Canterbury, Auckland, and Otago Acclimatisation Societies. For reasons unknown to the author, this venture did not proceed and the imported stock quickly hybridised with the common variety of goats.

Goats were possibly first used to control blackberry and other weeds as early as 1906 in both the Marlborough and Nelson districts. This form of mobile weed control quickly spread to other parts of the land. In 1950, K.A. Wodzicki wrote in *Introduced Mammals of New Zealand* that goats were still widely used for this purpose in Taranaki and Hawke's Bay. Inevitably, many goats simply wandered away, to link up with goats already feral and to revert all too quickly to a wild state.

During the First World War, the goat situation worsened in various parts of the country — for example, the Southern Lakes district of Otago. G.M. Thomson, writing in 1922, estimates conservatively that the wild goat population there at this time numbered 30,000. Mostly they were found on the more remote parts of large stations.

Desperate sheep farmers, faced with eventual ruin unless drastic action was taken, sought the aid of local hunters. In 1916, for instance, a runholder near Skippers (a deserted town site in Skippers Canyon) was offering one shilling for each token (a set of ears). During this period as many as 1,000 goats were being shot during the season (spring and summer) on some properties in Central Otago.

In 1930, the Department of Internal Affairs was given the awesome task of attempting to bring under control the various types of wild game — deer, thar and chamois — that were to be found in often prolific numbers in many parts of the country. Goat operations, under a special arrangement with runholders in the Marlborough district, were carried out during normal deer hunting forays by professional shooters as early as the 1930-1931 season. Records state that 277 goats were put down.

The department would not make any significant inroads into the ever-growing wild goat numbers, however, until the 1937-1938 season. Records state that government hunters accounted for 16,480 goats in the Marlborough-Canterbury districts. They were shot during regular deer control work.

In this same period a radio station was established on Sunday or, as it would become known, Raoul Island, in the Kermadec group. The department saw fit to send a field officer along with the expedition to 'investigate means of dealing with the goats, cats and rats which almost nullify attempts at growing fruit, vegetables and grain, and are inimical to the welfare of the bush and bird-life'. Presumably the field officer took his .303 rifle along with him, because annual reports for this year state that 699 goats were shot on the island.

The State Forest Service was at this time dismayed at the damage goats were causing in forests, both indigenous and exotic. Indeed, the annual report of 1929 made it clear that the 'browsing habits of these animals render them second only to deer as a destroyer of forest regeneration'. The annual report of 1940 stated that goats were 'reported to be plentiful in some of the North Auckland forests' and that they 'appear to be increasing in Wellington and Westland conservancies'. In fact, wild goats were on the increase wherever they could be found. The same trend continued as the years slipped away. A possible explanation for this was offered by K.A. Wodzicki (1950):

> Goat destruction is not enhanced with the same handsome returns as is the case with deer, opossum or rabbit. Until recent years wild goats had no commercial value at all, there being no market for the carcasses or skins. Further, the comparatively easy shooting of goats, particularly in some areas, does not appeal to the majority of New Zealand sportsmen.

That a good market had developed for goat skins by 1947 is reflected in the fact that of a total of 73,010 goats killed by government shooters for the 1946-1947 season, some 14,461 skins were recovered. The huge goat 'kill' for that particular year — with most animals being destroyed in the Marlborough and Otago districts — was far and away the largest ever recorded by the department. The second highest figure was 17,338 kills recorded for the 1937-1938 season. Overall, government hunters shot 115,865 goats for the period 1937-1947.

In 1946, the Department of Internal Affairs turned its attention to the Three Kings Islands. These are essentially three rocky islets, classed as the extreme northern frontier of New Zealand, which lie some 54 kilometres north-west of Cape Maria van Diemen.

The largest landmass in this group is Great Island (Manawa Tawi), which is 354 hectares in size. The other main islands of the group are North-East Island, South-West Island, and West Island; the last two are actually joined by a narrow chain of rocks known as the Princes Islands. In structure they consist of basic volcanic rocks resting on a base of greywacke. Goats had been released only on Great Island. The most likely number was four animals.

Before their introduction the botanist T.F. Cheeseman twice visited the Three Kings Islands. On Great Island, for instance, he posited (in papers and notes published in 1888 and 1891) that there were 143 different species of flora there. But when W.R.B. Oliver went there for the same purpose in 1934, some 44 years after goats had been released, he could identify only 70 species.

By the time the government shooting party stepped ashore on Great Island all low branches had been destroyed except, it was observed, for those of plants growing in places inaccessible to goats — steeply formed cliffs facing the sea. There was also a definite thinning out of the bush and consequent wind damage as a result. The grasslands appeared to have extended, too. All in all, it contrasted dramatically with the lush green vegetation that could be observed on South-West Island.

After consulting the annual reports of the Department of Internal Affairs I feel certain that an expedition to Great Island 'for the purpose of exterminating the goats thereon' would have taken place in the winter of 1944. Up to three months would have been allocated for the task.

During the shooting operations, stomach contents of dead animals revealed that they had been mostly feeding on 'grazing materials'. K.A. Wodzicki (1950) comments:

> An indication of the extent of the impact of this goat population on the vegetation is provided by the fact that by the end of the expedition's stay on the island when the majority of animals had been killed, regrowth of some plants was already occurring.

This would indicate that the party was there for several months at least.

A total of 393 goats were eventually shot. The party were convinced that they had achieved a total success and they were right. Since then a spectacular increase in the vegetation found on Great Island has taken place. By the late 1960s, a mixed forest had established itself, with endemic species eliminated by the goats re-invading from other islands in the group.

On 1 April 1956, the New Zealand Forest Service, for better or worse, relieved the Department of Internal Affairs of the 'wild animals' problem. It was no closer to being solved than it had been 26 years before. In their last reports pertaining to wild goats the department had this to say:

A disturbing factor common to many goat problem areas is the reinfestation that takes place from adjacent properties. Some land owners are opposed to goat destruction on the grounds of this animal's value in blackberry and weed control. In view of the modern effective chemical hormones now available for weed eradication such contentions are largely untenable. Goats are in many areas a definite and increasing forest menace, and further measures to counteract this problem are at present under consideration.

The goat bounty schemes operating in the Taranaki, Marlborough and Nelson provinces resulted in large numbers of these animals being destroyed. It is, however, unlikely that such schemes are doing more than maintaining the present goat population levels. Bounty schemes on any noxious animal are merely interim steps affording some relief to the problem until more effective eradication can be evolved.

The shooting arm of the Forest Service was known as the DPF (Division Protection Forestry). Naturally enough, they employed the same field staff that had worked for the deer control section of the Department of Internal Affairs. In effect, then, only the name of the responsible office had been changed.

With admirable determination, government hunters waged war on goats from one end of the country to the other. They hunted them in the scorching temperatures of Central Otago. They used teams of dogs in the tightly packed bush flanking Mount Taranaki's lower slopes — a dreadful business by all accounts in the depths of winter. They sped up the Wanganui River in jetboats, shooting scores of goats on the steep bluffs overlooking this most picturesque of waterways. They also pressed on with steely determination to eradicate goats from Raoul Island, where, as already mentioned, culling operations had started years ago.

Situated some 1,000 kilometres north-east of Auckland and blessed with a delightful sub-tropical climate, the 3,000-hectare landmass that is Raoul Island climbs to 520 metres above sea level. Largely forested, with pohutukawa being the dominant canopy tree, much of the terrain is steep and bluffy, bisected by deep, cauldron-like cavities where only the brave and foolhardy would dare venture. No problem for the goats, of course.

By 1956 estimates of the number of goats there varied. Two years previously, L.C. Bell of the Wildlife Service estimated they numbered around 2,000. A year later, N. Bonnington of the same department made a more conservative estimation, judging that they ranged between 800 and 1,000 animals. Either way, it was still far too many. Just one goat on Raoul Island would be considered that.

During 1956 two Forest Service hunters — Doug Harmon and Merv Bonis — culled 1,100 goats during a six-month stay. There were still a good number of animals remaining, however. So much then for Bonnington's calculations.

In the aftermath of such a bloodbath the wild goats of Raoul Island were granted a reprieve by the New Zealand government and they would experience a period of comparative peace. Then in 1970 the Forest Service again considered the situation. They decided that a long-term policy of hunting would be the only way to completely eradicate the goats.

So in 1972 the first of what would become an annual hunting expedition to Raoul Island came into being. From that date on between three and six hunters, each with up to three dogs, spent from two to eight months on the island, gradually whittling down the numbers of wild goats.

This war on the goats proved a daunting task for the hunters. Much of the terrain was dangerous. The bush was heavy, tangled, and alive with a thick, thorny growth introduced by the early settlers to deter goats from attacking their crops. The humidity, especially towards the end of the year, was energy-sapping for men used to working at high altitudes. Moreover, the multi-coloured goats were unlike any other of the same species they had ever hunted.

Ray Wise, leader of a five-month expedition in the early 1970s, was astounded at how swiftly the goats could move when escaping. Their ability to cope with the steep cliffs overlooking the sea was amazing. They were in that respect, he told me, the equal of thar or chamois. This opinion was also shared by Ray's two shooters — Vince Duckett and Errol Clince. Bill Nikl, who hunted there in 1976, regarded the goats as 'tougher than deer'.

It was noticeable to those hunters on Raoul Island in later years that, as their numbers steadily declined — 1,286 were killed in 1972 as against 341 in 1982 — the goats retreated to steeper coastal bluffs, where they were even more wary of man and dog.

Dogs of course were essential on Raoul Island, just as they were on Mount Taranaki when goat-culling teams worked there. The same thing could be said of the Wanganui River headwaters. Ray Wise believes that the goats would have been impossible to eliminate on Raoul Island without dogs.

Not that the dogs always won. Frequently a smart goat was able to shake them off on the bluffs. On several occasions a dog would lose its footing and suddenly plunge headlong, twisting, into space. A sheer drop of perhaps 180 metres. Yes, that particular dog had very definitely chased its last 'hairy'.

Then there were 'diversions' for keyed-up canines. Ray Wise recalls that on more than one occasion his dog — out of sight and possibly 80 metres away — would start to bark frantically. Obviously a goat was bailed. Up a tree, perhaps, poised on the gnarled, twisting limb of a mighty pohutukawa, possibly urinating in its fear. Easy meat for a well-placed shot from the old 'treble-two' (.222 Remington).

But when Ray linked up with his near-demented hunting mate and stared wonderingly up into the tree, there was no goat to be seen. A rueful Ray could only presume that his dog had latched onto one of the smelly wild cats that plagued the island, and that the cat, after taking to the heights, had leaped into the interlocking branches of another tree and vanished.

The April-to-December goat campaign on Raoul Island in 1983 proved a particularly arduous one. Goats were few and all were highly elusive. Still, the hunters accounted for 147. Towards the end of their time on the island they were experiencing great difficulty in even finding signs of goats, let alone seeing one on the hoof. At long last extermination seemed close at hand.

In December 1984 the New Zealand Forest Service, in the person of Andy Leigh, a senior environmental officer in Auckland, announced that the very last wild goat had been shot on Raoul Island. As he put it: 'We think we have got them all. The party knew there were two left and they got both.'

According to the *New Zealand Herald* report, (December 1984) the killing of the very last wild goat on Raoul Island proved a hazardous undertaking:

Wild goats are mostly found in the Forest Parks. This is the southern end of the Tararua Forest Park, where they are "lightly scattered".

Numerous wild Angora goats were seen on this sun-drenched hillface east of the Roxburgh River, near Alexandra. The big white billy (*left*) is a typical mature male found in this region where feral goats have been established for over a century.

The changing face of wild goat habitat in the North Island. The rugged peaks within the Coromandel Forest Park brood under a blanket of mist.

The valley of the Maraehako Stream sweeps back to heavily forested foothills flanking the westernmost regions of the vast Raukumara Ranges.

The serious wild goat hunter needs strongly constructed footwear to gain access to this little mob's rocky haunts, and catch this photograph.

Death Also Stalked the Hunter

Seconds before it died from a high-velocity bullet, the last wild goat on Raoul Island almost had its revenge.

It had been a classic duel: three crack Forest Service hunters, tough rugged terrain that suited animals, not men, and a swift quarry that had eluded its killers for six weeks.

A Wairarapa hunter, Mr Andy Rostenburg, clinging to the soaring cliff face at Smith's Bluff, saw his target.

But somehow he slipped. From a distance, his companions, Mr Norm McDonald, of Auckland, and Mr Ross Whiting, of Benneydale, feared their friend would be killed.

Mr Rostenburg, acting instinctively, jabbed his rifle barrel into the soft pumice cliff and stopped his fall.

Cut, bruised and shocked, he got up and fired off a .222 calibre round.

The bullet struck home, killing the goat and ending a costly 50-year battle against the destructive inhabitants of New Zealand's northern-most possession.

It has been estimated that government hunters killed an estimated 15,000 goats on Raoul Island between 1937 and 1984. Spending by the Forest Service for 1979-1983 came to $330,000. The budget for 1984 was $62,000.

Subsequent expeditions to the island have proved conclusively that Andy Rostenburg did in fact kill the last goat there. According to Auckland-based conservation officer, Dick Veitch, who was one of a party that visited the island as recently as 1988, there has been a 'wonderful recovery' in vegetation and forest growth now that goats no longer forage there.

But one problem on Raoul Island has been replaced with another — or should I say, another two — rats and cats. They are at the time of writing creating havoc with ground-nesting birds. Can they be eradicated? Dick Veitch thinks so, with a long and concentrated effort. We can only hazard a guess at how much that might cost. And certainly in the summer of 1989 the Department of Conservation — hindered by limited financial resources and personnel — is in no position to seriously consider such an expensive undertaking.

Today, wild goats have a wide distribution on the mainland. Possibly the largest concentrations still occur in the upper Wanganui River and Taranaki-King Country regions, areas where they have always been prolific. Offshore, they exist on D'Urville and Great Barrier Islands (where the Forest Service started shooting operations in 1976). On Arapawa Island about 40 animals (May 1988) are found within a 121-hectare sanctuary established by the Arapawa Wildlife Trust in the aftermath of Forest Service eradication campaigns in the 1970s. They still occur on Chatham Island, as well as on Auckland Island, where a herd of around 60 animals (April 1988) are found in the drier and warmer parts of the main island in the group. But DOC field personnel believe that they no longer exist on Great Mercury Island — where about seven animals were living in 1977.

It is, I think, well worth commenting further on the goats found on Auckland Island, which is the largest in the Auckland Islands group, some 466 kilometres south of Bluff. As already noted, goats were first liberated there in 1850. Further releases were made in the following decade, a significant one in 1865 by the Victorian Acclimatisation Society (Australia) at both Enderby and Erebus Cove. This practice, mostly with stock from Britain and Australia, was carried on until about 1907.

Of 10 documented liberations only one herd survives today on Auckland Island. They are thought to have descended from the 1865 liberations. Significantly, they are considered to be the southernmost goat population in the southern hemisphere (latitude 50. 32⁰ South). They are in fact surviving within a few degrees of what is considered the minimum temperature for the species.

In 1976 the goat population on Auckland Island was estimated to number about 100 animals (M.R. Rudge & D.J. Campbell, 1977). Nine years later the ecology division of the Department of Scientific and Industrial Research pressed the Department of Lands and Survey to eradicate the goats. The latter administered the Reserves Act and, after all, the Auckland Islands were gazetted as 'nature reserves' as far back as 1934. Importantly Section 20(b) of the Reserves Act 1977 couldn't be any clearer: 'except where the Minister otherwise determines,. . .exotic flora and fauna as far as possible be exterminated'. At any rate, the extermination of the Auckland Island goats — carried out by the Forest Service — was to be completed by 1990.

Realising that a scientifically interesting and possibly unique herd was under death sentence, the field division of the Department of Lands and Survey sought approval from the Outlying Islands Reserves Committee — an inter-departmental sub-committee reporting to the National Parks and Reserves Authority on management of New Zealand's outlying islands — to both study and live-capture some of the remaining animals. This request was granted, with the stipulation that live capture be carried out over the summers of 1986/87 and 1987/88. Complete extermination would of course still take place in 1990. McIvor and Sherley continue the story:

> In January 1986, the HMNZS *Waikato* visited the Island. The Field Division took advantage of the visit to send a small team to explore the feasibility of a large scale capture exercise, and to capture a small number of goats for assessment. Allan Kinnis, Lands and Survey Field Division, Christchurch, Paul Muir from the Animal Sciences Group, Lincoln College, and Dr Mike Rudge of DSIR Ecology Division were chosen. Dr Rudge was employed for his local knowledge of the area. In addition, the Reserves Division of the department employed Dr John Campbell of Ecology Division to accompany a NZ Forest Service hunter to shoot any goats found on the Hooker Hills. The hunting party failed to find any goats either in the upper reaches of Laurie Harbour or the Hooker Hills.

During the three days allocated to the operation, Kinnis, Rudge, Muir, plus 10 sailors, were able to capture 11 animals. In colour they ranged from grey to black. The two heaviest adults, a male and female, were grey. Captured inland, they weighed 127½ pounds (male) and 103 pounds (female). The other black and brown-toned animals were trapped on a coastal cliff site. Interestingly enough, they were first observed eating kelp. All the goats were in fine condition, with the mature animals remarkably large framed.

The goats, under the care of Allan Kinnis, were transported safely to New Zealand on the MAF vessel *James Cook*, which was calling to collect MAF fisheries research personnel from Enderby Island.

Thirteen months later, the second live-capture operation took place. To return to McIvor and Sherley's report:

> The main capture team led by Allan Kinnis (Field Division, Christchurch) comprised four shepherds: Lyn Morris (Manager Okuku

Pass Station), Jason Morgan, John Van Buren, and Steven Pauling and five of their dogs. This team left on the HMNZS *Canterbury* on 9th February.

Captain Jacques Cousteau generously offered to transport the three man study team to the Auckland Islands departing Stewart Island on 24th January 1987. This team comprised Aldous McIvor (Expedition Leader — Dept of Lands and Survey Field Division), Greg Sherley (Scientist — Dept of Lands and Survey Natural Sciences Unit) and Bob Willis (Reserves Ranger — Timaru).

In total, 56 animals were captured by the expedition. Four of these were captured by the study team during the three days prior to the arrival of the capture party. Three were caught by bush stalking and surprising the animals. The fourth, a mature buck, was caught at night using torches. It proved impossible to run the animals down in the forests during the day. The easiest, and least stressful technique for the animal was night spotlighting. In that instance the buck, bewildered by the light, and standing shielding its head behind a tree, was simply caught and chained to the tree, to be led blindfolded back to camp the next morning.

Of the 56 goats captured, 13 would die at capture or before they arrived at the department's farm at Ahaura, Westland. Also, two bucks would escape while in captivity — one by breaking a tether chain (he weighed 91½ pounds) and the other, a much smaller fellow, seized the opportunity to break away prior to being taken on board the *James Cook*. The party and its animals left for Dunedin on 20 February; the animals in the care of Allan Kinnis and Jason Morgan.

Again we return to McIvor and Sherley's report:

The captured animals have been located in Westland and Southland. The female flock and half of the males are based at Ahaura, Westland, while the remaining males are located at Te Anau. Both flocks have been augmented with 200-300 mainland feral females. The breeding programme which is under the guidance of Dr Geoff Nicoll (a Landcorp geneticist) has set up three flocks.

● A purebred Auckland Island flock;
● A crossbred flock mating Auckland Island bucks to mainland feral does; and
● A control flock of ferals against which the characteristics of the purebreds and crossbreds can be measured. The likely commercial contribution of these goats to New Zealand is in providing a genetic resource of meat goats.

Survival of purebred kids has been difficult and indeed, the sensitivity of the captured mature animals to stress and trauma of change has required fastidious skilled management. In the light of this knowledge, the survival of the animals on the Auckland Islands can only be described as remarkable.

So what, you might well ask, is so important about a purebred Auckland Island flock? They are after all only feral goats, right? No different from those in New Zealand? Wrong. Studies carried out by animal scientists at Lincoln College have revealed some interesting facts about Auckland Island goats. Firstly, they are genetically different from other types of feral goats in New Zealand. Intriguingly, the blood typing of the plasma proteins indicates that they are remarkably similar to Spanish Serrara Andaluga and Hungarian Saanen goats. This is substantiated by the three distinct colour groupings that occur — blue-grey, black and white, and black and tan. The more upright nature of the shortish horns further strengthens the case for the true ancestry of these animals.

Scientists McIvor and Sherley are of the opinion that the surviving goats, estimated to number no more than 60, were confined to about 0.5 per cent of the island's overall area. They also believe that the animals — considered at the extreme end of their ecological range — were unlikely to expand. In closing their report, they stated:

> The remnant flock on Auckland Island is sufficiently important to warrant protection. The safest plan to preserve the resource with its own natural random mating, and response to the environment free from man's influence is on Auckland Island. In fact, the uniqueness of this flock stems from this factor.
>
> The most practical management option that will retain the historical and scientific values of this flock is to retain the remnant flock on Auckland Island, where it can be studied and monitored. Failing this, the remaining animals should be captured and joined with the other captured animals in Westland. This however is not the preferred option. The remnant flock should not be destroyed.
>
> The authors of this report request the Department of Conservation to review the recommendations of the management plan with the view to requesting the Minister to give approval for the flock to remain on the Island as provided by Section 20(b) of the Reserves Act 1977. The flock however should continue to be studied and monitored, and if necessary, confined to the present range.
>
> Alternatively if protection is not granted, eradication by shooting should be deferred to enable Land Corporation to complete the capture of the remaining animals.

Despite this plea to save the remaining goats on Auckland Island for both historical and scientific reasons, the Minister of Conservation, Helen Clark, was reported as saying in the *Southland Times* (30 June 1988) that she had not chosen to exercise her discretion under the Reserves Act which would allow her to provide protection for the goats. And: 'Landcorp will have the opportunity to capture as many goats as it wishes before the Department of Conservation eradication programme starts early next year.' Moreover: 'Allowing the goats to remain when they destroy flora and fauna contravenes the spirit and purpose of the reserve.'

To bring this story up to date, I personally contacted Aldous McIvor at Landcorp's Wellington office. In correspondence, he replied:

> Mr George McMillan, Chief Executive for the Corporation, has advised the Hon Helen Clark, Minister of Conservation, on 22 December 1988 that the Corporation will not be able to take advantage of the live capture opportunity within the time constraints as defined by the Minister. However, he indicated that the Corporation would appreciate further consideration should the Minister defer the shooting beyond 1990.
>
> The Corporation staff investigated the cost and practicality of chartering a Ministry of Agriculture and Fisheries research vessel, as well as boats from Stewart Island and Bluff. The least cost option which is based upon a charter of the MAF vessel *Kaharoa* is in the range of $60,000-$63,318. The costs are comprised of $6,000 per day hire, $40 per hour fuel, with six to seven days steaming (MAF estimate) from Wellington plus GST, less 15% discount.
>
> It is clear that we are faced with a race against time in our breeding programme for the purebred Auckland Island animals. Reproduction rate during the first year following capture produced seven kids (5 male and 2 female) with a further difficult kidding due to the extraordinarily wet spring in Westland in 1988. The crossbreeding upgrade programme is running very well but is dependent upon a continued source of purebred bucks. For this reason the supplementing of the purebred flock from the Auckland Island was needed.

Noting the huge expense involved here, it is interesting to reflect that a Forest Service report dated 30 May 1986 estimates that a two-phase eradication of the goats on Auckland Island would cost $90,780 using naval transport or $182,780 using private chartered vessels; a cost per goat of $900 and $1,820 respectively.

How much then would it cost to carry out this operation in 1990 or even later than that? And all for a 'static' population of uniquely fascinating goats that, even if left completely alone in a windswept, freezing wilderness few of us will ever visit, might never exceed 100 in number.

Surely this case illustrates the need for someone in authority to get their priorities right. What is gained by sending at huge cost, and for no apparent good reason, a .222-equipped DOC hit-team 400 kilometres south of Bluff? What do you think?

Physical Description
A mature male goat will stand about 34-36 inches high at the shoulder, will have a body length of between 46-60 inches, and will weigh in the vicinity of 120-150 pounds. In this country he would be fairly classed as a small-to-medium game animal — in the same bracket, say, as a fallow or whitetail buck. He will have a rather 'blocky' appearance. His limbs will be stout, designed with climbing in mind.

The female of the species, as with the other game animals found in this country, is considerably smaller. But the difference is not as marked as it is between a male and female thar.

No animal encountered in New Zealand, if not the world, has so many variations in colour as does *Capra hircus*. They may be a pure or an off-white (the angora lineage clearly revealed), black, grey, or brown. Frequently they are a striking combination of colours — not altogether flattering where some individual animals are concerned. They may also be spotted, dappled, or saddled. Interestingly enough, the author, during 1985-1986, observed several goats in the southernmost reaches of the Rimutaka Range that from a distance appeared very much like miniature deer in their bright reddish-brown garments of high summer.

The pelage tends to be long and rather coarse to the touch. It is possibly longer — a simple case of adaptation — if the animals range 'high' country, such as, for example, certain parts of the Ruahine Range. For extra insulation, a fine woolly 'down' — not a great deal unlike that which a sika deer grows during the winter — can be found near the base of the hairs.

Both adult sexes may have manes. Only the male, however,

has a distinct ruff of hair at his throat — a beard, if you like. As the animal ages, so his beard grows even longer and thicker. Both sexes also grow horns which, unlike the antlers of a deer, are retained for life. The horns of a nanny are unimpressive when compared with the wide, heavy, corkscrew-like horns of a big 'trophy' male. Horns vary in colour, depending on localities; from bone (a yellowish-brown) through to dark brown.

Habitat and Habits
As a generalisation, it is true to say that wild goats normally inhabit low-lying terrain rather than high altitudes — ie, above the bushline. It is also true that goat habitat is as varied as that of wild pigs. But then, the story of the introduction and distribution of both species in this country bears a remarkable similarity.

And with no fear of contradiction, we can state that the wild goat is among the most versatile of wild animals. Indeed, when one considers its origins, it displays an admirable trait in being able to adapt to completely different terrain and weather conditions.

It is essential, I think, to elaborate on that point. We know that in origin goats are animals of dry, scrubby wastelands. Given a choice, it is sure they much prefer a dry climate where the temperature frequently ranges high — this explains why they have done so well in parts of Otago, Marlborough, and on the East Coast of the North Island. An even better example can be found over much of the sun-blasted Australian hinterland. However, goats were not given any choice on the type of habitat they were liberated into or, for that matter, what lay invitingly on the far side of a broken-down fence or through an open gateway. The end result was that many goats found themselves in areas of high rainfall — such as, for instance, parts of Taranaki, the Tararua Ranges, or the West Coast. Nevertheless, goats had no problems in coping with the often excessive rainfall such areas are noted for.

In 1987, I visited the Mangapurua Valley, located in the upper reaches of the Wanganui River — an account of that eventful trip can be found in *The Hunting Experience*. At any rate, this proved a comparatively warm valley, the bush-clad ridges above it reaching around 600 metres, the valley itself perhaps 300 metres lower. Rainfall here is extreme, therefore the growth is prolific — a veritable riot of jungle-like greenery.

Despite such rainfall, goats have thrived in this soggy environment. Possibly the first ones moved into the valley — via the Wanganui River frontal country — after the last settlers abandoned the area in the early 1940s. Gradually they built up their numbers, ignored by the mounted hunters who infrequently hunted the valley for pigs. Eventually the goats numbered many thousands, and remained so until Forest Service helicopter search-and-destroy missions started in the late 1970s. Commercial live-capture operations — once farming goats had become a viable proposition — later took an even bigger toll of their overall numbers.

Apparently goats are able to breed all year round. A nanny can successfully mate before she is one year old. The gestation period is around 180 days. She may produce three litters in two years. Twins are common; triplets far from extraordinary. A herd of wild goats — if left unchecked — is capable of doubling (and possibly more) its numbers every two years.

On Auckland Island, however, it is thought that goats are not as productive as this. It seems that the generally poor grazing has, over a very long period, affected their ability to breed — a slowing-down process, as it were — which explains why the population has remained fairly static. Also, they tend to be slower growing than mainland animals; the does, for example, do not kid until four-tooth. But when they do mature to full size — and a full-grown Auckland Island billy is a most handsome fellow — they are at least equal to, and in most instances larger than, feral goats found in New Zealand.

Of a marked gregarious nature goats, especially when found in large herds of 40 to 50 animals, will virtually eliminate all vegetation because of their sustained, non-selective browsing and tramping habits. In 1935, G.F. Yerex, then in charge of the deer control section of the Department of Internal Affairs, undertook a detailed inspection of goat damage in Egmont National Park, where goat control was first carried out in 1925. In an unpublished report that year, Yerex described the nature and effect of what he observed:

1. The killing by barking of the following trees and shrubs: *Nothopanax colensoi, Coprosma grandifolia* and *C. tenuifolia,* and *Pseudopanax crassifolium.*
2. The eating of fern fronds, grasses, supplejack, vine tips, the leaves and shoots of a very wide variety of trees and shrubs, and also seedlings of such major species as rimu, miro, kamahi, totara, etc. Some of these species in a later stage were rubbed and twisted by the horns.
3. The grazing of snow tussock and other alpine plants and the making of tracks.

It was Yerex's conclusion that the first type of damage led to an opening of the forest, and that the third facilitated slips and generally accelerated erosion.

The battle to save many North Island forests from the disastrous effects of too many goats reached unprecedented levels in the latter part of the 1970s and the early 1980s. In 1978, for example, as many as 50 men, most of them using .222s and dogs, were working on goat control operations in Pureora, Pirongia, and Whareorina forests. Helicopters were used where the animals largely ranged inaccessible regions. Total kill came to around 20,000. In the Ruakumara Forest Park in 1982 the goat situation was so bad that 1080 poison was used. At the time, the district ranger, Mr I.C.W. Glennis, was reported as saying: 'Goats have severely modified the forest in some areas with the result that very little, if any, of the lower forest canopy remains.' And: 'In these regions accelerated erosion is apparent, threatening the forest structure as well as the stability of rivers and streams.'

To sum up, goats are the most destructive animals found within a forest environment. They are born survivors with the ability, because of their non-selective browsing habits, to exist in a comparatively healthy state in a badly denuded area where many other types of wild animals would eventually die out. Also, their high birthrate makes them an extremely difficult proposition to control.

WILD SHEEP
(*Ovis aries*)

Male: Ram   Female: Ewe   Young: Lamb

Range

All of the world's wild sheep are related. Domestic sheep are thought to have descended from two different types of wild species — the urial and the mouflon. Various breeds of sheep, especially the merino, have been introduced into many countries. Due to their hardiness and general adaptability they have fared remarkably well.

The most commonly known wild sheep in North America is the Rocky Mountain bighorn. It is relatively widespread throughout the principal mountains of the west. A number of subspecies are known. Strains of bighorn occur in parts of Kamchatka and Siberia. More plentiful in numbers than the bighorn is the dall sheep. It ranges from the mountains of northern Alaska into northern British Columbia. The Alaskan population alone was estimated in 1986 to number between 30,000 and 50,000 animals. It is also in British Columbia where the largest numbers of stone sheep are found.

Native to Corsica and Sardinia is the mouflon. Over the past 150 years this species has been transplanted successfully into the mountainous regions of Germany, Austria, Czechoslovakia, Hungary, Romania and Poland. Today it is a highly rated game animal in those countries.

The largest of all wild sheep — the argali — is found in Asia. Largest of all is the Siberian argali. Incredibly, this species has the body size of a large donkey and its massive horns may have a spread of nearly four feet. The front curve of an exceptionally large horn measured 62½ inches and the circumference of another trophy-sized horn added up to 21½ inches (taken at base of horn). The mighty Siberian argali, due to extensive hunting pressure, is not as widespread as in previous years and is now mostly restricted to the Altai Mountains.

Found only in the Alatau Mountains is the Alatau argali. Further south we find Marco Polo's argali, commonly called Marco Polo sheep. This species is only slightly smaller in body size than the Siberian argali and its horns, while rather slender in comparison, are noted for their extreme spread. A tip-to-tip spread of 56 inches has been recorded. Marco Polo's argali is found only on the Pamir Plateau, the so-called 'roof of the world', much of which is over 5 kilometres above sea level.

Four species of wild sheep occur in Iran. The urial sheep is found in the foothills east of the Alborz Range, just south of the Caspian Sea. Also in the same range lives the Alborz red sheep, which is sometimes referred to as the Asiatic mouflon. The Armenian urial ranges the north-western parts of the country, while in the south-western regions lives the Larestan sheep.

Near the India-Tibet border one can find the Ladak urial. The Punjab urial is found in the Punjab and the Sind and extends its range west into Afghanistan, while the Afghan urial inhabits parts of Afghanistan, Baluchistan, and bordering territory.

Two breeds of wild sheep have definite goat-like tendencies. They are the bharal or blue sheep of the more remote regions of the mountains of central Asia, and the Barbary or maned sheep, which inhabits the mountains of North Africa from Morocco to Egypt, and northern Sudan to Tchad and Mali.

Feral sheep are also found on the islands of Soay, Boreray, and Hirta in Scotland. They occur in south-western Norway and parts of Sweden, and are established on the Channel Islands off the southern coast of California. They range, too, on parts of Hawaii, Kerguelen, and a number of oceanic islands. In Australia, they are found on Big Green Island in the Furneaux group in Bass Strait, and also in a small part of Western Australia (Kimberley Range). They are, however, much more widely distributed in New Zealand.

Liberations and Distribution in New Zealand

Not surprisingly, Captain Cook was responsible for the first attempt to bring sheep to New Zealand. His intentions were sound — meat, milk and hides were all vital future provisions.

During his second voyage to New Zealand, Cook brought two rams and four ewes from the Cape of Good Hope, South Africa. By the time the *Resolution* entered Dusky Sound in March 1773, only one ram and one ewe had survived. They were in a terrible state, suffering, it is recorded, from inveterate scurvy. Indeed, their teeth were so loose that they were unable to eat the green food that was given to them. Forster in his journal states they 'were in so wretched a condition that their further preservation was very doubtful'.

However, they must have improved, for, considering that the terrain around Dusky Sound was far too rough and forest-clad for them, Cook took them to Queen Charlotte Sound, on May 18. In his journal, Cook wrote:

> On the 22nd, in the morning, the ewe and ram I had with so much care and trouble brought to this place were both found dead, occasioned, as was supposed, by eating some poisonous plant. Thus my hopes of stocking this country with a breed of sheep were blasted in a moment.

It seems likely that the sheep had eaten tutu, a poisonous plant quite common in the Marlborough Sounds district.

In later years the early settlers brought sheep, cattle, horses, and all sorts of livestock with them to the new bolt-action Cook had written so glowingly about. Because of a lack of fences in the initial stages, many of the animals were allowed to roam freely. Naturally some of them, including sheep, wandered off into the bush, which, at that time, extensively covered the landscape.

By the mid-1800s, sheep could be found living in a feral state in various parts of the country. The same situation applied where several offshore islands were concerned, too.

As a means of providing food for castaway sailors, sheep were liberated on both Chatham and Pitt islands (together they form the Chatham Islands) in the early 1840s. By 1885 there were an estimated 200 sheep on these islands. Grazing rights were granted there in 1866, at which time the sheep numbered about 2,000. By the turn of the century this figure had topped 60,000. Many, living in more inaccessible regions — ie, cliff faces — had reverted to a feral state.

Apparently sheep first arrived on Campbell Island between 1888 and 1900. In 1896 the island was taken up as a sheep run. Farming continued there until 1931, when the lease was relinquished. The sheep, said to number over 4,000, were left to their own devices.

Between 1890 and 1900 sheep were also set free on the Auckland and Antipodes islands. None of these animals survived for any length of time; either the conditions there were too severe or they were killed by castaways. One would suspect the former as the most likely explanation.

Domestic sheep were first recorded on Arapawa Island in 1867. They are believed to have come from the Wairau Valley. If this is true, then they were almost certainly Australian merinos shipped from Sydney in the early 1840s. They in turn were descended from Flaxborne stock, considered to be the oldest Australian line, imported from Spain via England about 1795. Feral sheep were first noted on Arapawa Island in 1901, when they were said to be 'very numerous'.

At the present time wild sheep are found on Campbell Island. In 1970 the southern part of the island was fenced off so that a long-term study could be carried out on the effects of sheep on sub-antarctic vegetation and seabirds. A small number of sheep — apparently well spread — occupy Chatham Island. Those found on Pitt Island are now behind a fence, again for scientific research. These animals have been self-reliant for more than 70 years. Man they do not need. A small number of feral animals also inhabit Mason Bay on Stewart Island's west coast.

On the 'mainland' it is rather difficult to define precisely where wild sheep are. Certainly they are well spread around the country with clusters, rather than a general spread, occurring in most places. Suffice to say there are stable populations in the Hokonui Hills of central Southland and in the Oxford Forest in Canterbury (mostly on the true left of the Waimakariri River). They are also found in certain parts of the Waianakarua River (south-west from Oamaru), the Clarence River (Marlborough), and the Wairau River (Nelson Lakes district).

In the North Island the sheep mostly range high, central parts. This takes in the north-eastern portions of the Ruahine

Range, especially near the Ngaruroro River, and extends, via the river, through the Kaweka Range. They also inhabit numerous locations within the vast watershed of the Mohaka River, either living in small numbers on the 'frontal' river faces or in well-scattered groups in side-streams where, in most instances, they are seldom bothered by man.

Physical Description
From the extremely limited research material available, it does appear that wild sheep in this country originated from three specific types — merino, romney, and the puzzling animals found on Arapawa Island. Apparently the Raglan Peninsula flock originated from farmed romneys in the area.

Those animals inhabiting Arapawa Island are a mysterious lot. To the best of my knowledge they have not yet been positively identified. Superficially they resemble the merino type — they have unusual eyes, curly horns, and unkempt fleeces either brown, black, or a patchwork mixture of both colours. However, the sheep found on Arapawa Island do not match with descriptions of the many species in K. Ponting's *Sheep of the World*.

Only those sheep stemming from merino stock, which originated in Spain, are now found on mainland New Zealand. So imagine a domesticated merino sheep in a decidedly dishevelled state and that pretty much sums up the general appearance of one running in the wild.

Most wild sheep have tangled coats and a fair length tail. They have short ears and an oval-shaped face, lightly covered with a fine wool. The wool covering the body is not as densely packed together as is the 'tight' fleece of a farmed animal. Some sheep moult quite heavily in summer, particularly about the chest and shoulders, where the wool is often rather thick. The wool only grows to a certain manageable length and is frequently absent about the belly and other underparts. Nor are true feral sheep wool-blind. They have indeed adapted well to their environment.

With a 'rangier' build than the farmed counterpart, the legs of the wild merino appear longer. Actual body weight and general condition will vary from district to district. By and large sheep fare well in this country. The young animal I photographed in the upper Mohaka River region was obviously in top shape. Apart from its long tail, and the fact that the nearest fence was miles away, you would never have known it was feral. Similarly the small flock I observed and photographed in the Oxford Forest appeared to be faring well. This was to be expected. Sheep are most adaptable creatures. They can rough it with the best of them. As a matter of interest, merino sheep were first introduced into this part of inland Canterbury as early as 1853 and the wild herd found there now may have had its beginnings soon after.

Like goats, sheep retain their horns for the duration of their lives. Horns vary dramatically in both size and shape from species to species and even among subspecies. Basically, however, the structure of all horns is similar — a core of bone arising from the frontal plate of the skull which is covered with keratin, the main ingredient of hooves, hair and nails. Horns are weapons which either serve as a solid defence against predators or are used (their prime function) in highly ritualised combat with other males of the same species for the right to mate.

The heavily ringed horns of a feral merino sheep are impressive in trophy-sized animals. They are usually a light-brown or brown-yellow in colour and may have one or more full curls.

Habitat and Habits
Like other wild animals in this country, sheep favour terrain with a north-westerly aspect — such country receives ample sun and the resulting growth is sufficient for their needs. Adequate shelter is essential. Caves and recesses in overhanging rocks — quite common in the Mohaka River country and parts of Marlborough where sheep are still found — are ideal. Like a goat, a wild sheep will foul its resting place.

Ideal sheep habitat is usually steep — ie, river faces. Sheep walk upon hoofs divided into two toes, their ankles are slim, and the upper part of their legs are muscular. Consequently, they traverse such difficult terrain with ease. Indeed, they are excellent mountaineers. Even domestic sheep cope very well where the terrain is steep and the air is thin.

Wild sheep found on Arapawa Island (*below*) superficially resemble
the merino type: they have unusual eyes, curly horns and unkempt
fleeces, either brown, black, or a patchwork of both colours.

This rugged terrain is typical of the upper Mohaka River country, fringing Hawke's Bay. Wild sheep, seldom bothered here, are generally easy to approach. The young one (*below*) is seen on the banks of the Poamoko Stream.

A hunting guide, Joe Houghton, checks the horns of a wild ram taken
by Philip Holden in the upper Mohaka River region in early 1986.

Looking across the Waimakiriri River, Canterbury, to the
Puketeraki Range, where wild sheep occur in small numbers.

A small mob of wild sheep
pause on the scrub-dotted,
tussocky slopes above the
Waimakiriri River.

Once wild sheep have found a stretch of country very much to their liking they tend to remain there. They both graze and browse; essential requirements in the survival stakes. They will eat tussock to virtually ground level, are able to feed on the wickedly barbed spear-grass, and will destroy such trees as ribbonwood by eating the bark.

This non-selective habit, coupled with over-browsing, proved catastrophic on various sub-antarctic islands, where some species of plants are said to have been completely destroyed. The growth of young trees and shrubs was severely retarded, which in turn opened up the forest interior to the ravages of the seldom-absent wind. (The similar habits of wild cattle on these islands also played a part in this destruction.)

In the previously mentioned upper Mohaka River country, I watched for some length of time a young sheep — an 18-month-old ewe, I judged — feeding with vigour on regenerating beech forest. This particular spot had a good sheep trail leading into it; a sort of miniature bush highway located about 90 metres above a creek flowing through a large watershed. The type of terrain, for instance, that you can find in the Urewera country, which was no great distance to the north.

Noticeably, the sheep were occupying a rather narrow belt of country running parallel to the creek. Within it the forest floor was mostly exposed, rich, dark earth once thick with secondary growth. The results of over-grazing meant that every time it rained heavily more topsoil would slip down to the creekbed. It was all too typical of a wild sheep stronghold.

Little, if anything, of note has so far been published on the habits of wild sheep in this country and therefore I shall draw on my own observations for the rest of this segment.

In the early 1960s, I was fortunate enough (particularly in light of writing this chapter) to be on a hunting block where there were many wild sheep. This was the 'north-eastern' block in the Ruahine Range. Naturally government hunters shot wild sheep. In parts of Marlborough and Nelson, where they had once numbered in their many thousands, they were designated as top priority in the years following the Second World War. For the financial year ending 31 March 1947, for example, the deer control section of the Department of Internal Affairs accounted for 5,074 feral sheep, the majority of which were reported to have been taken in Marlborough and Nelson. On the north-eastern block in the Ruahines, however, we were never put under any pressure to shoot them. Deer, pigs, and goats all rated much higher in the field officer's eyes than did a feral sheep! And while I did put down a fair number of sheep on that block, most of the time I simply trained my 8x30 fieldglasses on them and watched what they got up to.

The country where they were mostly found had once been part of a sheep run, abandoned, I believe, during the depression years of the 1930s. That accounted for the broken-down fences one frequently saw. Generally speaking, the sheep lived close to the Ngaruroro River. The upper limit of their range was about 150-215 metres. Between this level and the turbulent river the terrain was decidedly steep and very rocky in places. Much of it was covered with a forest of tall manuka scrub and the sheep very often rested in there when they were apparently weary of the sun. Within easy striking distance were big grassy clearings — the growth, intermingled with clover, was lush and vividly green. Few, if any, sheep could resist such fodder in the early spring.

Certainly, the wild sheep I observed were a gregarious bunch, appearing to enjoy the happy atmosphere of an extended family group. They made the most of the warming rays of the sun, particularly after a frosty night. Heavy rain mostly had them making sure-footed steps, even on slimy rocks, to their snug retreats — big caverns, trampled hard by the passage of countless hoofs; bone dry and dusty, the kind of primitive shelter where our ancestors might have hopefully rubbed two sticks together.

One spring morning I watched young rams sparring with each other. These were vigorous but playful encounters when they butted each other with immature horns. We could, I suppose, class these as training sessions for the more serious battles of later life. Also in spring (and as early as mid-August) I had seen ewes with energetic lambs at foot. Only once did I see one with twins. The gestation period of a merino sheep is said to be about 5 months which would be consistent with a successful mating taking place in late summer or early autumn — the time when true wild sheep mate.

While a ewe may conceive when she is much younger — as early as 4-5 months in rare cases — the normal age is 18 months. Thereafter a ewe will give birth each year, normally to one offspring. Similarly, the ram may mate in his first year, but, again, he is a much more potent force from the age of 15 months. By the time he is about seven years of age a ram is past his prime.

Domesticated merino sheep may live until they are 13 years old. In the wild state I doubt very much that such an age could be attained.

8 STALKING WILD GOATS AND SHEEP

Wild Goat

Organised goat hunting took place in this country long before the first deerstalking parties 'legally' ventured into the hills. By the early 1850s, for example, goats freely ranged the lowish hills about Banks Peninsula in Canterbury. The *Lyttelton Times* of 18 September 1952 reported that:

> . . . a Mr Piper — a recently arrived pilgrim — hearing that there was good goat shooting on the neighbouring hills, had gone out for a day's sport and 'bagged' a very fine one valued at £4, and captured another.

In the closing paragraph of an article titled 'Wild Goat Hunting in the Tararua Ranges', A.H. Messenger (1901) wrote:

> Compared to deer stalking, wild-goat hunting may be considered by some very poor sport, but I have heard an accomplished deer stalker speak highly of it, and noticed that he had amongst his collection of heads some fine specimens of wild billy goats which had, he affirmed, afforded him excellent sport.

Soft-skinned, goats are wellnigh perfect game for such light, flat-shooting calibres as the .222, .223, .22/250, and .243. I also found the 7x57 a fine goat calibre.

My own experiences with feral goats provide more than ample material upon which to base this short section. Before coming to this country, I hunted them in several parts of central and northern New South Wales — up in lightly timbered high country where rocky outcrops and escarpments provided ideal habitat, through which a keen 19-year-old manfully shouldered a heavy, military-issue .303 while wedgetailed eagles soared and swooped with the air currents way above the tan-coloured landscape.

Later on, employed by the New Zealand Forest Service as a hunter, I came up against wild goats in quite a few locations.

These are the calibres I used: .303, .222, .243, 7x57, and .270. Fellow cullers, working from Northland to Central Otago and beyond, grassed them with anything from a .22 Magnum through to a .30-06. Interestingly enough, for the financial year 1961-1962, (at which time I was on the Forest Service payroll) government shooters accounted for more than 25,000 goats.

Despite their obvious intelligence (a reason they make such good pets) wild goats, in comparison with deer, are remarkably easy to hunt. They are perfect game for a young hunter to begin with; and an excellent choice for a bowhunter, who, because of the range limitations of his equipment, needs to be very close to his target before releasing an arrow. Exceptions to this do occur, however, and that is normally when goats within a certain area have been relentlessly harrassed over a long period. Only then do the 'gun-shy' remnants, virtually living on their nerves, abandon their strong 'territorial' instincts and, as with thar in the same grim predicament, seek new range.

As the Forest Service has discovered over its 30-odd years of turbulent animal control, and as the Department of Conservation undoubtedly will, the act of eliminating the last goats within a specific stretch of country is an almost impossible task. Indeed, only when wild goats have been confined to an island situation has the government's shooting arm of the day achieved this aim — the previously mentioned Raoul, Kapiti, and Three Kings islands are all examples of islands where feral goats no longer exist.

One thing that works to a hunter's advantage is that goats are rather noisy animals in the forest. Frequently they dislodge stones on steep faces. Often they are vocal — a kid bleeting apprehensively, an unseen mother's reassuring reply, a billy snorting as though something were blocking his nasal passages. Goats forage noisily, too. Billies in particular make a fair sort of commotion when they rear up on their chunky hindlegs and browse on low-hanging foliage. A particularly large goat can easily reach to almost six feet in this manner.

And always remember that where there are nannies, then so too there are billies in close proximity. Adult male goats — rank-smelling fellows that they are — seem to think with their reproductive organs. Certainly they will mount a nanny the

197

instant she is so inclined. Also, a billy goat, like an adult wild ram, is quite capable of mating with many females within a short period of time.

When fired at, goats will normally mill together or simply stand there as the shot rings out unless they are pretty sure where the marksman is. When they do run, it is often at a speed — a fast gait — that a fleet-footed hunter can keep up with providing, of course, that the terrain isn't too steep. Also, goats are apt to pause at regular intervals, to peer back in a terrified manner over a hunched-up shoulder. The nannies in particular show their distress by urinating. All this means that a fit hunter is quite often given more than one opportunity to put down the billy of his choice before it finally vanishes. Forget all about taking out nannies and young stuff unless you are a runholder with a goat problem or you are in the employ of one. Control operations are the responsibility of DOC.

Essential equipment for the serious goat hunter includes a scope for his rifle — a 4x is ideal. The rifle can be sighted-in for 200 metres — few, if any, shots will exceed this range. Naturally, he will use a fast-expanding projectile on such thin-skinned game, that will kill as humanely as possible. And a shot in the vital parts — neck, shoulders, lungs, etc — is essential. A wounded goat is to be avoided at all costs. Very simply, they scream and cry like a human being; a sound to chill one's very soul. The first time I gutshot a big nanny I was so badly upset by her distressed cries that, as I clambered up a rocky scree to where she lay screaming like a pain-tormented baby, I broke out in a cold, clammy sweat and felt sick to my stomach at what I had caused her to suffer.

A compact pair of binoculars — my own Nikon 7x35s are just dandy for this game — are required for ascertaining the 'trophy' potential of a distant billy. On the other hand, a spotting scope, indispensable when hunting the higher-climbing thar and chamois, is not really needed in this instance because trophy goats are generally observed within easy striking distance. What is essential, however, is a strong pair of boots with a thick 'vibram' rubber sole. They allow one to move quietly in the forest and also provide sufficient support in rough terrain.

Stalking wild goats, and, for that matter, wild sheep, often

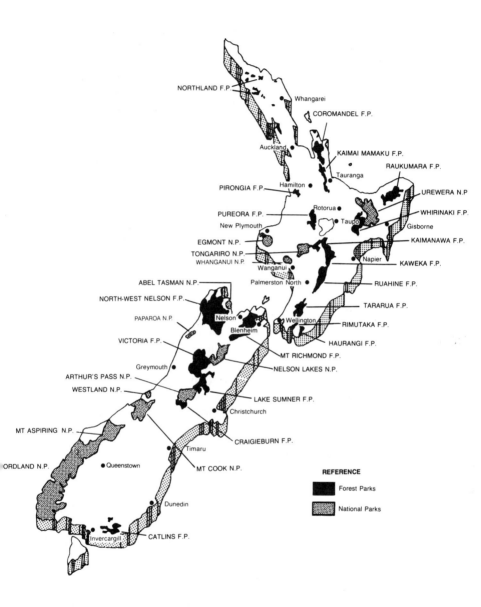

NORTHLAND F.P.

Whangarei

COROMANDEL F.P.

Auckland

KAIMAI MAMAKU F.P.

RAUKUMARA F.P.

Tauranga

PIRONGIA F.P. Hamilton

UREWERA N.P

PUREORA F.P. Rotorua

WHIRINAKI F.P.

New Plymouth Taupo

Gisborne

EGMONT N.P.

KAIMANAWA F.P.

TONGARIRO N.P.

WHANGANUI N.P. Wanganui

Napier

KAWEKA F.P.

ABEL TASMAN N.P. Palmerston North

RUAHINE F.P.

NORTH-WEST NELSON F.P.

TARARUA F.P.

PAPAROA N.P. Nelson

Wellington

RIMUTAKA F.P.

Blenheim

VICTORIA F.P.

HAURANGI F.P.

MT RICHMOND F.P.

Greymouth

NELSON LAKES N.P.

ARTHUR'S PASS N.P.

WESTLAND N.P.

LAKE SUMNER F.P.

Christchurch

MT ASPIRING N.P.

CRAIGIEBURN F.P.

Timaru

ORDLAND N.P. Queenstown

MT COOK N.P.

REFERENCE

Forest Parks

National Parks

Dunedin

Invercargill

CATLINS F.P.

FOREST PARKS AND NATIONAL PARKS

199

takes a hunter into truly wild country. A topographical map should never be overlooked. They may be the NZMS 1 1:63,360 series (1 inch to 1 mile), with which most of us are familiar, or the more recent NZMS 260 1:50,000 metric series. A folding brochure entitled 'Maps of New Zealand' is a handy reference to which maps are required for a certain area.

Because they are so widespread, wild goats are found in many forest parks, namely Northland, Coromandel, Kaimai Mamaku, Pirongia, Raukumara, Kaweka, Ruahine, Tararua, Rimutaka, Haurangi, Mount Richmond, North-west Nelson, and Victoria. Strong concentrations of goats are also found in some national parks, in particular Mount Egmont and Wanganui.

Following a few basic rules when stalking goats will greatly improve your success. Watch the wind. All wild animals have a keen sense of smell and your big-horned variety is no exception. Wear dull clothing that blends in with the general colour of the terrain — 'camo' hats, shirts, jackets and pants are ideal. Certainly it pays to spend more time glassing or simply using the naked eye than it does to move too swiftly through likely country. Keep off the skyline whenever possible. When you have to cross a distinct ridge or high point it makes sense to move in a stooped, non-human-like position.

Always remember that wild game are easier to approach from above than they are from lower ground. A sentinel, for instance, will invariably keep a wary eye on the terrain below — the direction in mountain terrain from which the wind mostly comes — or on the slopes on either side of it. Get high up quickly, then, and glass below. Chances are you will move in on a trophy beast with the breeze in your face.

This attention to detail, of knowing the habits of one's chosen quarry, invariably pays off in no uncertain way and can of course be applied to every species of gamebird and animal included in this book.

Trophies
To gain acceptance into the NZDA National Trophy Listings a set of goat horns needs to attain 100 points on the Douglas Score system of measuring trophies or, alternatively, have a spread of horns more than 30 inches.

OWNER .... *F. LAAS*

KILLED BY ....

LOCALITY & DATE .... *AKATORE FOREST,*
.... *OTAGO , APRIL, 1988 .*

Steel Tape Measurements of	Left	Right	SCORE Shorter measurement dbld.
LENGTH	31¼	31	62½
Girth at Base of horn	8⅛	8⅛	16¼
SPREAD			36
		TOTAL SCORE	114¾

MEASURED BY:

ASSISTANT:

Of nine 'trophy' goat heads entered in the NZDA National Trophy Competitions in 1987, a surprisingly high percentage (seven) exceeded 100 points. It is also interesting to note where they were taken.

Name	DS on Entry	Locality Taken
George Fleming	120 2/8	Pio Pio
Craig Ferguson	118 6/8	Ratahei
Ian J. Hogg	115 5/8	Catlins Coast
Brent Johnson	114 6/8	Tolaga Bay
Murray Cramond	111	Owaka
G. Te Kahika	107 5/8	Waihuna
Russell Noble	105	Pureora

A significant fact relating to the NZDA list of top 10 wild goat heads is that they were all obtained in the North Island.

New Zealand's Top Ten Wild Goat Trophies

Ranking	Douglas Score	Taken by	Owner	Locality	Date shot	Length longest horn	Spread	Girth at base
1	141¾	W. Oliver		Hawke's Bay	—	39½	47¼	8
2	140¼	A. Kitto		Wanganui	—	39¾	49¾	7
3	136⅛	J.A. Grimshaw		Northland	1969	38⅛	47⅞	7¼
4	131	Pick up in bush	L.A. Wilson	Nth Auckland	1915	37¼	43¼	7¼
5	130⅝	K.M. Purdon		Whangarei	1975	39⅞	44⅜	7¾
6	130	A.J. Bower		Nth Taranaki	1958	35⅜	46	7½
7	128⅜	T. Barrett		Tuturi	1971	36⅞	43⅝	7⅛
8	127½	A.J. Bower		Urenui	1985	34⅞	44¾	6¾
9	126	V. Purdon		Matapouri	1979	40⅞	33½	7⅜
10	124¾	A.J. Gregory		Waitakere	1965	38	36¼	7

Wild Sheep

All things being equal a wild sheep is not a difficult customer to grass. The one I shot in the upper Mohaka River — shown in the photographic section — fell instantly after being struck in the shoulder with a 100-grain Norma soft-point bullet fired from a .243 at a range of about 70 metres. This particular ram, however, had moulted rather extensively about the shoulder region that summer and the fast-expanding slug hadn't met the 'woolly' resistance that it undoubtedly would have at other times of the year.

When government hunters Jim Stegmann and Hank Christensen came across a flock of wild merinos high on the tussock tops of the Kaweka Ranges in the early 1960s (sheep were first grazed here about 130 years ago) they were armed with a .222 BSA and a .270 Husqvarna respectively. While Jim, a deadly shot with 'light' calibres, hit the sheep where he was aiming for he discovered, to his immense dismay, that the pacy 50-grain bullet did not have sufficient striking power to penetrate much further than the wool — ie, it blew up more or less on the surface of the skin. On the other hand, Hank, who usually had 130-grain loads up the spout of his rifle, dropped his feral targets on the spot and then did the same thing with those that Jim had wounded. Jim wasn't that rapt, I recall.

I can't really remember just how many wild sheep I eliminated on that same North Island block; it could, I suppose, have numbered about 50 animals. What I am certain of, though, is that I used a BSA 7mm, topped off with a 4x Nikel scope in Parker-Hale mounts. Also I know that I mostly used 150-grain Norma slugs, and that some of the shots taken at long range were with 139-grain Federal rounds (an excellent Canadian load). One damn good thing about that particular 7x57: it had a pleasing habit of putting either bullet weight in pretty much the same spot when you were sighting the piece in — something most .270s will do with 130/150 projectiles.

At any rate, both rounds proved devastating killers of wild sheep, dropping them in almost all instances like half-filled sacks of wheat. That type of sterling performance is very reassuring, you know. Makes a man feel almighty confident of his particular firepower.

While most sheep will drop very quickly when hit solidly with a 'light' calibre — particularly those unaware of the rifleman's presence — today's sheep hunter, stalking primarily with a trophy in mind, would be well-advised to use a suitably heavy cartridge with long-range potential, ie 300-350 metres. As I stressed in *A Guide to Hunting in New Zealand*, the emphasis today is on 'selective' shooting, either for trophies or meat, and the opportunity to take the animal of one's choice might present itself once at long range.

Insofar as bullet weights are concerned, I consider a 139/140-grain load ideal. Such a bullet weight, even when the design of the projectile is fast-expanding, will have sufficient weight and energy to penetrate deep into the animal's vital organs. If I were using a .270, for instance, I would feel a mite happier loading up with 150-, as against 130-grain bullets.

A top class scope — forget the cheap inferior brands — is an integral part of the sheep hunter's rifle. A 4x scope is a good choice, as, for that matter, is a compact variable power — a 2x7 Leupold, say.

Once I would have stressed quite dogmatically, and with good reason in the early sixties, that one must always use a scope of steel construction because of their rugged reliability. Such excellent scopes were, and still are, manufactured by Pecar, Kahles, and, until quite recently, Weaver. Today's alloy-tubed scopes, however, are a far cry from those on sale when I first started hunting professionally for a living.

In fact, I cannot praise them enough. I have used alloy scopes for over 20 years, the first being a Leupold 3x in 1967. I have used other scopes of the same brand in the intervening years without a single problem. Today there is a brand new 4x Leupold scope fitted to the steel mounts of my Sako .243 rifle. Also, my small game rifle — a 1949 Brno ZKW465 .22 Hornet in marvellously original condition — is fitted with a 4x Leupold 'compact' scope. Enough said, I think.

Naturally a sling should be fitted to the sheep hunter's rifle, so that, in tough country, he is able to use both hands when climbing or, perhaps, descending a particularly nasty cliff face.

Because of the nature of the country sheep inhabit — seldom less than rough and much like that inhabited by goats — close attention must be paid to one's footwear. Forget all about sandshoes, which offer the vulnerable ankle no support whatsoever, and ankle-high rubber boots, a downright liability

(DOUGLAS SCORE)

OWNER .... *P. N. COMMINS*

KILLED BY ....

LOCALITY & DATE ...*WAIMAKARIRI RIVER, CANTERBURY, FEB, 1988*

Steel Tape Measurements of	Left	Right	SCORE Shorter measurement dbld.
LENGTH	30⁶	31⁶	61⁴
Girth at Base of horn	8³	8²	16⁴
SPREAD			
	TOTAL SCORE		78

MEASURED BY:

ASSISTANT:

on slimy rocks. Settle instead for a type of boot with solid leather uppers and a thick, deeply cleated rubber 'vibram' sole.

Today, there is a wonderful range of this sort of boot available. Some of the models imported from the United States and Europe — Austria and Italy, in particular — are perfect for general hunting conditions in New Zealand. They are also more comfortable than the locally made product, which tend to be rather stiff and inflexible in comparison. Sure the imports are expensive, but what isn't if it's any good? Take a tip from me and go check them out at any of the shops specialising in tramping, climbing and skiing gear.

The basic rules that apply to stalking goats also apply to stalking sheep. See pages 196 to 200.

Trophies

To gain acceptance into the NZDA National Trophy Listings a wild sheep head requires a score of 70 points.

At the 1987 NZDA National Trophy Competitions four wild sheep heads exceeded 70 points:

Name	DS on Entry	Locality Taken
John Sanders	77 4/8	Takanui Mts
Vern Pearson	76	Tarawera
Grant Taylor	71 7/8	Herbert Forest
Frans Laas	71	Wainakarua

By glancing through the top 10 list of wild sheep taken in this country, one can see that virtually every area where they are found has produced a top 10 head.

New Zealand's Top Ten Wild Sheep Trophies

Ranking	Douglas Score	Taken by	Owner	Locality	Date shot	Length left horn	Length right horn	Base left horn	right right horn
1	106½	M. Rapson		Kakanui Mts	1978	43¾	44	9½	9½
2	93½	K. Heneghan		Ngamatea	1983	37¾	37¾	9	9
3	88¼	C.R. Nicholson		Mohaka River	1980	34¾	34¾	9⅜	9½
4	87¼	R. Beman		Dunback	1983	33½	34¾	10⅛	10¼
5	86½	S. Perfect		Tarawera	1980	36⅜	36⅜	6⅞	7⅛
6	86¼	K. Henaghan		Ngamatea	1983	34¾	35⅜	8½	8⅜
7	85¾	O.P. Reed		Chatham Is.	1982	33⅞	35⅛	9	9⅛
8	84¾	A.K. Severinen		Nth Ruahine	1984	34¾	37⅞	7¾	7⅝
9	84	C. Drysdale		Hokonui	1969	33	33	9¼	9
10	83	J. Rudd		Marlborough	1975	34¾	34	7½	7¾

Postscript

The NZDA National Big Game Trophy Records Committee would like to hear from anyone who has accounted for an 'unrecorded' wild goat or wild sheep trophy scoring high enough to be included in their trophy records. Address an envelope to either the Wild Goat or Wild Sheep Convener, C/- NZDA, PO Box 6514, Wellington.

A high-scoring big-horned sheep or goat is a prize to treasure. We can say the same thing about a resplendent cock pheasant. Any of the taxidermists listed in Appendix 6 will be more than pleased to inform you how best to prepare your trophy in the field. Charges for mounting trophies are available upon request.

APPENDICES

Appendix 1: Acclimatisation Society Directory

The information in Appendix 1 is correct at time of going to press. To check for changes to the Acclimatisation Society directory, contact the National Executive in Wellington.

Ashburton
84 Belt Road
Ashburton
PO Box 113
Telephone: (053) 87 490

Auckland
7th Floor, Westpac Building
Hamilton
PO Box 1432
Telephone: (071) 491 666

Bay of Islands
PO Box 484
Kerikeri
Telephone: (0887) 79 164

Hawera
PO Box 92
Hawera
Telephone: (062) 85 088

Hawke's Bay
C/- Gardiner, Reaney & Swinburn
Maritime Building
Browning St
Napier
PO Box 259
Telephone: (070) 343 385

Hobson
Victoria Street
Dargaville
PO Box 404
Telephone: (0884) 8374

Mangonui-Whangaroa
2 Redan Road
Kaitaia
PO Box 390
Telephone: (010) 200

Marlborough
75 Seymour Street
Blenheim
PO Box 603
Telephone: (057) 84 762

National Executive
10 Ganges Road
Khandallah
Wellington 4
PO Box 22 021, Johnsonville
Telephone: (04) 797 325

Nelson
1st Floor
Clifford House
38 Halifax Street
Nelson
PO Box 190
Telephone: (054) 84 894/ 81 873

North Canterbury
61 Bealey Avenue
Christchurch 1
Telephone: (03) 669 191

Otago
35 Hope Street
Dunedin
PO Box 76
Telephone: (024) 779 076

South Canterbury
PO Box 150
Temuka
Telephone: (056) 57 584

Southland
14 Kelvin Street
Invercargill
PO Box 159
Telephone: (021) 44 501

Stratford
PO Box 78
Stratford
Telephone: (0663) 7254

Taranaki
PO Box 662
New Plymouth
Telephone: (067) 510 790

Tauranga
PO Box 20
Te Puke
Telephone: (075) 738 366

Waitaki Valley
6 Coquet Street
Oamaru
PO Box 167
Telephone: (0297)
47 991/ 47 992

Wanganui
PO Box 7112
Wanganui
Telephone: (064) 55 480

Wellington
10 Ganges Road
Khandallah
Wellington 4
PO Box 22011, Johnsonville
Telephone: (04) 792 538

West Coast
Werita Street
Greymouth
PO Box 105
Telephone: (027) 5403

Westland
PO Box 179
Hokitika
Telephone: (0288) 58 546

Whangarei
49 James Street
Whangarei
PO Box 3
Telephone: (089) 483 109

Appendix 2: Gundog and Specialist Breed Clubs

NORTH ISLAND

The Gundog Society
Mrs M. Schofield
PO Box 37121
Stokes Valley
(04) 636 574

Whangarei Gundog Club
Mr M. L. Allen
215 Fairway Drive North
Kamo
Northland

North Auckland Gundog Club
Mr S. Lake
71 Metcalfe Road
Ranui
Auckland
(09) 833 7237

Golden Retriever Club
Mrs H. Spencer
19 Tonkin Drive
Forrest Hill
Auckland 9
(09) 410 4531

**The Auckland & Regions
German Shorthaired Pointer
Club**
D. Griffin
PO Box 21323
Henderson
Auckland 8
(09) 836 0489

The Labrador Club
Mrs P. Drake
64 Quadrant Road
Onehunga
Auckland 6
(09) 665 526

Waitemata Gundog Club
Mrs M. Dickey
89 Angelo Avenue
Howick
Auckland
(09) 534 9619

South Auckland Gundog Club
Mr A. Levien
Taraire Drive
RD 1
Drury
South Auckland
(09) 294 8171

Waikato Gundog Club
Mr B. W. Newport
Driver Road
RD 1
Taupiri
(071) 246 745 or (081746) 745

Irish Setter Club
Mrs D. Paterson
215 Te Rapa Road
Hamilton
(071) 494 994

Pahiatua Gundog Club
F. E. Petersen
PO Box 120
Pahiatua

Rotorua Gundog Club
Mr U. M. Forrester
PO Box 806
Rotorua
(07339) 774

The Pointer and Setter Club
Mrs J. Broughton-Mortensen
Wingfield Farm
Old Taupo Road
RD 1
Tokoroa
(0814) 68 688

Wairoa Gundog Club
Mrs M. O'Connor
12 Osler Street
Wairoa
(0724) 6186

East Coast Gundog Show Society
Mrs M. E. Fulton
513 Frederick Street
Hastings
(070) 66 225

Hawke's Bay Gundog Club
Mrs D. O'Connor
217 St Leonards Avenue
Hastings
(070) 68 462

Central Hawke's Bay Gundog Club
Mrs D. Mehrtens
19 Tavistock Road
Waipukurau
(0728) 88 848

Taranaki Gundog Club
Mrs K. Pepperell
50 Cummings Street
Okato
Taranaki
(067) 24 030

Wanganui & District Gundog Society
Miss N. D. Minnell
41 Durie Street
Durie Hill
Wanganui
(064) 54 691

Horowhenua Gundog Club
Mrs K. Malmo
Kingston Road
RD 4
Palmerston North
(069) 27 361

Manawatu Gundog Club
S. Nicholsen
112 Salisbury Street
Ashhurst
(0632) 68 365

Upper Hutt Gundog Club
N. J. Alexander
12 Walker Grove
Stokes Valley
(04) 63 825

The Continental Gundog Club
Mrs R. L. Radich
5 Carroll Street
Ngaio
Wellington 4
(04) 795 836

Central Golden Retriever Club
Mrs S. Stevens
50 Laings Road
Lower Hutt
(04) 666 357

Wellington & District Labrador Retriever Club
Mrs R. Woodhouse
20 Latitude Close
Whitby
Wellington
(04) 359 588

SOUTH ISLAND

Seddon Districts Gundog Society
Mr B. Shepard
Ranzau Road East
Hope
Nelson
(054) 48 107

Marlborough Gundog Club
Mrs B. L. Phillips
7 Rushleigh Crescent
Renwick
Blenheim
(057) 28 477

Canterbury & Regions German Shorthaired Pointer Club
Mr I. Thomson
128 Idris Road
Christchurch
(03) 518 470

The Weimaraner Club
Mrs B. Rusbridge
PO Box 21198
Christchurch
(03) 427 599

Southern Irish Setter Club
Miss T. Roberts
PO Box 8249
Riccarton
Christchurch
(03) 897 406

English Setter Club
Mr C. Graham
64 Francis Avenue
Christchurch 1
(03) 857 001

Canterbury Cocker Spaniel Club
Mrs S. M. Byrne
14 Fitzroy Place
Christchurch 5
(03) 599 214

Southern Gundog Society
Miss J. Hamilton
76 Marshland Road
Christchurch 6
(03) 857 981

Southern Golden Retriever Club (Inc.)
Mrs S. Scales
9 Walnut Avenue
Christchurch
(03) 523 229

Canterbury Labrador Retriever Club
Mrs R. Mattson
16 Bracebridge Street
Kaiapoi
(0327) 7776

Canterbury Gundog Club
Mrs M. C. Dobson
Moorfield
Hoskyns Road
RD 5
Christchurch
(03) 478 408

South Canterbury Gundog Club
M. Race
11 Bridge Street
Timaru
(056) 81 039

Waimate Gundog Club
Mrs J. Robertson
65 Belt Street
Waimate
(0519) 8186

North Otago Gundog Club
M. E. Beattie
6 Wye Street
Oamaru
(0297) 68 406

Otago Gundog Club
C. R. Medlin
22 Stephen Street
Dunedin
(024) 67 497

Otago-Southland German Shorthaired Pointer Club
Mr F. Stent
59 Kirkaldy Street
Dunedin

Otago-Southland Gundog Society
Mrs G. Shields
6 Brunel Street
Dunedin
(024) 30 889

South Otago Gundog Club
Mrs A. Alexander
29 Wakefield Street
Balclutha
(0299) 80 875

Southland Gundog Club
Mr W. A. Hannah
179 Lamond Street
Invercargill
(021) 76 525

Western Southland Gundog Club
Mrs V. Dockerty
8 Dryfe Street
Nightcaps
Southland

Westland Gundog Club
N. F. Andrews
81 Fitzgerald Street
Cobden
Greymouth
(027) 4543

Appendix 3: Associated All-Breed Obedience Societies

NORTH ISLAND

Whangarei Dog Obedience Association
Mrs F. Norgate
PO Box 269
Whangarei
(089) 489 878

All-Breeds Dog Training Club
L. Hancox
PO Box 12682
Penrose
Auckland

Auckland Central Dog Training Club
Miss D. M. Sheehan
5/50 Gray Avenue
Mangere East
Auckland
(09) 276 8313

East Auckland Dog Obedience Club
N. Girling
PO Box 86
Clevedon
South Auckland
(09) 292 8743

North Shore Dog Training Club
Mrs S. Fleming
11 Andelko Place
Henderson
Auckland 8
(09) 836 0580

Dog Agility Training Association
Mr I. Gray
14 Sylvan Avenue
Northcote
Auckland
(09) 418 1789

Hibiscus Coast Obedience Dog Training Club
The Secretary
PO Box 133
Whangaparaoa
(084620) 883

Akarana Dog Obedience Association
Mrs L. Dormer
PO Box 57081
Owairaka
Auckland 3
(09) 863 333

Manukau Dog Obedience Club
Ms L. Blackmore
PO Box 407
Papakura
Auckland
(09) 299 9750

Tuakau Districts Dog Training Club
Mrs A. H. Robinson
C/- Pacific Chicks
Paparata Road
Bombay
South Auckland
(085) 20 714

Thames Valley Dog Obedience Club
Mrs B. Verram
14 Kennedy Street
Paeroa
(0816) 7737

Cambridge Dog Obedience Club
Mrs M. G. Anderson
Tarr Road
RD 1
Ohaupo
(071) 296 864

Hamilton Dog Obedience Club
Mrs E. A. Scott
PO Box 10440
Hamilton
(071) 247 012

Waikato Canine Obedience Club
Mrs M. Fraser
26 Mears Road
Hamilton
(071) 493 067

Tokoroa Canine Obedience Association
Mrs J. L. Edgar
PO Box 621
Tokoroa
(0814) 67 016

Rotorua Dog Obedience Club
Mrs L. Windelborn
PO Box 2009
Rotorua
(073) 479 361

Kawerau Dog Obedience Club
The Secretary
Mrs K. Ngatai
PO Box 66
Kawerau
(076) 37 594

Taupo Canine Obedience Club
Mrs G. Oliver
PO Box 624
Taupo
(074) 89 165

Gisborne Dog Training Club
Mr T. Hollis
Waihora Road
Te Karaka
Gisborne
(079) 23 735

Tauranga Canine Obedience Club
Lynn Quinn
PO Box 9038
Greerton
Tauranga
(075) 441 654

Mount Maunganui Dog Training Club
L. Hibberd
PO Box 4119
Mt Maunganui
(075) 57 450

Napier Dog Training Club
Mr N. E. Wood
158 Marine Parade
Napier
(070) 358 077

Hawke's Bay Canine Obedience Club
Mrs J. Young
6 Spencer Street
Greenmeadows
Napier
(070) 446 113

Havelock North Dog Training Club
Miss A. Capper
16 Glen Park Place
Havelock North
(070) 778 543

North Taranaki Canine Obedience Club
Mrs A. Cowlard
15 Cowling Road
New Plymouth
(067) 35 193

Hawera Dog Obedience Association
Mrs C. Kirk
C/- 3 Cameron Street
Hawera
(062) 85 612

Wanganui Dog Obedience Club
Mrs B. Dickson
37 Rimu Street
Wanganui
(064) 44 529

Feilding Dog Training Club
Miss L. Chilcott
PO Box 26
Bunnythorpe
(063) 39 020 or (063) 292 620

Zone 3 Trials Training Club
J. A. Garwood
57 Norbiton Road
Foxton
(069) 38 405

Zone 3 Dog Agility Club
Mrs C. Parker
Shannon Road
Foxton
(069) 38 533

Tararua All-Breeds Dog Training Club
Mrs J. M. Wilson
PO Box 571
Palmerston North
(063) 294 860

Horowhenua Obedience Dog Training Club
Mrs C. Parker
PO Box 163
Levin

Kapiti Dog Obedience Club (Inc.)
Mr P. Heald
PO Box 96
Paraparaumu
(058) 86 497

Titahi Bay Canine Obedience Club
Mrs M. A. Atkins
PO Box 50595
Porirua
(04) 324 687 (a/h) or
(04) 735 766 (w)

Wellington Canine Obedience Club
Mrs C. Bridge
PO Box 14032
Kilbirnie
Wellington
(04) 325 855 (a/h) or
(04) 872 147 (w)

Central All-Breeds Dog Training School
J. Morrow
14 Earls Terrace
Mount Victoria
Wellington
(04) 842 489

Upper Hutt Dog Training School
Mrs V. Williams
42 Whitechapel Grove
Stokes Valley
Lower Hutt
(04) 635 203

Avalon Canine Obedience Club
Mrs D. Livingstone
PO Box 31224
Lower Hutt
(04) 664 708

Wainuiomata All-Breed Canine Obedience Club
Mr M. Johansen
PO Box 42141
Homedale
Wainuiomata
(04) 646 568

SOUTH ISLAND

Nelson Canine Obedience Club
Mrs N. E. Bond
PO Box 1024
Belgrove
Nelson
(054) 28 568

Blenheim Canine Obedience Club
Mrs S. F. Kenny
PO Box 259
Blenheim
(057) 82 282

Canterbury Canine Obedience Club
Mrs G. C. Bouterey
PO Box 9085
Addington
Christchurch
(03) 382 261

Canterbury Canine Agility Training Society
Mrs B. Rusbridge
PO Box 21198
Christchurch
(03) 427 599

Christchurch Dog Training Club
Mr R. Sheppard
PO Box 27017
Christchurch
(03) 842 432

Mid-Canterbury Canine Obedience Club
Mrs J. McMullan
RD 5
Ashburton
(053) 26 809

South Canterbury Canine Obedience Club
Mrs T. J. Kennedy
Seadown Road
RD 3
Timaru
(056) 82 752

Obedience Trials Association
Mrs M. Godfrey
PO Box 5
Pareora Via Timaru
(05626) 636

North Otago Dog Training Club
Miss D. J. Thwaites
4 Arrow Crescent
Oamaru
(0297) 46 366

Otago Canine Training Club
Ms J. Oliver
PO Box 5373
Moray Place
Dunedin
(024) 761 479

Taieri Canine Training Club
G. Oudemans
102 Argyle Street
Mosgiel
Dunedin
(02489) 7983

South Otago Dog Training Club
C/- Mrs J. Mathewson
26 Essex Street
Balclutha

Southland Dog Obedience Club
Mrs T. Little
PO Box 210
Invercargill
(021) 64 100

Appendix 4: Gun Clubs affiliated to the New Zealand Clay Target Association Inc.

New Zealand Clay Target Assn Inc.
PO Box 603
Napier
Telephone: (070) 58 909
National Secretary: Sid Hanson

Alexandra Gun Club
Miss J. Stewart
PO Box 293
Alexandra

Amberley Gun Club
Mrs G.C. McCombe
67A Rockinghorse Road
Christchurch

Ashburton Gun Club
Mrs J.P. Rogers
119 Racecourse Road
Ashburton

Auckland Met Gun Club
Mrs L. Craig
PO Box 23-017
Papatoetoe
Auckland

Awatere Gun Club
Mrs A.M. Leslie
Rowley Crescent
Grovetown
Blenheim

Balfour Gun Club
Mr F.J. McGarvie
Wendon RD 7
Gore

Banks Peninsula Gun Club
Mr L. Graham
PO Box 10
Duvauchelle

Belfast Gun Club
Mrs S. Isitt
PO Box 63
Belfast
Christchurch

Cambridge Gun Club
Mr J. Blyth
No. 4 RD
Hamilton

Central Southland Gun Club
Mrs S.A. Miller
158 Findlay Road
Invercargill

Chatham Islands Gun Club
Mr T. Brown
PO Box 77
Chatham Islands

Christchurch Gun Club
Mrs A. Sears
107 St James Avenue
Christchurch

Dannevirke Gun Club
Mr G.E. Cheer
PO Box 26
Norsewood

Darfield Gun Club
Mrs D.J. Woodward
Hartlea
Wards Road
Darfield RD

Dunedin Gun Club
Mr N.S. Tutty
PO Box 172
Mosgiel

Eketahuna Gun Club
Mrs G.E. Hansen
No. 3 RD
Eketahuna

Ellesmere Gun Club
Mrs I.H. Winchester
Lakeside No. 3 RD
Leeston

Fairlie/McKenzie Gun Club
Mrs R.F. Wills
Cricklewood RD 17
Fairlie

Geraldine Gun Club
Mrs G. Leary
Orari Station No. 22 RD
Geraldine

Gisborne Gun Club
Mr I. Watson
PO Box 4
Gisborne

Golden Bay Gun Club
Mr R.L. Tunstall
140 Commercial Street
Takaka

Greymouth Gun Club
C/- V. Markland
418 Main South Road
Greymouth

Haast Gun Club
Miss N. Craig
PO Box 25
Haast

Hamilton Workingmen's Gun Club
Mr M. Moon
21 Rhonda Avenue
Hamilton

Hari Hari Gun Club
Mr H. Wilson
164 Brittan Street
Hokitika

Hawke's Bay Central Gun Club
Mrs C. Rowland
76 Riverbend Road
Napier

Huntly Gun Club
Mrs E. Beddis
PO Box 164
Huntly

Hutt Valley Gun Club
Mr W. Pym
16 Moffit Street
Vogeltown
Wellington

Kaeo Gun Club
Mrs L. Dangen
PO Box 117
Kaeo

Kaikohe Gun Club
Mr P.J. Washbourne
Monument Road
Kaikohe

Kaitaia Gun Club
Mrs J Edlin
State Highway 1, RD 2
Kaitaia

Kawerau Gun Club
Mrs J. Craill
85 Fenton Mill Road
Kawerau

Kokatahi Gun Club
Mr M. Havill
Ford Road, Kowhitirangi
Hokitika

Kopuku Gun Club
K.W. Fielder
Wairere Road
Manurewa RD

Levin Gun Club
Mr A. Webby
11 Maire Street
Otaki

Maniototo Gun Club
Mrs R. McPike
21 Dungannan Street
Ranfurly

Matamata Gun Club
Mr H. Rhodes
PO Box 323
Matamata

Mataura Gun Club
Mr R.W. Dickie
15 Burns Street
Mataura

Mead Te-Pirita Gun Club
Mr C. Crossen
68 Elizabeth Street
Rakaia

Methven Gun Club
Mr P. Boal
Windwhistle School RD 2
Darfield

Moa Creek Gun Club
Mrs N. Nevill
Moa Creek RD
Oturehua
Central Otago

Nelson/Waimea Gun Club
Mr D. Hill
PO Box 409
Nelson

New Plymouth Gun Club
Mr D. Gilliland
16 Leon Place
Waitara

Nightcaps Gun Club
Mr R. Brash
Scotts Gap RD 10
Invercargill

Nilo Gun Club
Mrs M. Hynds
PO Box 190
Tauranga

North Canterbury Gun Club
Mr G. Leaper
PO Box 268
Rangiora

Northern Wairoa Gun Club
Mr S. McCully
PO Box 114
Dargaville

Oamaru Gun Club
A.C. Kingan
15 D RD
Oamaru

Ohingaiti Gun Club
Ms M. Chaney
144 Ikitara Road
Wanganui 5001

Opotiki Gun Club
Mr A. Swanson
Paerata Ridge RD 2
Opotiki

Palmerston North Gun Club
Mrs D. Stern
3 Elliott Street
Palmerston North

**Palmerston/Waikouaiti Gun
Club**
Mr M. Stewart
49 Ronaldsay Street
Palmerston

Patangata Gun Club
Mr A. Fargher
32 Bibby Street
Waipawa

Pihama-Oeo Gun Club
Mr T. Bewick
8 Rimu Street
Hawera

Porirua Gun Club
Mr J. Varley
66 Old Porirua Road
Ngaio
Wellington

Puketiro Gun Club
Mr A.F. Berney
Settlement Hill
PO Box 51 Owaka
South Otago

Putaruru Gun Club
Mrs P. Coatham
PO Box 173
Putaruru

Rangitikei Gun Club
Mr J. Tavener
No. 1 RD
Bulls

Rifle Rod & Gun Club
Mrs J. Wasley
PO Box 24
Feilding

Rodney Gun Club
Mr J.R. Noakes
19 Snells Beach Road
Warkworth

Rotorua Gun Club
Miss A. MacPherson
PO Box 2138
Rotorua

Roxburgh Gun Club
Mr D. Burton
6 Leitholm Place
Roxburgh

Southland Gun Club
Mr R. McIlwain
PO Box 601
Invercargill

**South Canterbury Simulated
Field Club**
Mrs D. Weastall
Mt Nessing RX
Albury
South Canterbury

South Otago Gun Club
Mr M.D. Farquhar
210 Clyde Street
Balclutha

South Taieri Gun Club
Mrs R. McDiarmid
137A Martin Road
Fairfield
Dunedin

Stewart Island Gun CLub
Mrs J.K. Langdon
PO Box 144
Half Moon Bay
Stewart Island

Taumarunui Gun Club
Mr G. Brears
PO Box 14
Taumarunui

Taupo Gun Club
Mrs F. Clark
PO Box 1091
Taupo

Te Anau Gun Club
Mrs J. McHardy
38 Mokonui Street
Te Anau

Te Aroha Gun Club
Mr W.J. Farmer
PO Box 151
Te Aroha

Te Kuiti Trapshooters Club
Mr D.P. Cole
PO Box 165
Te Kuiti

Thames Gun Club
Mr C. Judd
318 Hill Street
Thames

Thunderbird Gun Club
Mr J. Worth
Ryburn Road RD 4
Ruakura
Hamilton

Timaru Gun Club
Mr M.T. Munro
40 Hopkins Street
Timaru

Tokoroa Gun Club
Mr L.K. Murphy
Maraetai Road RD 1
Tokoroa

Tongariro Gun Club
Mrs N. Flight
41 Hirangi Road
Turangi

Tuatapere Gun Club
Mr J.W. Munro
Groveburn Road
Tuatapere

Waihi Gun Club
Mr D.S. Wharry
No. 1 RD
Waihi

Waihora Gun Club
Mrs D.E. Johnston
Weedons Road RD 4
Christchurch

Waikato Gun Club
Mr H. Oliver
Marychurch Road RD 4
Hamilton

Waimate Gun Club
Mrs J. Forsyth
1 Belt Street
Waimate

Wairarapa Gun Club
Mrs J. Behl
RD 2
Featherston

Wairau Firth CTC
Mrs B. Marshall
Aberhart Road
Grovetown
Blenheim

Wairoa Rod & Gun Club
Mr K.J. Worsley
PO Box 2078
North Clyde
Wairoa

Waitemata Gun Club
Mr J. Kelly
PO Box 275
Kumeu

Wakatipu Gun Club
Mrs A. Shaw
'Barnhill' No. 1 RD
Queenstown

Wanaka Gun Club
Mr W.J. Gillespie
18 Wiley Road
Wanaka

Wanganui Gun Club
Mr D. McGovern
PO Box 4218
Wanganui

West Otago Gun Club
Mrs P.J. Morrison
Knapdale No. 3 RD
Gore

Western Lake Gun Club
Mrs V.M. Parker
Western Lake RD 3
Featherston

Western Southland Gun Club
Mr D.G. Brown
Papatotara
Tuatapere RD

Whakatane Gun Club
Mr R. Drayson
30 Henderson Street
Whakatane

Whangamata Gun Club
The Secretary
202 Graham Street
Whangamata

Whangarei Gun Club
Mrs A.L. Hollister
No. 1 RD
Hikurangi
Northland

Whatitiri Gun Club
Mrs G. Bourke
Otangarei Fish Supply
William Jones Drive
Whangarei

Whitianga Gun Club
Mrs L. France
Hot Water Beach Road RD 1
Whitianga

Woodbourne Clay Target Club
Mr R. Carmody
71 Inkerman Street
Renwick
Marlborough

Woodville Gun Club
Mrs J. Mabey
PO Box 25
Woodville

Appendix 5: Gun Club Information

Alexandra
Main Road North
4 Trap, 1 Skeet
Circuit programme
Contact Alan Craig
Tel: 8679

Amberley
Innes Road
2 Trap, 1 Skeet
Circuit programme
Contact M. Hartnell
Tel: 8040

Ashburton
Alford Forest Road
2½ km from main town
3 Trap (DTL), 2 Skeet
1st Sunday
Contact Mrs J.P. Rogers
Tel: 4773

Auckland Metropolitan
Cnr Helvetia & Gun Club Roads
Tel: (085) 86 408
1km to Pukekohe
1 Ball Trap, 4 DTL Traps
3 Skeet Fields
1st & 3rd Sundays
Contact Ray Moorhead
Tel: 278 0939

Balfour
Balfour-Glenure Road
4 Trap, 2 Skeet
Circuit programme
Contact Fraser McGarvie
Tel: Lumsden, 2R

Belfast
Main Road West
Tel: 429 544
10 DTL, 6 Skeet
2 Ball Trap, 1 Trench
Circuit programme
Contact Trevor Isitt
Tel: 8956

Cambridge
Ringers Road, Tauwhare
Cambridge 12km
Hamilton 18km
2 DTL
3rd Sunday (except May)
Contact John Blyth (071 295) 840
or Rex Calder (071) 65 337

Chatham Islands
Te One Road
6km from Waitangi
1 DTL, 1 Skeet, 1 Ball Trap
2nd Sunday
Contact T. Tuahui
Tel: 93

Dannevirke
Laws Road
2 DTL, 1 Skeet
2nd Sunday
Contact John Farrell
Tel: 7837

Eketahuna
Cullen Street, Eketahuna
1km from Eketahuna
2 DTL, Simulated Field
2nd Sunday
Contact G. Hansen
Tel: 4083

Ellesmere
Beethams Road, Leeston
60km from Christchurch
1 Skeet, 3 DTL
Circuit programme
Contact Mrs I.H. Winchester
Lakeside RD No. 3, Leeston
Tel: 242-659

Fairlie/MacKenzie
Connors Road, Cricklewood
1 Skeet, 2 DTL
1st Sunday
Contact D. Wills
Tel: ABY 730

Geraldine
Tipladys Road
2 DTL, 1 Skeet
4th Sunday
Contact Peter Jones
Tel: 913

Gisborne
Willows Road, Matawhero
3km from Gisborne
Tel: 74 126
2 Skeet, 2 DTL, 1 Ball Trap
2nd Sunday
Contact Nina Stahel
Tel: 23 696

Golden Bay
PuPu Valley Road, Takaka
1 DTL
4th Sunday
Contact Mark Page
Tel: (0524) 59 980

Greymouth
Taylorville Road, Coal Creek
1 DTL
2nd Sunday
Contact V. Markland
418 Main South Road

Haast
Turnbull River Road
10km to Haast Beach
DTL & manually operated trap
Last Sunday
Contact Ian Rendall
Tel: 825

Hamilton Workingmen's
Cambridge Grounds
Ringers Road
10km from Hamilton
2 DTL
1st Sunday
Contact Morty Moon
Tel: 437 509

Hari Hari
Lower Poerua Valley Road
5km from Hari Hari
2 DTL, 1 Skeet
1st Sunday at 10.30 a.m.
Contact Lindsay Bell
Tel: 33 190

Hawke's Bay Central
Maraekakaho Road, Hastings
3 DTL, 2 DTL/Ball, 4 Skeet
3rd Sunday
Contact Mrs Carol Abbott
Tel: 798 845

Huntly
McVie Road
5km from North Huntly
Tel: 87 536
2 Skeet, 3 DTL
4th Sunday
Contact E. Beddis
Tel: 87-755

Hutt Valley
Swamp Road, Whitemans Valley
2 DTL, 1 DTL/Ball, 2 Skeet
3rd Sunday
Contact Wayne Pym
Tel: 897 076 Well.

Kaeo
Matauri Bay Road
8km from Kaeo
2 DTL, 1 Ball Trap, 1 Skeet
ISU Skeet
Last Sunday
Contact John Richardson
Tel: (0327) 231 or
Linday Dangen, Tel: (0887 75)
854

Kaikohe
Reservoir Road
2 DTL, 1 Skeet
2nd Sunday
Contact Frank Jones
Tel: 149 or 310

Kaitaia
Okahu Road
4km from Kaitaia
1 DTL, 1 Skeet
1st Sunday
Contact Mrs J. Edlin
Tel: 1523

Kokatahi
Signposted from Kokatahi Store
1.6km from Hokitika
1 Skeet, 2 DTL
3rd Sunday
Contact Mike Havill
Ford Road, Kowhitirangi
Tel: 835 or 525

Kopuku
Kopuku Landing, Maramarua
2 DTL
2nd Sunday
Contact John Blake
Tel: 806

Levin
Lindsay Road, Levin
2 Sporting, 2 DTL
2nd Sunday at 10.00 a.m.
Contact A.R.D. Webby
11 Maire Street, Otaki
Tel: 48 021

Maniototo
Ranfurly
2 DTL
Contact K.G. Kearney
Tel: (0294) 434

Matamata
Mangawhero Road
5km from Matamata
3 DTL, 1 set Skeet towers
4th Sunday; Skeet 5th Sunday
Contact Eyvonne Aspin
Tel: (0818) 606

Mataura
Waimumu Road, Mataura
1 Skeet, 3 DTL, 1 Ball Trap
Southland programme
Contact R.W. Dickie
Tel: 8592

Mead Te-Pirita
Burns Road
off North Rakaia Road
Rakaia
1 Skeet, 1 Ball Trap, 3 DTL
Canterbury programme
Contact C. Crossen
Tel: (053) 27 343

Methven
Trotting Club Grounds, Methven
2 DTL, 2 Skeet
Contact Peter Boal
Tel: (0516 66) 828

Moa Creek
Behind old Moa Creek Hotel
44km from Alexandra
1 Skeet, 4 DTL
Shoot nine days annually
Contact Donald Matheson
Tel: 421

Nelson/Waimea
Upper Motueka Valley Road
Golden Downs Forest
50km from Nelson
3 DTL, 2 Skeet
2nd Sunday
Contact Paul Black
Tel: 81 516
or Dave Hill Tel: 75 587

New Plymouth
Beach Road, Omata
10km to PO at New Plymouth
1 Skeet, 2 DTL
2nd Saturday (practice)
4th Sunday (club day)
Contact R. Dollimore
Tel: 47 980 Waitara

Nightcaps
Wreys Bush
3 DTL, 2 Skeet
Circuit programme
Contact Robin Brash
Tel: (0225) 5213

Nilo
Tara Road off Papamoa
Domain Road
15km from Te Puke
3 DTL, 1 Skeet
1st Sunday
Contact Allan Ebbett
Tel: 88 413 B or 66 577

Northern Wairoa
Finlayson Park, State Highway 14
1km from Dargaville
2 DTL, 1 Ball Trap, 1 Skeet Field
3rd Sunday
Contact Mr S. McCully
Tel: (0884) 7429

Oamaru
Works Road, Pukeuri
6km north of Oamaru
2 DTL, 1 Skeet
Last Sunday
Contact David Hay
Tel: 48 374

Ohingaiti
1km north Ohingaiti
2 Trap, 1 Skeet
2nd Sunday
Contact Chris Renshaw
Tel: 28 042 Hunterville
Marion Chaney, Tel: (064) 38 027
Gordon MacPhee
Tel: (0652) 28 130

Opotiki
Main Whakatane Road
2 DTL, 2 Skeet
3rd Sunday
Contact Barbara Swanson
Tel: 1017R

Palmerston North
Longburn-Rongotea Road
Tel: (063290) 893
Approx. 10km from
Palmerston North
1 Skeet, 2 DTL
3rd Sunday
Contact J. Wilkinson
Tel: 71 467 or Mrs D.M. Stern
Tel: 87 939

Palmerston/Waikouaiti
Edinbourgh Street, Waikouaiti
2km from PO at Waikouaiti
2 DTL
Saturdays monthly
Contact C. Stewart
Tel: (024) 851 241

Patangata
Patangata
12km from Waipawa
1 Trap, 1 Sporting Field
1st Sunday
Contact A.A. Fargher
Tel: 78 839

Picton
Picton Airstrip, Waikawa Road
1 DTL
3rd Sunday
Contact Betty Marshall
Tel: (057) 89-436

Pihama/Oeo
Oeo Road
25km from Hawera
2 DTL, 1 Skeet
2nd Sunday
Contact Tony Bewick
Tel: 85 149

Porirua
Sievers Grove, Porirua
1 DTL
1st Sunday
Contact A.R.D. Webby
Tel: (069) 48 021

Puketiro
Puketiro
12km from Owaka
3 DTL
Last Sunday
Contact Graeme Browne
Tel: (020) 58 106 or
Albert Berney
Tel: (020) 58 176

Putaruru
Overdale Road
2 DTL
2nd Sunday
Contact John Coatham
Tel: (0814) 68 985

Rangitikei
State Highway 3
2km north of Bulls
2 DTL, 1 Skeet
1st Sunday
Contact A. Anderson
Tel: (063293) 798

Rifle, Rod & Gun
Tiritea Road
close to Palmerston North
1 Skeet, 2 DTL
4th Sunday
Contact Mrs J. Wasby
Tel: 34 820

Rotorua
Atiamuri Highway
2km from Rotorua
3 Skeet, 4 DTL, 1 Ball Trap
1 Simulated Field
1st & 3rd Sundays
Contact Ann MacPherson
Tel: 83 780

Roxburgh
Roxburgh Trotting Club
2km from Roxburgh
2 DTL
Contact Alan Christie
Tel: 48 299

South Canterbury
Connors Road
off Timaru/Fairlie Highway
50km from Timaru
Simulated Field
Contact David Wills
Tel: 730 Albury, or
Von McRae, Tel: (056) 89-746

South Otago
Aerodrome
Glasgow Street, Balclutha
2 DTL, 1 Skeet
Otago/Southland Official
Programme
Contact Murray Farquher
Tel: (0299) 82 726

South Taieri
Momona Airport
2 DTL, 1 Skeet
2nd Sunday
Contact M. Tudor
Tel: 7692 Mosgiel

Southland
Pacific Avenue, Oreti Beach
5 DTL, 3 Skeet, 2 Ball Trap
Contact Joe Wilson
Tel: 393-055

Stewart Island
Airstrip Access Road
1 DTL, 1 DTL/Ball, 1 Skeet
Contact Ron Dennis
Tel: (021) 58

Taumarunui
Echolands Road
2km from Taumarunui
Tel: 8927
4 DTL, 2 Skeet, 1 Ball Trap
1 Sporting
Contact Steve Redmayne
Tel: 8354
or Gavin Brears Tel: 7509

Te Anau
Te Anau/Mossburn Highway
1km from Te Anau
Tel: (0229) 8098
1 Skeet, 2 DTL
Contact P. Sinclair
Tel: (0229 6) 637

Te Aroha
Mikkelsen Road, RD 3, Te Aroha
1 DTL
1st Sunday
Contact R.A. Herbert
Tel: 48 137 or (a.h.) 48 483 Darg.

Te Kuiti
Lees Block Road
8km north of Te Kuiti
Tel: 87 580
2 DTL, 1 Ball Trap
2nd Sunday
Contact D.P. Cole (0813) 88-165
or a/h 86-731

229

Thames
Main Road
1km from Thames
2 Skeet, 3 DTL, 1 Ball Trap
Skeet practice 1st Saturday
shoot day 3rd Sunday
Contact D. Leonard
Tel: 77 062 (Ngatea)
or C. Judd, Tel: 87 869

Thunderbird
Hamilton
1 DTL
Last Sunday
Contact Jack Worth
Tel: 64 372

Timaru
Richard Pearse Airport
Falvey Road, Levels, Timaru
Tel: 82 501
3 Skeet, 6 DTL, 1 Ball Trap
3rd Sunday
Contact M.J. Munro
Tel: 61 377

Tokoroa
Maraetai Road
1km from Tokoroa
2 DTL, 1 Skeet, 1 Ball Trap
1st Sunday
Contact K. Silcock
Tel: 67 210

Waihi
Tauranga Highway
3km from Waihi
1 Trap, DTL & Ball Trap
2nd Sunday
Contact Don Land
Tel: (0816) 8085

Waihora
Main Tai Tapu/Akaroa Highway
2 DTL, 1 Skeet
Circuit programme
Contact G. Woods
Tel: (03) 252 534

Waikato
Holland Road, Eureka
8km from Hamilton
Tel: 291 785
10 DTL, 5 Skeet, 3 Ball Trap
1 ISU Skeet
Club day 2nd Sunday
skeet practice 4th Saturday
Contact H.R. Oliver
Tel: (0819) 3826

Wairarapa
Norfolk Road, Masterton
2 DTL, 1 Ball Trap, 2 Skeet
4th Sunday
Contact D. Hathaway
Tel: (0593) 8360

Waitemata
Great North Road, Kumeu
6 DTL, 4 Skeet, 1 Trench
2nd & 4th Sundays
Contact Vic Ball
Tel: (09) 596 246

Wakatipu
Shotover Bridge
6km from Queenstown
1 DTL, 1 Skeet
Contact John Hillock
Tel: 27 369

Wanaka
Horseshoe Bend, Hawea River
8km from Wanaka
4 DTL, 1 Skeet
Central Otago circuit
Otago/Southland programme
Contact W.J. Gillespie
Tel: 8132 or C.M. Burdon
Tel: 7045

Wanganui
Marangai Road
8km from Wanganui
Tel: 26 841
3 DTL, 1 Skeet, 1 Trench
3rd Sunday
Contact D.P. McGovern
Tel: 57 706

Western Lake
Western Lake, Featherston
1 DTL
Contact Bob Parker
Tel: (08228) 745

West Otago
Station Road, Tapanui
2 DTL, 1 Skeet
Contact A.C. Gunn
Tel: (02022) 868

Whakatane
Golflinks Road
2 DTL
1st Sunday
Contact Lloyd Dennis
Tel: 87 190

Whangarei Combined
McAllister Road, Mangapai
13km from Whangarei
2 Skeet, 2 DTL
1st Sunday
Contact D. Jecentho
Tel: 483 134 (Bus)

Whatitiri
McBeths Road, Poroti
13km from Whangarei
1 Skeet, 2 DTL, 1 Ball Trap
3rd Sunday
Contact Mrs G. Bourke
Tel: 481 921, or I. Mitchell
Tel: 62 030

Whitianga
South Highway
2km from Whitianga
1 DTL
4th Sunday
Contact Ian Marshall
Tel: (084363) 762

Woodville
Dodds
1km from Woodville
2 Skeet, 1 Ball Trap, 4 DTL
1st Sunday
Contact Alan Mabey
Tel: 48 386

Appendix 6: Taxidermist Directory

NORTH ISLAND

Wayne & Sue Bennet
Huntly West Road
Ngaruawahia
Telephone: (07124) 7167

Paul Blackley
38 Whakarau Street
Turangi
Telephone: (0746) 8476

Gordon Clark
50 Birch Street
Taupo
Telephone: (074) 89 267
or
4 George Street
Paeroa
Telephone: (0816) 7237

Terry Doyle
200 Taupehi Road
Turangi
Telephone: (0746) 8306

Goudswaards Taxidermy
PO Box 246
Cambridge
Telephone: (071) 5382

Terry Jenkins
Main Road
Clevedon
Telephone: (092928) 767

John McCosh
RD 1
Featherston
Telephone: (0553 27) 853

Max Motley
52 Upham Street
Havelock North
Hawke's Bay
Telephone: (070) 775 611

Doug Mould
3 Rotokawa Street
Taupo
Telephone: (074) 88 710

Ken Thomas
39 Raihara Street
Kaikohe
Telephone: (0887) 81 340

Wildlife Taxidermy Studio
9 Skinner Road
23 RD
Stratford
Taranaki
Telephone: (0663) 6944

SOUTH ISLAND

Terry Jacobs
PO Box 4058
Christchurch
Telephone: (03) 384 266
a/h 428 322

G. D. O'Rourke & Sons Ltd
Main Road
Pleasant Point
Timaru
Telephone: (056) 27 737

Gary Pullar
Mosgiel Taxidermy Studio
25 Severn Street
Mosgiel
Telephone: (024 89) 894 494

Peter J. Ritchie
Mountain Top Taxidermists
51 Ngaio Street
Christchurch
Telephone: (03) 326 258

Southern Taxidermy
Victoria Court
Dee Street
Invercargill
Telephone: (021) 83 617

Widescope Taxidermist
11 Market Place
Twizel
Telephone: (056 20) 823
a.h. (056 823) 476

Appendix 7: New Zealand Smallbore Rifle Association Directory

New Zealand SB Rifle Assn
PO Box 89
Tauranga
Secretary: G.D. Dawson

NORTH ISLAND

Auckland SB Rifle Assn
C/- Miss A. Dickey
PO Box 2136
Auckland

Bush SB Rifle Assn
C/- Mr A. A. Duckett
Konini
RD 7
Pahiatua

Gisborne SB Rifle Club
C/- Mr F. McGarva
99 Main Rd
Makaraka
Gisborne

Hawke's Bay SB Rifle Assn
C/- Mrs J. A. Johnson
PO Box 897
Hastings

Horowhenua SB Rifle Assn
C/- Mr S. G. Arnott
Taikorea Rd
RD 3
Palmerston North

Hutt Valley SB Rifle Assn
C/- Mr R. Mason
PO Box 38633
Petone

Mana Outdoor SB Rifle Assn
C/- Mrs H. Bates
45 California Drive
Totara Park
Wellington

Manawatu SB Rifle Assn
C/- Mrs S. J. Carne
PO Box 6063
Palmerston North

Sth Hawke's Bay SB Rifle Assn
C/- Mr I. J. Sigvertson
Barnsdale Farm
RD 1
Takapau

Taranaki SB Rifle Assn
C/- Mr R. L. Peterson
19 Brookes Tce
Waitara

Valley Air Rifle & Pistol Club
C/- Mrs B. Newton
4 Manuka St
Miramar
Wellington

Waikato SB Rifle Assn
C/- Mr J. Stuart
71 Queen St
Te Kuiti

Wairarapa SB Rifle Assn
C/- Mrs N. Wilton
PO Box 363
Masterton

Wanganui SB Rifle Assn
C/- Mrs J. Travers
PO Box 582
Wanganui

Wellington SB Rifle Assn
C/- Mrs P. Hastings
PO Box 772
Wellington

Whangarei SB Rifle Club
C/- Mr G. S. Herman
120 Hospital Rd
Whangarei

SOUTH ISLAND

Ashburton SB Rifle Assn
C/- B. L. Hunter
4 Hefford Place
Ashburton

Ashley SB Rifle Assn
C/- B. W. Blackie
103 West Belt
Rangiora

Central Otago SB Rifle Assn
C/- T. Davis
Gimmerburn
RD 1
Ranfurly

Christchurch SB Rifle Assn
C/- Mr R. Wl Taylor
PO Box 776
Christchurch

Central Southland SB Rifle Assn
C/- V. J. Wilson
29 Albert St
Winton

East Otago SB Rifle Assn
C/- Mr D. J. Gillan
PO Box 4011
Dunedin

East Southland SB Rifle Assn
C/- C. S. Robinson
22A Main St
Gore

Ellesmere SB Rifle Assn
C/- R. J. Gardiner
RD
Dunsandel

Geraldine SB Rifle Assn
C/- Mr L. J. Smith
25 Lyall Terrace
Temuka

Invercargill SB Rifle Assn
C/- Mr E. Herman
34 Gimblett Street
Invercargill

Mackenzie SB Rifle Assn
C/- Mr R. D. Irving
Marahau
Albury

Malvern SB Rifle Assn
C/- Mrs D. Oakley
Halkett Rd
No. 1 RD
Christchurch

Marlborough SB Rifle Assn
C/- Mr V. Wadsworth
PO Box 412
Blenheim

Nelson SB Rifle Assn
C/- Mrs L. Waters
230 Nayland Rd
Stoke
Nelson

North Canterbury SB Rifle Assn
C/- Mr D. W. Shanks
64 Beach Rd
Kaikoura

North Otago SB Rifle Assn
C/- Mrs J. L. Wallace
PO Box 115
Oamaru

North Southland SB Rifle Assn
C/- Mrs R. Collins
RD 1
Balfour

Otago Provincial Assn
C/- H. M. Lester
RD 4
Balclutha

South Canterbury SB Rifle Assn
C/- C. L. Hall
Waipopo Rd
RD 3
Timaru

South Otago SB Rifle Assn
C/- Mr P. Orr
Moneymore
RD 2
Milton

South Southland SB Rifle Assn
C/- Mr A. R. Maxwell
RD 3
Wyndham

Timaru SB Rifle Assn
C/- Mrs Y. L. Gray
61 Tawa St
Timaru

Waimate SB Rifle Assn
C/- Mr S. Campbell
No. 9 RD
Waimate

West Coast SB Rifle Assn
C/- Mr P. McVicar
80 Blake St
Blaketown
Greymouth

West Southland SB Rifle Assn
C/- Miss E. L. Andrews
39 Richard St
Riverton

Appendix 8: New Zealand Small Game Shooters Sporting Association Inc. Directory

Auckland
CPO Box 3278
Auckland 1

Bay of Plenty
3 Snowden Street
Ohauiti
Tauranga

Cheviot
PO Box 12
Cheviot

Franklin
PO Box 290
Papakura

Kapiti
PO Box 51
Waikanae

New Plymouth
C/- 81 Riversdale Drive
New Plymouth

Otago
102 Gladstone Road
Mosgiel

Whangarei
120 Hospital Road
Whangarei

Appendix 9: Selected Reading

BOOKS

Allison, C. with Coombes I. *The Australian Hunter*. Cassel, Melbourne, 1969.

Allison, C. *The Hunters' Manual of Australia and New Zealand*. Reed, Australia, 1980.

Ashby, C.R. *The Centenary History of the Auckland Acclimatisation Society, 1867-1967*.

Barnes, F.C. *Cartridges of the World*. DBI Books, Northfield, Illinois, 1980.

Brander, M. (Editor). *The International Encyclopaedia of Shooting*. Pelham Books, London, 1972.

Brown, W.F. *How To Train Hunting Dogs*. A.S. Barnes & Co., New York, 1942.

Burton, M. & R. *The Animal World*. Macmillan, London, 1977.

Byrne, J. *Wing Shooting in New Zealand*. Reed, Wellington, 1982.

Cubitt, G. & Mountfort, G. *Wild India*. Collins, London, 1985.

Donne, T.E. *The Game Animals of New Zealand*. John Murray, London, 1924.

Gooders, J. & Lambert T. *Collins British Birds*. Collins, London, 1982.

Harris, L.H. *A Hunting Guide*. New Zealand Forest Service, 1973.

Holden, P. *Backblocks*. Hodder & Stoughton, Auckland, 1974.

Holden, P. *The Golden Years of Hunting in New Zealand*. Hodder & Stoughton, Auckland, 1983.

Holden, P. *New Zealand: Hunters' Paradise*. Hodder & Stoughton, Auckland, 1985.

Holden, P. *The Deerstalkers*. Hodder & Stoughton, Auckland, 1987.

Holden, P. *A Guide To Hunting in New Zealand*. Hodder & Stoughton, Auckland, 1987.

Lamb, R.C. *Birds, Beasts & Fishes*. The North Canterbury Acclimatisation Society, 1964.

Lever, C. *Naturalised Mammals of the World*. Longman Group Ltd, England, 1985.

Lockley, R.M. *The Private Life of the Rabbit*. Andre Deutsch, London, 1964.

Lockley, R.M. *Man Against Nature*. Reed, Wellington, 1970.

Long, J.L. *Introduced Birds of the World*. Reed, Australia, 1981.

Marlow, B. *Marsupials of Australia*. The Jacaranda Press, Brisbane, Australia, 1965 (Revised edition).

Merne, O.J. *Ducks, Geese and Swans*. Hamlyn, London, 1974.

Monk, J. *Gun Dogs*. Reed, Sydney, 1969.

Morecombe, M. *Australian Marsupials*. Lansdowne Press, Sydney, 1972.

Mochi, U. & Carter, T.D. *Hoofed Mammals of the World*. Lutterworth Press, London, 1974.

New Zealand Birds. Reader's Digest, Sydney, in association with Reed Methuen Publishers, Auckland, 1985.

Ogilvie, M.A. *Wild Geese*. Poyser, England, 1978.

Oliver, W.R.B. *Birds of New Zealand*. Reed, Wellington, 1955.

Ponting, K. *Sheep of the World*. Blandford Press, Dorset, 1980.

Reed, A.H. & A.W. *Captain Cook in New Zealand*. Reed, Wellington, 1951.

Rene, P.B. *The Guinness Guide to Mountain Animals*. Guinness Superlatives, Middlesex, 1975.

Ricciuti, E.R. *Wildlife of the Mountains*. Harry N. Abrams, New York, 1979.

Roberts, G. *Game Animals in New Zealand*. Reed, Wellington, 1968.

Rolls, E.C. *They All Ran Wild*. Angus & Robertson, Sydney, 1969.

Salmon, J.T. *Native Trees of New Zealand*. Reed Methuen, Auckland, 1980.

Smith, H.G. *Tutira*. William Blackwood & Sons, Edinburgh & London, 1935.

Soothill, E. & Whitehead, P. *Wildfowl of the World*. Blandford Press, Dorset, 1978.

Sowman, W.C.R. *Meadow, Mountain, Forest and Stream*. Nelson Acclimatisation Society, 1981.

Thomson, G.M. *Wild Life in New Zealand. Part I: Mammalia*. Government Printer, Wellington, 1921.

Thomson, G.M. *Wild Life in New Zealand. Part II: Introduced Birds and Fishes*. Government Printer, Wellington, 1926.

Thomson, G.M. *The Naturalisation of Animals and Plants in New Zealand*. The University Press, Cambridge, England, 1922.

Troughton, E. *Furred Animals of Australia*. Angus & Robertson, Sydney, 1967.

Wild New Zealand. Reader's Digest Services, Sydney.

Wises New Zealand Guide. Wises Publications Ltd, Auckland (revised edition), 1987.

Wodzicki, K.A. *Introduced Mammals of New Zealand*. Dept of Scientific & Industrial Research, Wellington, 1950.

ARTICLES AND REPORTS

Adams, C. 'Call and Crawl for Canadas'. *Petersens' Hunting*, February 1987.

'Auckland Island Goats to go.' The *Southland Times*, 30 June 1988.

Bryant, C. 'Been there done that' (Myxomatosis rabbits released by 50s government). *Weekend Star*, 7 November 1987.

Byrne, J. *Getting Started in Upland Game Hunting*. Acclimatisation Societies of New Zealand, Wellington, 1987.

Caithness, T. *Gamebird Hunting*. (Fish and Fowl series No. 2) The Wetland Press, 1982.

Canada Goose Hunting, Lake Ellesmere, New Zealand. New Zealand
Acclimatisation Societies.

Cheeseman, T.F. 'Notes on the Three Kings Islands.' *Transactions of the New
Zealand Institute,* Vol. 20.

Coe, B. 'Mallards Galore.' *Rod & Rifle,* March/April 1980.

Cummins, J. 'Possum: pest or profit?' *New Zealand Listener,* 16 July
1977.

'Death Also Stalks the Hunter.' *New Zealand Herald,* December 1984.

'Death Mars Start of Duck Shooting.' *Sunday Times,* 8 May 1988.

Douglas, N. *The Douglas Score: A Handbook on the Measuring of
Antlers, Horns & Tusks.* The New Zealand Deerstalkers' Association,
1959.

Fetherston, J. 'If we allow tragedies like this to happen. . .' *Women's Day,*
11 April 1988.

Ford, M. 'Our New Game Bird — the Red-Leg.' *New Zealand Outdoor
Golden Jubilee Album,* 1987.

Gunshot. New Zealand Clay Target Association, October/November
1988 and December/January 1989.

Harris, L. *Forest Wildlife.* Government Printer, Wellington, 1985.

Harris, L. *The New Zealand Firearm Handbook* (Mountain Safety
Manual No. 2). New Zealand Mountain Safety Council Inc., Dept of
Internal Affairs, Wellington, (revised edition 1985.)

'How to get rid of the rabbit?' *Straight Furrow,* 20 April 1988.

Howard, P.J. *Red-Legged Partridge Introductions & Subsequent Reports:
Appendices to Annual Reports.* Auckland Acclimatisation Society,
1979-1984.

Hunting In Wellington Conservancy. New Zealand Forest Service,
Wellington, 1984.

Hunting the Canada. New Zealand Wildlife Service, Wellington, 1981.

Imber, M.J. 'Canada Geese studies in Canterbury.' *Ammohouse Bulletin,*
Vol. 1, No. 30, 1971.

Introduction To Canada Goose Shooting. Compiled by T. Pierson, D.
Potts, and P. Armitage. North Canterbury Acclimatisation Society,
1984.

Johnson, J.A. 'Snake River Chukar.' *Petersens' Hunting,* January 1988.

Kean, R.I. 'Wallabies in New Zealand.' *New Zealand Outdoor,* August
1954.

Kircher, A. 'Honkers in the Moonlight.' *Rod & Rifle,* July/August 1984.

'Landcorp Protecting Auckland Island Goats.' The *Southland Times,* 8
April 1988.

McIvor, A. & Sherley, G. *A Study and Live Capture of Auckland Island
Goats.* Landcorp, 1988.

Mankelow, D. 'Chukar: New Zealand's Forgotten Gamebird.' *Rod &
Rifle,* March/April 1985.

Marshal, G. *Possum Hunting in New Zealand*. The Halcyon Press, Auckland, 1984.

Messenger, A.H. 'Wild Goat Hunting in the Tararua Ranges'. *The New Zealand Illustrated Magazine*, May 1901.

Moresby, D.J. *Commercial Opossum Hunting*. Published by the author, 1984.

Nelson, N. '50 Gimmicks that Get Geese.' *Petersens' Hunting Annual*, 1986.

New Zealand Journal of Forestry: 1949-1956.

New Zealand Farmer Weekly 3 June 1943; 13 June 1946; 10 July 1947.

Parkes, B. *Getting Started In. . .Waterfowl Hunting*. Acclimatisation Societies of New Zealand, Wellington, 1987.

Parkes, J.P. 'Feral Goats on Raoul Island.' *New Zealand Journal of Ecology*, Vol. 7, 1984.

Parkes, J.P. *Hare Control in the High Country*. Protection Forestry Division, Forest Research Institute, Rotorua, 1981.

'Poison Blitz on Wild Goats.' *New Zealand Herald*, 17 March 1982.

Pracy, L.T. & Kean, R.I. *The Opossum in New Zealand: Habits and Trapping*. New Zealand Forest Service, Wellington, 1969.

'Productive control of geese favoured.' *The Press*, 5 February 1988.

Ross, F.M. *The Canada Goose*. New Zealand Wildlife Service, 1984.

Rudge, M.R. and Campbell, D.J. (1977) 'The History and Present Status of Goats on the Auckland Island (NZ Sub-Antarctic) in relation to vegetation changes induced by man,' *New Zealand Journal of Botany*, 15:211-253.

Sheep Production Guide (The Livestock and Grain Producers' Association of New South Wales). New South Wales University Press, Australia, 1976.

Smith, R.V.F. *Rifle Sport in the South Island*. Pegasus Press, Christchurch, 1952.

Thompson, F. 'Field Survey for Wild Red-Legged Partridge at Waiterium'. Annual Reports, Auckland Acclimatisation Society, 1988.

'Two shooters injured.' The *Southland Times*, 9 May 1988.

Upland Gamebirds: A Discussion Paper. Gamebird Management Section, Dept of Conservation, 1987.

'Wallaby Drive (1,825 Animals Shot).' The *Christchurch Press*, 16 August 1965.

Waterfowl Hunting in Southern New Zealand. Southland Acclimatisation Society, Invercargill, 1984.

Westerskov, K.A.J. *The Pheasant in New Zealand*. Dept of Internal Affairs, Wellington, 1962.

Westerskov, K.A.J. *The Pheasant in Nelson*. Dept of Internal Affairs, Wellington, 1957. (Reprinted from 89th Annual Report of the Nelson Acclimatisation Society, pp. 15-24).

Williams, G.R. 'Chukar in New Zealand'. *New Zealand Science Review*, Vol. 8, Nos. 1-2. Wildlife Division, Dept of Internal Affairs, 1950.

Williams, G.R. *The California Quail in New Zealand*. Wildlife Publication No. 15, Wildlife Division, Dept of Internal Affairs, 1952.

Williams, M. *The Duckshooter's Bag*. The Wetland Press, 1981.

Williamson, G.M. 'Observations On the Behaviours of Red-Legged Partridges.' Annual Report, Auckland Acclimatisation Society, 1988.

Yerex, G.F. 'Unpublished Reports on Goat Damage in Egmont National Park.' Dept of Internal Affairs, 1935.

ANNUAL REPORTS

Agricultural Department: 1901-1904, 1941.

Ashburton Acclimatisation Society: 100 years 1886-1986, 1987, 1988.

Auckland Acclimatisation Society: 1916-17, 1986, 1987, 1988.

Hawera Acclimatisation Society: 1987, 1988.

Hawke's Bay Acclimatisation Society: 1987, 1988.

Hobson Acclimatisation Society: 1985, 1986, 1987.

Internal Affairs Department: 1916-1957.

Mangonui-Whangaroa: 1985, 1986, 1987.

Nelson Acclimatisation Society: 1988.

North Canterbury Acclimatisation Society: 1987, 1988.

Otago Acclimatisation Society: 1987, 1988.

South Canterbury Acclimatisation Society: 1987, 1988.

South Canterbury Wallaby Board: 1988.

Southland Acclimatisation Society: 1966-67, 1987, 1988.

State Forest Service: 1920-1951.

Stratford Acclimatisation Society: 1987, 1988.

Taranaki Acclimatisation Society: 1987, 1988.

Tauranga Acclimatisation Society: 1987, 1988.

Waimate Acclimatisation Society: 1902-1932.

Wellington Acclimatisation Society: 1986, 1987, 1988.

West Coast Acclimatisation Society: 1987, 1988.

Westland Acclimatisation Society: 1985, 1986, 1987, 1988.

INDEX

245